Microcredit Guarantee Funds in the Mediterranean

Palgrave Studies in Impact Finance

Series Editor: **Mario La Torre**

The *Palgrave Studies in Impact Finance* series provides a valuable scientific 'hub' for re-searchers, professionals and policy makers involved in Impact finance and related topics. It includes studies in the social, political, environmental and ethical impact of finance, explor-ing all aspects of impact finance and socially responsible investment, including policy issues, financial instruments, markets and clients, standards, regulations and financial management, with a particular focus on impact investments and microfinance.

Titles feature the most recent empirical analysis with a theoretical approach, including up to date and innovative studies that cover issues which impact finance and society globally.

Titles include:

Paola Leone and Pasqualina Porretta
MICROCREDIT GUARANTEE FUNDS IN THE MEDITERRANEAN
A Comparative Analysis

Roy Mersland and R. Øystein Strøm (*editors*)
MICROFINANCE INSTITUTIONS
Financial and Social Performance

Palgrave Studies in Impact Finance series
Series Standing Order ISBN: 978-1-137-38961-9
(outside North America only)

You can receive future titles in this series as they are published by placing a standing order. Please contact your bookseller or, in case of difficulty, write to us at the address below with your name and address, the title of the series and the ISBN quoted above.

Customer Services Department, Macmillan Distribution Ltd, Houndmills, Basingstoke, Hampshire RG21 6XS, England.

Microcredit Guarantee Funds in the Mediterranean

A Comparative Analysis

Paola Leone
Professor of Banking and Finance, Sapienza University of Rome, Italy

and

Pasqualina Porretta
Senior Lecturer in Banking and Finance, Sapienza University of Rome, Italy

Contents

List of Figures and Boxes

Figures

Boxes

List of Tables

Acknowledgements

The book is the result of progressive research over time on microcredit guarantee funds and institutions; it is the outcome of considerations and analysis developed over years, by authors and co-authors, in the field of guarantee schemes and credit risk mitigation, in several conferences, seminars and research projects on this topic. This book is part of a research project (promoted by Sapienza University of Rome) related to "Sustainable microfinance: guarantee funds and securitization", that aims to analyse the conditions for expanding the "future of sustainable microfinance" in Mediterranean countries.

The book has been designed and developed within the Department of Management at the Sapienza University of Rome, thanks to support and suggestions from an academic team (P. Leone and P. Porretta) and the editor Mario La Torre who, in the last few years, developed huge expertise in research on the microcredit sector. In a context of collaboration and discussion, new research questions have been identified in order to build a logical scheme of analysis to address and comprehend the peculiarities of the microcredit sector (regulation, operator, business models, financial instruments used, and so on) in three European (Italy, Spain and France) and three African (Morocco, Tunisia and Egypt) countries, as well as the peculiar aspect of guarantee funds and institutions operating in the microcredit/microfinance sector in selected countries. The logical scheme, built by the academic team, offers a comprehensive comparative analysis of the most significant models operating in the microcredit sector along with the guarantee funds and institutions adopted in the above-mentioned countries.

The book has been developed thanks to a reciprocal intellectual exchange among authors and co-authors (S. Leo, F. Mango and I. C. Panetta) in different areas of the microcredit sector. The co-authors gave significant support in this research and in writing some chapters on different countries; the authors want to express to them their gratefulness.

The work, in particular, addresses the issue of guarantee funds and institutions as a response to the trade-off between the promotion of policies facilitating the access to credit for the poor and "non-bankable" customers/beneficiaries and risk profile reduction of the corresponding portfolios.

The need for financial sustainability is more urgent in North African countries and, more generally, in those countries where contributions and aid from international agencies and self-financing are the main sources of funding. However, because of the international financial crisis, developed countries (i.e., European countries) also have recently had to face the same issues. In this research, the relevant topic of financial sustainability looks at guarantee schemes as instruments able to open the microcredit sector to the dynamics of the market and, ultimately, to improve access to credit.

The academic research team from the Sapienza University of Rome worked together, reasoning and sharing their expertise in the field of microcredit, credit risk mitigation and guarantee schemes to achieve the aims of this research project: to satisfy the operational needs of supervisors, microcredit institutions/operators and other financial intermediaries (guarantee intermediaries, financial intermediaries, microcredit institutions) for the programming activities related to financially sustainable microcredit projects.

Furthermore, the authors wish to express their gratitude to many colleagues and practitioners with whom they shared discussion and opinions. The authors are also grateful for the assistance and support received from Italian *Ente Nazionale per il Microcredito*, which provided the monitoring data related to microcredit sector and operators in Italy.

Finally, the authors and coauthors wish to express thanks to their families and ask for their forgiveness for the time taken up in the preparation of this book.

Any errors and omissions that will be encountered by readers are attributable to authors and co-authors.

About the Authors

Sabrina Leo (PhD) is research fellow in financial intermediaries at Sapienza University of Rome. Her main research interests are lending, credit contraction, microcredit, microfinance, social impact investment, and non-banking financial institutions/operators.

Fabiomassimo Mango (PhD) is permanent lecturer and assistant professor in banking and finance at Sapienza University of Rome. He has more than a decade of experience conducting training courses, research and consultancy in the banking and finance sector. In the last years, he has made a significant contribution to the disciplines of banking and finance thanks to his studies in the fields of financial crises, international financial markets, and ratings and ratings agencies.

Ida Claudia Panetta (PhD) is associate professor at Sapienza University of Rome, where she teaches International Financial Institutions and Capital Markets and Fund Industry and Pension Funds. She is a member of the academic board of the PhD in banking and finance at Sapienza University of Rome. She is economic sciences working group coordinator at Sapienza Research Center for Cyber Intelligence and Information Security. Her main research interests are liquidity risk management, banking regulation and supervision, and corporate governance and cyber-security in the financial system. She acted as a consultant and trainer for various banks and mutual credit guarantee institutions.

1
Introduction

Paola Leone and Pasqualina Porretta*

1.1 Microfinance: definition, products and services

There is no internationally accepted definition of *microfinance*; however, the term is used to indicate a range of financial services/ products (of small amounts) offered to low-income/non-bankable customers and micro-enterprises. Microfinance covers a wide range of financial services that include savings, credit, insurance and remittance. Microfinance targets those people who are denied credit by formal financial and banking institutions because of lack of knowledge as well as formal rules which they have to follow to get a credit from these institutions.

In fact, microfinance, according to Otero (1999, p. 8) is "the provision of financial services to low-income poor and very poor self employed people". These financial services generally include savings and credit but can also include other financial services such as insurance and payment services. Schreiner and Colombet (2001, p. 339) define microfinance as *"the attempt to improve access to small deposits and small loans for poor households neglected by banks"*.

Generally, microfinance[1] is associated with developing countries, where large segments of the population need to access these types of financial services, although microfinance includes a variety of activities that extend to developed countries, where – especially after the international economic and financial crisis – an increasing number of people face poverty due to factors such as immigration, unemployment, inactivity and marginalization.

Traditionally, those people who benefit from microfinance are citizens of developing countries who struggle to provide for themselves; they are known, unfortunately, as "the poorest of the poor". Within this category, women are of particular significance since they constitute the group that is most affected by financial exclusion in many developing countries. More recently, microfinance has turned its attention to self-employed workers and individuals in charge of small, often family-owned businesses which are unable to obtain bank credit. For micro-entrepreneurs, microfinance represents an alternative to credit given by lenders, and often constitutes a way out of the money-lending system (La Torre and Vento, 2006, p. 3).

From this perspective, it's important to underline that at the EU level, a definition for microcredit focuses on microbusiness and entre-preneurs who have limited access to conventional banking loans. The Commission Communication "A European initiative for the development of microcredit in support of growth and employment" has stated this definition (ESBG, 2009, p. 1). The EC did not clearly define their target groups, and did not focus on start-ups and micro-enterprises or on financially excluded[2] enterprises or individuals. Those two target groups have different requirements and call for different, and therefore adapted, financial solutions.

Microfinance defines an area of activity that includes all those economic/financial relationships that financial institutions may establish with their customers. In particular, the term refers to a range of financial products and services, often accompanied by social intermediation services, offered to customers who struggle to access the traditional banking system because of their weak economic and social conditions. Microfinance is thus broadly viewed as an activity that can be potentially carried out by a wide array of institutions providing financial services such as lending, deposits, insurance and so on. Microfinance institutions (MFIs) is simply a generic term including an estimated diverse entities such as commercial banks, non governmental organizations (NGOs), credit unions, financial companies and so on. In some countries, the term "microfinance institution" is used to refer to NGOs or other entities whose main activity is the delivery of microcredit, or entities requiring a minimum level of microfinance activity from a specialised microfinance provider.

In many countries, a variety of institutional types engage in micro-finance; many of these operators are supervised by banking regulators and authorities. In line with their different activities, these entities are characterised by different licensing and prudential standards; some institutions may not be supervised at all. In particular, the following can operate in the microfinance sector:

- *Banks,* the definition includes traditional commercial banks and similar financial institutions (for example savings bank). Generally speaking, the extent of the banks' engagement in microfinance varies considerably within and across countries. In particular, commercial banks have been increasingly active in micro-lending over time, which may reflect enhanced competition, social responsibility concerns, government policies, or a combination of these. In some countries, this situation may simply reflect that the bulk of the retail market is low-income;
- *Co-operative,* such as credit co-operatives, co-operative banks, construction companies, mutual savings and loans associations and so on. Co-operatives that engage in business with non-members are normally prudentially regulated and supervised, just like co-operatives that lend to and take deposits only from their members (member-only) in high-income countries, regardless of their size. In low and middle-income countries, the regulatory and supervisory system for member-only co-operatives varies, but tends to fall under non-prudential regulators. Financial co-operatives that engage in business only with their members tend to be licensed or registered by a government agency other than the banking authority or the central bank, such as the ministry of finance, ministry of labour or ministry of co-operatives, and normally are not prudentially supervised;
- *Microcredit Institutions* (MCIs), these are entities whose sole activity is lending to low-income individuals and small or micro-enterprises[3] and they are not allowed to take deposits. These entities are subject to a wide variety of supervisory systems, ranging from simple registration requirements to prudential supervision. They may take on a variety of commercial (for example limited liability or joint stock companies) and non-profit (for example associations, foundations) forms. Few countries impose a licensing or authorization requirement to MCIs. In some countries, the license is issued by a public agency or authority other than the banking authority, Central Bank or Ministry of Finance, and in two of them there are no minimum licensing criteria, only simple registration procedures. (BCBS, 2010, p. 36–38)

Microfinance can be seen from three different angles: its social component, which means tackling social and financial exclusion, reducing unemployment and helping the reintegration of excluded citizens into the community; its economic component, which defines microfinance as an economic tool potentially enabling economic growth; the provision of aid, an instrument used in developing countries.

Microcredit is often confused with microfinance, but it is actually only one of the products of the latter (though the most important), which also includes a number of other financial products/services that can be synthetically grouped in the following areas:

- Small loans (microcredit)
- Micro-insurance products/services
- Micro-leasing instruments/products
- Social housing products/services
- Forms of deposit collection and management
- Payment services
- Remittance services

Over the past decade, many changes have taken place in the overall microfinance landscape.

Microfinance has strongly expanded in many countries, assisted by technological advances, new opportunities emerging alongside the traditional microcredit model and new players entering the industry to capitalise on these opportunities. Today's situation is characterised by increasing involvement by Development Finance Institutions, investment funds and other institutional investors in microfinance business (European Commission, 2008).

Microcredit, and microfinance in general, could be seen as a political tool in some countries, tempting politicians to demand forbearance or forgiveness of loans granted to poor customers during times of economic stress. Microfinance can be an appropriate solution to tackle financial and social exclusion, as it provides lending, financial management and other financial products or services. For instance, the EU has set up several policies on social inclusion, which highlight the role and benefits of micro-loans in reducing poverty, boosting economic growth and creating jobs.

The beneficiaries of microfinance products/services constitute a category which generally includes economically and socially vulnerable subjects. The target varies according to practices followed by the MFIs and the countries they operate in. However, the recipients are usually low-income individuals or people with irregular income, the unemployed, non-homeowners, migrants, residents in depressed or marginal areas and/or women (especially in developing countries), all subjects who have one characteristic in common: financial exclusion.[4] Microfinance offers products/services that often allow for or facilitate their financial inclusion, which the European Commission defines as *"[...] The process by which people are able to access and/or use financial services/products in the mainstream market that are appropriate to their needs and enable them to lead a normal social life in the society in which they belong"* (European Commission, 2008). The European Commission, therefore, regards financial exclusion not just as a lack of access to financial instruments, but also the inability/impossibility to actually use them.

Different reasons may lead to financial exclusion (La Torre and Vento, 2006, p. 4). First of all, there is so-called *self-exclusion*, which mainly originates from a perception of inadequacy of the single individuals to meet the requirements set forth by the financial intermediaries; this category includes *the poorest of the poor*. We then define *access exclusion* as resulting from a *risk assessment* process conducted by financial intermediaries on customers, which indicates their poor creditworthiness; this category includes the *"poor"*. The *"poor"* and the *"poorest of the poor"* are two categories that have traditionally represented the targets of microcredit programmes.

However, financial exclusion may also result from an exclusion from the social-political system; this is the so-called *political exclusion*, which usually affects migrants and all those subjects who are not bankable, as they are *not included in the census*.

Then, there are subjects whose existence is known but who fail to gain access to the financial system because they cannot afford the costs and conditions of the financial products offered; in this case, we can speak of *"penalised"* subjects, affected by the so-called *condition exclusion*. Finally, we can identify a form of *financial exclusion* affecting customers who are considered *"marginal"* by the financial intermediaries (mostly small entrepreneurs), as they represent a low-value target according to traditional *customer valuation* models; in this case, we can talk about *marketing exclusion* (Figure 1.1).

1.2 Microcredit: a brief overlook

As mentioned above, microcredit is one of the instruments used by microfinance to meet the need for access to credit by so-called *non-bankable subjects*. The term is normally used to indicate two types of financial activities: the *social microcredit* (mainly aimed at the social inclusion of *excluded* subjects by supporting their current expenditure and providing

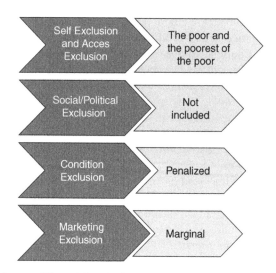

Figure 1.1   Forms of financial exclusion
Source: Author's elaboration based on La Torre and Vento, 2006, p. 4.

social services, training courses, and so on) and *microcredit for businesses* (supporting start-ups and self-employment initiatives), which obviously have different objectives.

This microcredit market segment goes by the definition of *nearly bankable*, and in this perspective, microcredit services are seen as highly important to stimulate economic growth, create jobs and tackle financial exclusion.

Microcredit can be provided in any of the technical formats used for ordinary credit. Yet, when compared to ordinary credit, microcredit shows a number of peculiarities that can generally be defined as follows:

- *Reduced size of the loans.* Loans are usually very small, short-term and unsecured, with better repayment rate and higher interest rates if compared to traditional bank loans. Many microcredit providers charge higher interest rates to offset higher operational costs involved in the labour-intensive micro-lending methods;
- *Support lending with non-financial services (tutoring, monitoring, technical assistance, and so on).* Supporting loans with a number of ancillary and instrumental services is key for the success of any microcredit programme. Effective links need to be put in place between providers

of these support measures, both within schemes where support services are integrated in a single programme and in those focusing uniquely on lending;

- *Beneficiaries are non-bankability or financial exclusions.* Microcredit providers usually cater to low-income customers, both underemployed individuals and entrepreneurs running informal family businesses (e.g., petty traders). Borrowers are typically concentrated in limited geographic areas, social segments or entrepreneurial sectors;
- *Creditworthiness assessment should take into account the peculiarities of the borrowers* (absence of credit history, absence of collaterals to be provided to financial intermediaries, no written accounting practices, no solid business plans, no information databases showing an adequate business structure and significant statistical data). Loan documentation is largely generated by the microcredit provider officers through visits to the borrowers' business and home. Borrowers often lack formal financial statements, so loan officers may help in the preparation of documents by using expected cash flows and net worth to determine the amortisation schedule and the amounts of loans. The borrower's personality and willingness to repay is also assessed during field visits. Credit bureau data are not always available for low-income clients or all types of microfinance providers, but when they exist, they are used, too. Credit scoring, if applicable, complements rather than replaces this process (BCBS, 2010, p. 16). In general, we can say that the process of evaluation of microcredit loans should be characterised by (1) a specific evaluation model; (2) a tutoring activity dedicated to the borrowers during all phases of lending; (3) possible partnership with highly skilled support and tutoring institutions;
- *Microcredit lending often is supported by risk mitigation instruments (guarantees).* The same promoters of microcredit programme often take care of creating guarantee funds to support access to microcredit by micro-borrowers. It is a well-known fact that for a number of reasons, micro and small enterprises usually face difficulties in accessing the traditional financial system. These enterprises often look opaque indeed: not adequately capitalised, lacking the collateral traditionally required by banks and, more generally, considered too risky by financial intermediaries. For all these reasons, the financial system may not always able or willing to screen such firms adequately, thus determining their failures on the market. On the other hand, a large group of different stakeholders may have an interest in sustaining the development of these micro and small firms, such as central and local

governments, entities in charge of fostering local economies, but also large companies sharing concerns for their business sector and the health of firms operating in the same chain.

The traditional banking sector regards lending to microcredit target groups, as defined above, as too risky and cost-intensive. Commercial banks argue that they face unacceptably high risks of default against low profit margins. As a result, they are not interested in providing their services to some customer segments, which thus end up being *non-bankable*.

This means that the business of microcredit is quite different from traditional banking. It includes innovative and subjective elements such as different guarantee requirements or no collaterals at all, as well as alternative methods for creditworthiness evaluation. In many cases, microcredit is granted not only for economic reasons and not just to make a profit, but also to serve a broader social cohesion purpose by trying to reintegrate disadvantaged people into the society to which they belong.

In fact, different kinds of credit guarantee schemes and institutions have been developed in several countries to facilitate access to credit; they generally offer guarantees to small and medium enterprises (SMEs) that borrow from banks or other financial intermediaries. In financial systems where micro and small enterprises have no substantial alternatives to traditional bank loans, mutual guarantee schemes and institutions may significantly contribute to facilitate their access to credit, by reducing the information asymmetries between lenders and borrowers and, in some cases, by decreasing the cost of funding. In this perspective, it is important to explain the nature of guarantee funds as well as their objectives in the microcredit industry.

1.3   Microcredit guarantees

The presence of mutual guarantees (and, possibly, co-guarantees and counter-guarantees) accompanying the requests for micro-loans allows, on one side, to improve access to credit for those micro-borrowers who generally do not have the collaterals required by bank intermediaries and, on the other side, to mitigate the banks' credit risk and, possibly, facilitate capital management for the bank intermediaries that enjoy the guarantees and provide the micro-loans.

As is known, in fact, microcredit programmes activated by the various MFIs are exposed, like any forms of financing, to the risk that borrowers might not be able to refund the amount received (so-called credit risk[5]). Credit risk represents one of the greatest risks faced by the promoters of microcredit programmes, due to the high level of risk perceived, which originates from the peculiar conditions and characteristics of the micro-borrowers. Their poor creditworthiness has prompted the MFIs to resort to alternative instruments to hedge against this risk; the solutions adopted vary depending on the environment where the microcredit takes place and the practices followed by the individual microfinance institutions; the most common instruments are insurance products, guarantee funds and micro-loan securitization.

The presence of mutual guarantees, therefore, besides being a fundamental factor in the implementation of microcredit programmes, allows, in many cases, lenders to practice a lower *pricing* on microcredit, thanks to a reduced risk of the operations; secondly, it improves the sustainability of microcredit programmes. Finally, it has a positive impact on the *outreach* – the ability to offer financial services to segments of the population who are traditionally excluded from the traditional banking system.

The provision of microcredit entails higher operational costs, due to the small size of the loans, the lack of (sufficient) collaterals, as it is often difficult to reach customers physically and to build a wide (and expensive) network of operators able to provide ancillary or instrumental support services to these borrowers and to work closely with their target groups.

But even if the provision of microcredit is not profitable, it makes economic sense to support it, as generally the cost of funding self-employment initiatives is generally lower than the cost of unemployment, at least in the medium- and long-term.

The importance of the mutual credit guarantee schemes for microcredit lending has increased thanks to the capital adequacy requirements established by the Basel II agreement and their further strengthening with the Basel III agreement.

Although microcredit beneficiaries are not required to provide any collateral, lenders need to hedge against the risk of non-repayment/default of the borrowers (so-called credit risk). Guarantee schemes, by providing adequate risk coverage to the lenders, often facilitate the provision of loans and contribute to the reduction of loan-related losses. In addition, guarantee funds, besides mitigating the credit risk of the lenders,[6] are useful instruments to achieve the social purposes and the financial sustainability that lay at the core of the MFIs' objectives.

MFIs, in fact, seek to combine their social mission with the pursuit of financial goals in order to be competitive on the market in the medium- to long-term. While the above social objective – namely facilitating the access to a number of financial products/services for a number of disadvantaged individuals who, for different reasons, are excluded from traditional banking – is the most obvious and constitutes the primary reason underlying the creation of the MFIs, they also need to consider economic aspects and rely on adequate resources to pursue their objective of social justice independently, ensuring continuity and sustainability of their actions over time.

The issue at the basis of microcredit guarantees is that they are often seen as not economically sustainable, because of high costs and low return.

In many cases, guarantee funds, by ensuring MFIs and banks against credit risk, may help reach a greater number of customers or groups affected by disadvantages without sacrificing the overall sustainability of microcredit programmes. In this sense, it is necessary that, on the one hand, the resources used for the creation of guarantee funds are sufficiently consistent so as to allow reaching a high number of customers and, on the other hand, fund managers must be in possession of the capacity and skills needed for a correct management of such instruments.

An adequate risk assessment/management process represents a critical aspect for any MFIs, yet a key factor to determine their survival and growth. The particular characteristics of the MFIs – traditionally dedicated to the achievement of the social objectives and relying on external aid – have never favoured the development of proper internal management and monitoring activities of the risks incurred. The recent development of such institutions also in industrialised countries, the impossibility of meeting the MFIs' financial needs only with funds provided by external subjects through donations, and the increased complexity of their operations, have prompted these institutions to improve their internal management processes to make the best use of available resources, through the definition of risk management models, in order to reduce the variability of results and avoid losses that might jeopardize their stability, pursuing a financial self-sustainability model. The adoption of adequate risk management models represents a key factor for the MFIs' success and may facilitate the attraction of external resources.

1.4   Microcredit guarantee funds: main general features

Before entering upon a comparative analysis following the above logic scheme (cf. Table 1.1), we believe it appropriate to present the main operational features of the microcredit guarantee funds as well as the benefits that they may bring to the microfinance/microcredit sector.

As it is well-known, the typical operating structure of any microcredit programme involves at least four main actors: the promoter, the lender, the guarantor and, finally, the beneficiary of the micro-loan, each one playing an important role in the implementation and the correct functioning of the programme itself.

Promoters are subjects who activate the microcredit initiatives, and they do not necessarily coincide with lenders. Promoters define the scope of microcredit programmes, identifying their target and objectives; they bear any costs related to the promotion of said programmes and work to find resources for the creation of guarantee funds. Promoters can be represented by public institutions, central governments or local authorities, universities or other private entities and by bodies such as banking or non-banking institutions and non-profit organisations. Public institutions are often the main actors looking for partnership agreements aimed at supporting such projects, thus creating a virtuous circle. Public institutions, also following lobbying initiatives by microfinance associations, usually try to involve banks, microcredit associations and guarantee funds into a sort of "social agreement", where a bank would typically sign a protocol under which it agrees to apply particular conditions to the target subjects, and the microfinance association carries out a selection process and monitoring of the borrowers. Along with the public institution, the association implements other instrumental and ancillary support activities.

In almost all cases, at least in more financially developed countries, the lenders of the microcredit programmes coincide with banks, because the law limits the lending activity to a number of regulated financial intermediaries, in order to ensure the stability of the financial system. In some cases, lenders may coincide with local public authorities, while in others, lending might be provided by some private institutions, such as authorised MFIs. Moreover, financial intermediaries/brokers may also help manage the guarantee funds created to activate the microcredit programmes.

Subjects providing the resources to create guarantee funds may coincide with public and private institutions, such as bank foundations and others, associations, NGOs, chambers of commerce, development banks, and so on.

The guarantee fund managers can be bank intermediaries or financial intermediaries who already manage guarantee funds on behalf of third parties and may have an interest in entering the microcredit sector.

Financial intermediaries working in the microcredit sector, especially in more financially developed countries, may be constituted by authorised credit guarantee institutions.

From an operational standpoint, microcredit guarantee funds guarantee a portion of the funding provided by the banks according to the agreements signed with the same banks (or funding bodies in general). If we consider 100 the initial established allocation of the guarantee fund, it is then possible to grant guarantees for an amount equal to x times (leverage) the fund itself.

The leverage ratio defines the maximum amount of guarantees issued, and its limits depend on the agreements signed with the banks, or the specifications of tenders for microcredit programmes issued by public institutions, the average risk of the parties secured, and the nature of the guarantees pledged, which can be both collateral and personal guarantees.

Microcredit guarantee funds may provide various technical-legal forms of guarantees. From a legal standpoint, we can have collateral or personal guarantees. *Collateral guarantees* are basically configured as earmarked funds with bank intermediaries that are intended to provide protection against losses deriving from micro-loans. Each time a guarantee is provided, the fund managers must set aside a percentage (no longer available for guarantee purposes) to be used in case the micro-borrower defaults. Personal guarantees are normally sureties (including secured or unsecured letters of credit). From a technical standpoint, guarantees may be represented by direct guarantees (immediately enforceable by the lender against the fund), secondary guarantees (enforceable only after payment has been sought against the principal borrower), co-guarantees, or counter-guarantees. The legal and technical form of the guarantees provided contribute to defining their *appeal* for the whole bank system and, in the countries adhering to the Basel framework on capital, also their validity in terms of loss absorbency mitigation (*Credit Risk Mitigation framework*[7]). With regard to mandatory loss absorbency requirements against credit risk, the Basel II Framework established a number of provisions specifically dedicated to guarantee instruments in order to mitigate their impact. Compliance with such requirements allows banks to reduce their exposure to credit risk and, consequently, facilitates the capital absorption of the micro-loans granted. Obviously, the lack of requirements under the above Regulatory Framework does not affect the validity of such instruments as protective measures for the benefit of the banks (in the credit recovery phase), but it does not allow them to reduce the absorption of capital required to cover the micro-loans granted.

Methods to access the microcredit guarantees, their activation, revocation and other technical-operational aspects related to guarantee funds management (provision, enforcement, maximum expansion of the activities) as well as the legal form of the guarantees provided are established in the agreements signed with the intermediary lenders. Generally, a *process of allocation* of resources must accompany the provision of guarantees to the fund, which are thus no longer available for guarantee purposes.

The provisions of the fund are designed to ensure that, in accordance to the extension of the micro-loans, the fund always possesses the liquidity needed to meet the redemption requests of the banks following the default of the parties secured. Logically, the provisions of the guarantee fund must be proportionate to the credit risk of the guarantee beneficiaries. In the microcredit sector, there is often a lack of available credit risk "instruments" for loans granted to subjects by virtue of their peculiar social, economic and financial conditions; a frequently used solution is to "immobilize" a fixed percentage of monetary resources for fund allocation purposes.

The request for refund is made by the bank after it has sought payment from the principal debtor first and then its guarantors, in case of secondary guarantee. In case of direct guarantee, payment will be sought directly against the guarantee fund, and then the latter could possibly claim it against the guaranteed party.

The operations of the microcredit guarantee funds will be comprehensively analysed in the third area of our research (Chapter 4), which will assess the operational characteristics of such funds within a number of microcredit programmes in the countries examined.

1.5 The research: methodology and logic analysis scheme

This work, part of a research project (by Sapienza University of Rome) related to *"Sustainable microfinance: guarantee funds and securitization"*, aims to analyse the conditions for expanding the "future of sustainable microfinance" in the Mediterranean countries. Specifically, the work addresses the issue of guarantee funds as a response to the trade-off between the promotion of policies facilitating the access to credit for the poor and "non-bankable" subjects and risk profile reduction of the corresponding portfolios.

In light of the above, our research offers a comprehensive comparative analysis of the most significant models operating in the microcredit sector, along with the guarantee funds adopted in three European countries (Italy, Spain and France) and in three African countries (Morocco, Tunisia and Egypt). Given that the Mediterranean area of North Africa consists of a non-homogeneous group of countries, the choice was made according to some distinctive features related to their economic, structural (trade, investment, banking structure) and institutional profiles. In particular, based on research conducted by Intesa San Paolo (2010), it appears that, when compared to nearby countries, Tunisia, Morocco and Egypt are characterised by more diversified economies that show moderate growth in high-labour-intensive manufacturing sectors and lively trade relations with Europe. In those countries, micro-, small- and medium-sized enterprises provide two-thirds of the total employed force, and constitute an important source of investment attraction, employment, economic growth and income redistribution; structural reforms, promoted by the recent deep changes in the political systems of such countries, have focused their attention on the achievement of specific targets, like the creation of job opportunities and improvement of the local business competitiveness. That has been implemented by encouraging the development of local initiatives and international microcredit projects.

In general, financial inclusion is a critical factor to enhance the competitiveness of the Middle East and North African (MENA) regions, create jobs, improve income levels and reduce poverty. Financial inclusion is implemented by favouring access to financial services such as credit, bank accounts, deposits, payment services, insurance, and pensions. Firms need access to financial services in order to be able to invest, innovate, take advantage of market opportunities, manage cash flow and costs, and reduce risks. Micro-enterprises constitute the vast majority of enterprises in the MENA countries as well as being significant employers. While most MENA countries have taken steps to improve financial inclusion, there has not yet been a comprehensive high-level commitment in this sense across much of the region. Although financial inclusion is a policy focus in several MENA countries, it does not yet appear to be a priority objective like stability for MENA financial regulators and ministries of finance (Douglas, 2011).

With regard to Southern Europe, Spain, Italy and France stand out among the group of countries on the Mediterranean Sea that devoted their attention to developing the Euro-Mediterranean Partnership. Spain, Italy and France are industrialised countries, characterised by a fabric of small- and medium-sized enterprises with significant experience in microcredit, especially due to the severe crisis in production and employment, which has affected their economies as a result of the international financial crisis. In light of such differences, we decided to carry out a comparative analysis between Italy, Spain and France separately from the group of North African countries: Morocco, Tunisia and Egypt. Although characterised by different levels of economic and social development, these countries share a common attitude and practice in their efforts to promote and achieve microcredit financial sustainability. Some of the features they have in common include an active role played by public agencies in funding and in capacity-building, and a certain opaqueness in the information available to the public with regard to microcredit programmes, operative methods, subjects involved and beneficiaries.

The need for financial sustainability is more urgent in North African countries and, more generally, in those countries where contributions and aid from international agencies and self-financing are the main sources of funding.

However, because of the international financial crisis, developed (European) countries, too, have recently had to face the same issues. In this research, the relevant theme of financial sustainability looks at guarantee funds as instruments able to open the microcredit sector to the dynamics of the market.

Tunisia and Morocco, along with Egypt, are characterised by more diversified economies, with moderate growth in highly labour-intensive manufacturing sectors and lively trade relations with Europe. With regard to Southern Europe, Spain, Italy and France are industrialised countries, characterised instead by a fabric of small and medium-sized enterprises boasting significant experience in microcredit, especially due to the severe crisis in production and employment, which has affected all three countries as a result of the international financial crisis. The structure and organisation of the microcredit/microfinance sector in the countries analysed are rather heterogeneous, as they originate from growth paths and development models that belong to different social-economic situations (country-specific guarantee systems); therefore, the comparative analysis between the aforementioned three European countries was carried out separately from the North African group.

The perspective adopted in this research intends to provide a clear picture of the microcredit sector/guarantee funds in the current scenario, in each macro Mediterranean area, focusing on three key investigation areas: analysis of the regulatory framework and supervisory authority in the microcredit/microfinance sector, mapping of microcredit/microfinance institutions operators, and analysis of the key features of the microcredit guarantee funds and institutions.

Finally, the study aims to highlight, in general terms, strengths and weaknesses of the different types of microcredit guarantee systems. In doing so, it helps shed a light on the borders of sustainable microfinance in the two macro-areas considered as well as proposing a number of regulatory or operative solutions which may improve the economic sustainability of the microcredit sector/institutions and, ultimately, contribute to facilitation of effective access to credit for micro-enterprises and micro-borrowers.

Within this framework, the book aims to answer the following questions:

- How does the regulatory framework of each country facilitate or hinder the development of a sustainable microfinance model?
- What are the structural configuration and the morphology of the microcredit sector in each country in the two Mediterranean basin areas? Do they constitute different business models?
- How do the different actors involved in the microfinance sector use guarantee funds?
- What are the main operational characteristics of these guarantee funds? Do they contribute to the development of sustainable microfinance?
- Is it possible to find out some similarities between guarantee funds used in North African countries and those used in South European economies? What are the implications for the financial and business systems in the countries analysed?

In order to respond to these questions, we carried out an analysis of each country, focusing on three key investigation areas: (1) regulatory framework and supervisory authorities in the microcredit sector; (2) mapping of microcredit institutions and operators; (3) main features of microcredit guarantee funds: types and key operational features. Each area of investigation was examined using a number of available information sources; these include documents issued by national regulatory and supervisory authorities, reports on the areas examined and literature available on these topics.

In this perspective, the analysis scheme was arranged by relying upon the most recent available data. Though the lack of data often prevented us from having a comprehensive historical outlook, nevertheless it was possible to highlight the key features and the similarities among the various microcredit guarantee funds.

This project aims to meet the operational needs of supervisors, microcredit institutions/operators and other financial intermediaries (guarantee intermediaries, financial intermediaries, microcredit institutions) for the planning of activities related to financially sustainable microcredit projects.

The analysis performed on each country kicked off with an investigation of the *Regulatory Framework and Supervisory Authority in the Microcredit, Sector* due to their influence on the legal and institutional provision of microcredit programmes as well as their role in defining both the scope of operations and the technical and legal characteristics of the mitigation tools provided. In fact, any microcredit/microfinance system requires a legislative and normative framework which relates to the state legislative power, where an interaction and cooperation process between the public, financial and business sectors should take place. In this perspective, governments focus their interests on the promotion of micro-enterprises, entrepreneurs, creation of wealth, jobs, and so on; entrepreneurs are interested in accessing financing opportunities under competitive conditions (costs, terms, and so on); financial institutions require quality and certified guarantees that may help mitigate their credit risk.

Within the regulatory framework, banks in EU countries play a particularly relevant role by the regulations on capital (Basel II[8]), which define the qualification requirements of the mitigation tools used to reduce the capital appropriation of the funding bank intermediaries against credit risk, and, therefore, influence the *modus operandi* of guarantee intermediaries. This influence is stronger where credit guarantee institutions have acquired the legal and institutional status of supervised intermediaries, while it is weaker where they do not enjoy such status. The rules of prudential supervision are different in line with the bank intermediaries using the Standard, IRB Foundation or IRB Advanced approach; in any case, they change the possibilities/chances for credit guarantee institutions to uniquely follow traditional logics and technical modalities. Yet, far from diminishing the requests for guarantees, Basel II produces the opposite effect, offering new and interesting opportunities to all guarantors who are able to comply with its requirements by providing eligible guarantees. This agreement thus enhances the operability of the credit guarantee institutions; their guarantees, if compliant with the above requirements, can be used by the funding banks to reduce credit risk, capital requirements, and, therefore, the very same cost of the funds granted to the guaranteed parties. In this context, guarantees, especially properly certified and Basel-compliant guarantees, are quite scarce.

The investigation area entitled *Mapping Microcredit Institutions/ operators: A Comparative Analysis* (Chapter 3) is aimed at mapping the number, typologies, legal status, ownership structure and some structural information of the microcredit institutions in each country analysed.

The investigation area entitled *The Microcredit Guarantee Funds and Institutions: A Comparative Analysis* is meant to investigate the key features of the microcredit guarantee funds (within a specific microcredit program) in terms of volume of guarantees, type and nature of guarantees granted, average coverage percentage of funding, leverage ratio, numbers of beneficiaries/projects, sectors involved, and so on (cf. Table 1.1).

Each individual investigation area was examined using accessible information sources; these include documents created by national supervisory authorities, reports on the investigation areas examined and specific literature on the subject.

The Table 1.1 illustrates the logic scheme used in our research work and its breakdown.

Table 1.1   Logic scheme

REGULATORY FRAMEWORK AND SUPERVISORY AUTHORITIES IN THE MICROCREDIT SECTOR	Specific microcredit regulations in each country Main content of regulations Presence/absence of specific supervisory authorities (for microcredit operators) Guarantee funds regulations
MAPPING MICROCREDIT INSTITUTIONS/OPERATORS	Origin/start date Numbers of MFIs/operators (most recent date) Types (banks, non-banking financial institutions, government bodies, NGOs, support organizations, co-operatives, others) What is their mission? (Social microcredit, microcredit for enterprise development, support services, and so on) Legal forms Ownership structure (public, private, mainly public, mainly private) Territorial penetration (national, regional, provincial) Target groups (rural population, urban population, unemployed people or people on welfare, women, ethnic minorities and/or migrants, youth, disabled people, people excluded from mainstream financial services, no client-specific targeting, others) Microcredit/Microfinance institutions' critical points/areas

Continued

Table 1.1   continued

MICROCREDIT GUARANTEE FUNDS/ INSTITUTIONS: MAIN FEATURES	Number and types of guarantee funds/ institutions and their development in recent years Type/nature of the mitigation instruments offered and their compliance with Basel II framework Issuers/lenders of microcredit funds Beneficiaries/client targeting Type of businesses supported Percentage of coverage Leverage ratio Guarantee granting process (how many subjects are involved, timing of lending, costs, etc.) Creditworthiness analysis and business idea feasibility: absence/presence of a credit scoring model (who does it, how, when) Guarantee management: sponsorship, financial education, monitoring, reporting, other complementary and collateral guarantee services (who, when and how implemented? What are the related costs?) Statistics of the guarantee funds: – Volume of the guarantees granted; numbers of beneficiaries/projects – Average amount of lending; average default rate recorded Fees/interests charged by micro-lenders; guarantee fees, repayment rate, etc. Costs and benefits analysis of the guarantee funds: sustainability

The book is structured in five chapters.

In the second chapter, we analyse the regulatory framework and the supervisory authorities in the microcredit sector in each country. In fact, according to the logic scheme used, the analysis of each country kicked off with the investigation area dedicated to the *Regulatory Framework and Supervisory Authority in the Microcredit Sector,* as it undoubtedly influences the legal and institutional layout of microcredit programmes and defines both the scope of operation and the technical and legal characteristics of the mitigation tools provided. In fact, the microcredit/ microfinance system requires a legislative and normative framework, which corresponds to the State legislative power, where an interaction and cooperation process between the public, financial and business sectors should take place. Chapter 2 ends with a comparative analysis of the microfinance/microcredit regulatory frameworks in the selected countries.

In Chapter 3, we provide a mapping of the different microcredit/ microfinance institutions in each country. In fact, according to the logic scheme used in this research, the investigation area dedicated *Mapping Microcredit/Microfinance institutions/operators* aims to provide mapping of the number, types, legal status, ownership structure and structural information of the microcredit institutions system in each country. This chapter ends with some reflections on the different intermediation models related to microcredit guarantee funds.

Chapter 4 is dedicated to the analysis of the main operational features of the guarantee funds in a number of microcredit programmes. This chapter, which relates to our investigation area dedicated *Microcredit guarantee funds,* as underlined before is meant to whereas microcredit programmes activated by the various MFIs are exposed to credit risk, it is important to understand the main operational features of the guarantee funds in the microcredit programmes of each country. This chapter is thus devoted to highlight the key operational features of the guarantee funds, providing a comparative analysis between them.

In Chapter 5, based on the results of the analysis conducted, we offer some reflections on the conditions for expanding the "future of sustainable microfinance" in these Mediterranean countries. We address the necessity of guarantee funds as a response to the trade-off between the promotion of policies that facilitate access to credit for the poor and "non-bankable" subjects and the risk profile reduction of the corresponding portfolios. This final chapter contains a number of suggested actions, policies and strategies to be implemented to promote the development of sustainable microcredit in other European or African countries.

Notes

* Although both authors have prepared the chapter jointly, Pasqualina Porretta has written sections 1.1 to 1.5, whereas Paola Leone and Porretta have written section 1.5.

1. Nobel Prize laureate Muhammad Yunus, who invented microfinance, was here last year when he received the Four Freedoms Award from the Roosevelt Foundation. In the 1970s, Professor Yunus was working at the Chittagong University in Bangladesh. At that time, he started experimenting with providing small loans to the people in the villages surrounding the university. In 1976, he started the now renowned Grameen Bank with help from the government. The goal was simple: providing small loans to the very poor. Regular banks would not grant such loans because they considered them too risky – poor people typically lack collateral – and too costly. The small scale

of the loans and high monitoring costs for each loan typically do increase operational costs.

2. For a definition of financial exclusion see: http://www.european-microfinance. org/index.php?rub=microfinance-in-europe&pg=microfinance-and-financial-exlusion.

3. Definition of Microenterprise: http://europa.eu/legislation_summaries/enterprise/business_environment/n26026_en.htm. The European Commission considers as micro-enterprises any businesses with fewer than 10 employees and a turnover under 2,000,000 EUR. Adopted by the European Commission on 1 January 2005, in EC Recommendation Article 2 of annexed recommendation 2003/361/CE.

4. Definition of social exclusion: http://www.european-microfinance.org/index.php?rub=microfinance-in-europe&pg=microfinance-and-social-exclusion. Definition of financial exclusion: http://www.european-microfinance. org/index.php?rub=microfinance-in-europe&pg=microfinance-and-social-exclusion.

5. The concept of credit risk in the microcredit and microfinance world as well as in traditional finance, refers to the possibility that an unexpected variation of the creditworthiness of a given party, which has been granted some credit, generates an unexpected corresponding variation of the value of the credit position itself. This definition includes both the possibility that the counterparty may become insolvent and, therefore, could be unable to fulfil its financial obligations, and also possible variations of its creditworthiness. Compared to traditional financing practices, the difference here is that microcredit attributes a greater importance to the probability of default of a given counterparty, rather than the deterioration of its creditworthiness.

6. For an in-depth analysis of the different types of mutual credit guarantee schemes in a number of countries in Europe and Latin America, see Porretta, P., Leone, P. (2012), pp. 147–86.

7. BCBS (2006), International Convergence of Capital Measurement and Capital Standards: A Revised Framework – Comprehensive Version, June, http://www.bis.org/publ/bcbs128.htm.

8. These are international agreements relating to the suitability of capital allocations of banking and credit companies against the risks undertaken. The agreement is structured on three pillars: the first relates to the minimum capital requirements, which must cover the unexpected losses related to credit risk, market risk and operative risk; the second relates to prudential control aimed at assessing suitability of capital allocations; finally, the third is related to the discipline and regulations of the market and the transparency of the bank's risk profile (BCBS, 2006).

2
Regulatory Framework and Supervisory Authorities in Microcredit Sector: A Comparative Analysis

Paola Leone, Fabio Massimo Mango, Ida C. Panetta and Pasqualina Porretta*

2.1 Regulatory Framework and Supervisory Authorities in Morocco

The microcredit system in Morocco is considered one of the best and most advanced in all North Africa. It is regulated by Law No. 18–97 (published in the *Official Gazette* of 1 April 1999), whose art. 1 establishes: "Microcredit associations are those created in compliance with the provisions of Dahir No. 1–58–376 of 3 January (15 November 1958), which regulates the right of association aimed at providing micro-loans". Articles 2 and 3 of Law No. 18–97:

- Define micro-loans as loans granted to economically disadvantaged individuals and aimed at starting or supporting enterprises, achieving thus their economic inclusion (art. 2);
- Set the maximum amount of micro-loans (established with special decree) in the amount of 50,000 Dirhams (DH, around 5,000 USD, art. 2);
- Establish that non-profit associations created pursuant the 1958 Dahir Act are entitled to engage in the microcredit business;
- All microcredit associations must be authorised by the Ministry of Finance to carry out the microcredit business as well as all complementary and instrumental activities, such as training, technical support and assistance, but they cannot engage in traditional banking services by receiving public money on current account, savings or

similar (in accordance with article 2 of the Dahir No. 1–93–147 of 6 July 1993).

The by-laws of any microcredit association (art. 5 of Law No. 18–97) must explicitly state that the sole purpose of the association is to carry out operations under articles 1 and 2 of the Law No. 18/97 and that microcredit must be provided without any sort of discrimination; that human and financial resources must be sufficient to pursue the association's business purpose; that its members do not intend to carry out any kind of political or union activity through the association.

Art. 5 of the Law No. 18–97 also states that the associations' development plan, the provision of micro-loans and their distribution among urban areas must be compatible with the national programmes of economic and social integration of low-income segments of the population. Associations involved in microcredit must achieve their financial independence and sustainability within the first five years of activity (art. 6) and carry out their business in a transparent way. In addition, they must: (1) create a mandatory (art. 14) internal supervisory committee entrusted with monitoring the activity and preparing an annual report; (2) inform the general public of terms and conditions applicable to microcredit operations, notably with regard to interest rates, commissions and fees charged to the borrowers. The above information must be clearly displayed at their premises (art. 9).

Looking at the provisions of this normative framework, it appears that microcredit is strictly regulated also with regard to some areas that, generally speaking, involve the associations' management strategies and internal policies. Art. 8 of Law No. 18–97 specifically indicates that the maximum and minimum interest rates applied to the micro-loans must be established by a specific decree of the Ministry of Finance after consultation with the Microcredit Advisory Committee. To date, however, despite over 17 years having passed from such provision, the Microcredit Advisory Committee and the Ministry of Finance have not yet issued any regulations on the matter; therefore, Moroccan MFIs are free to carry out their microcredit operations by applying interest rates following the most appropriate market trends. The Microcredit Advisory Committee, created by the same Law on microcredit (art. 19), is a consulting-only body; it offers advice and opinions on the main issues related to microcredit activities and operations, issues recommendations to the Ministry of Finance on the authorisation or revocation of licenses to operate in the microcredit sector and offers consulting services on accounting and prudential regulations of the microcredit associations.

The Ministry of Finance, following a consultation with the Microcredit Advisory Committee, establishes the minimum size of assets and liabilities for the microcredit associations (art. 16). The Moroccan MFIs carry out microcredit by financing themselves through one of the methods under art. 10 of Law No. 18–97 (Table 2.1): donations or public or private contributions, loans, interests and commissions charged on the micro-loans, funds made available under partnership agreements signed with central government authorities, agencies or local authorities, profits generated from financial investments made through available funds, and reimbursement of funds allocated. An additional funding source of the Moroccan MFIs is provided by art. 11 of the law (Table 2.1), which establishes that they can raise funds, without prior authorisation by the Ministry of Finance, by appealing to public generosity. However, the Ministry of Finance must be notified of conditions, circumstances and outcomes of any such appeal.

Article 21 of Law No. 18–97 lays out some provisions on the organisational structure of the MFIs in Morocco; it establishes, in fact, that Moroccan MFIs are to join the Federation of Microcredit Associations, a trade association entrusted with the functions of: establishing rules of conduct for the microcredit sector prior to authorisation of the Ministry of Finance; ensuring compliance with laws and regulations by its associates, including decrees and executive provisions; informing the Ministry of Finance of any violations of the above; issuing recommendations to the Ministry of Finance on actions to be promoted for developing the microcredit industry; appointing its representatives on the Microcredit Advisory Committee; designing and managing services for the development of microcredit (art. 23).

Moreover, article 26 of Law No. 18–97 provides that, in the event of liquidation of a microcredit association, the net proceeds of the liquidation shall be transferred to the government, which shall assign it to another association with the same purpose.

Table 2.1 Funding sources of the MFIs in Morocco according Law No. 18–97

Registered capital
Donations or public and private contributions
Public resources made available under partnership agreements, bilateral or
   multi-lateral cooperation agreements
Resources obtained from the reimbursement of the micro-loans granted
Loans with banks and financial institutions
Profits generated from financial investments made through available funds
Appeals to public generosity

Bank Law No. 34/03 of 14 February 2006 also regulates microfinance activity by banks and similar financial institutions (B.O. No. 5400, 2 March 2006); art. 53, para. 4 of that law establishes that all microcredit associations are subject to the supervisory and regulatory powers of the Central Bank (*Bank Al-Maghrib*), which is responsible for ensuring that all banks and financial institutions abide by the law, including executive regulations. The Central Bank also verifics the adequacy of their administrative, accounting and auditing systems through periodic inspections, requests for documentation, and useful information to be supplied for monitoring and control purposes (art. 54). Results and performances of microcredit activities are communicated to the Microcredit Advisory Committee. The microcredit associations must submit their financial statements to the Central Bank, according to terms and conditions set forth by the latter, as well as all documents (budget, and so on) and pieces of information needed for a comprehensive monitoring.

Law No. 58–03 of 6 May 2004 extended the application of the legislation on microcredit to loans granted for social housing and funding of work needed for connection to the national water supply and electricity networks. In 2007, a bill (Law No. 04/07) was passed to further extend the scope of the legislation to the marketing of insurance products and services (*micro-insurance*). In addition, a bill passed in 2010 (No. 53) established that microcredit can be carried out both directly by microcredit associations and indirectly through holdings in banks; it also issued provisions on methods and terms to be followed in case of mergers between microcredit associations.

In the analysis carried out, we did not find any specific regulations on guarantee funds supporting microcredit.

This initial overview of the normative framework of the microcredit in Morocco highlights some precise choices made by the national legislators, and specifically:

• Microcredit activity is limited to non-profit associations. This choice has some pros and cons; if, in fact, this legal form allows carrying out microcredit activity without the need to comply with the numerous legal and administrative requirements and constraints faced by financial intermediaries, on the other side, it prevents microfinance associations from accessing important funding sources available on the market and from carrying out traditional banking by receiving deposits from the general public (as previously highlighted, raising funds through appeals to the public generosity is strictly regulated);

- Microcredit development programmes of each MFI must be structured and implemented within the "perimeter" and in accordance with the national economic and social integration programmes;
- The choice of the regulators to prevent microcredit associations from carrying out traditional banking activity, such as deposits from the public, also restricts their chances of funding and performing proper brokerage activities;
- Microcredit in Morocco is a strictly regulated sector, although a number of legal provisions of Law No. 18–97 have not been followed by executive decrees (e.g., maximum applicable interest rates). The regulators adopted a typical structural approach, as they intended to establish the operational structure of the whole microcredit sector and the minimum capital requirements in relation to the size of MFIs. Finally, microcredit is subject to monitoring and control activity by several entities that have different functions and responsibilities:
- The Central Bank exercises inspection, information and sanctioning powers;
- The Ministry of Finance regulates the whole sector, including issuance of licenses and authorisations to operate, approval of the MFIs' by-laws and charters and their modifications, including the Federation of Microcredit Associations, and replacement and suspension of the microcredit associations' managers due to serious misconduct, appointment of liquidators, etc;
- The Federation of Microcredit Associations ensures its associates' compliance with the law and informs the Ministry of Finance of any violations;
- The Microcredit Advisory Committee, a consulting-only body, supports the regulatory and supervisory activity carried out on the industry by the Ministry of Finance.

2.2   Regulatory Framework and Supervisory Authorities in Tunisia

Microfinance in Tunisia was created and developed as a tool to fight poverty. These origins determined also its objectives: to improve the living conditions of the poor through income generated by activities supported by microcredit; to halt the rural exodus and depopulation of regions; to stimulate entrepreneurship and disseminate the "culture" of work as an "engine" for sustainable socioeconomic growth; to facilitate access to the credit system by non-bankable subjects; to promote social and economic integration of the poor. Operators/Institutions regard the

Tunisian microfinance system as one of the most advanced in North Africa, after Morocco's.

In Tunisia, Law No. 99–67 primarily sets forth the general rules for the exercise of microcredit. In particular, article 1 defines microcredit as those credit activities aimed at socioeconomic integration: loans granted to fund the purchase of material goods, capital goods, production goods or goods needed to improve social living conditions. The maximum amount of the micro-loans as well as conditions and terms for their provision are established by decree of the Ministry of Finance.

Article 2 of the aforementioned law identifies the following micro-credit beneficiaries: (1) subjects with the capacity to carry out economic activities who belong to needy families or vulnerable groups; (2) unqualified subjects who do not receive any salary and are able to carry out economic activities, professions or jobs in the agricultural sector.

Micro-loans are granted by associations created in accordance with Law No. 59–154 (art. 3), which cannot engage in traditional banking by receiving money from the general public on current deposits or savings, and therefore are not subject to regulations governing the activity of bank intermediaries (art. 4). These associations can grant micro-loans only when they are expressly authorised by the Ministry of Finance, which approves their requests provided the associations meet a number of specific requirements (art. 6): human and financial resources of the associations must be sufficient to achieve the objectives set, credit strategies must be compatible with national and regional programmes and policies for socioeconomic development. Microcredit providers finance their activity through the following channels (art. 9): public funds made available under partnership/microcredit programmes with public institutions/associations, public and private donations, resources from bilateral and multi-lateral cooperation programmes, interests/commissions from microcredit activities, sums collected from the recovery of micro-loans (Table 2.2).

The microcredit associations authorised to provide micro-lending must inform the public of terms and conditions applied to the micro-loans, mainly through prospectuses available at their offices (article 8).

The associations are subject to control and monitoring by the Ministry of Finance, which may revoke their authorisations to exercise the activity in the event of gross misconduct or failure to comply with the Law (article 12–14).

Ministerial Decree of 27 August 1999 established a maximum limit (5%) to the annual interest rate applicable by the associations authorised to provide micro-loans, which may also charge a commission of 2.5% on the

Table 2.2 Funding sources of the MFIs in Tunisia legislative according to decree No. 117/2001

Registered capital
Funds made available under agreements and contracts for microcredit
    programmes with companies, governments, public bodies or local government
    authorities
Resources from bilateral or multi-lateral cooperation programmes
Resources obtained from the repayment of the micro-loans granted
Loans in Tunisian dinars with banks
Funds from shareholders holding more than 10% of the capital for public
    companies subject to provisions of the Code of Commercial Companies
Yields on bonds and treasury bills, equity
Other resources from investments in private equity funds

---

amount of the credit granted. Such conditions are mandatory for micro-loans provided under the financing scheme promoted by the Tunisian Solidarity Bank (one of the main MFIs in the country). A following Ministerial Decree of 29 September 2010 cancelled these provisions.

In January 2011, a civil revolution ended 20 years of dictatorship in Tunisia. Government authorities, donors and MFIs then started to reconsider the logic underlying the traditional microcredit sector in the country (strong centralisation, strong public control), resulting in the creation of a number of smaller MFIs totally independent from public contributions and able to provide a restricted range of services (with the exception of ENDA). This process led to a new reference legislation approved in October 2011, accompanied by a new national strategy for microfinance development (Ministry of Finance, 2011).

The regulatory framework at issue (Legislative Decree No. 117/2011) introduced special provisions dedicated to activities carried out by microfinance associations (according to article 1 of the legislative decree, these are subjects performing operations authorised in accordance with the decree itself as their core business). In particular, the decree

- Establishes that microcredit associations must have a share capital no lower than three millions TND. Article 2 of Legislative Decree No. 117 recognises also those associations with an initial share capital of 200,000 TND regulated by Legislative Decree No. 2011–88 of 24 September 2011;
- Establishes that microcredit associations cannot engage in traditional banking activity by receiving money from the general public on current deposits or savings;

- Establishes that in the event of liquidation of a microcredit association, its board must indicate a subject to be assigned the remaining amounts following liquidation, namely associations with similar purposes that may be indicated in the association by-laws/charters;
- Establishes a number of provisions on methods and requirements to hold shares in other microfinance associations and in case of mergers;
- Provides for a number of mandatory standards in regard to internal governance and auditing of the microcredit associations;
- Sets out some mandatory requirements for the disclosure of the conditions applied to the micro-loans;
- Provides detailed provisions for the composition of the sources that can be used by microfinance associations to fund their activity (cf. Table 2.2);
- Establishes (article 7) that the maximum import of micro-loans is to be set forth by a memorandum of the Ministry of Finance;[1]
- Allows microfinance associations to operate, under certain terms and conditions, as agents of insurance companies;
- Establishes that microfinance associations must create and adhere to a microcredit trade association, aimed at representing their general interests and carrying out studies and researches on the sector as well as preparing a code of conduct for all its members and ensuring its correct application;
- Creates a regulatory and supervisory authority for the microcredit sector operating under the Ministry of Finance.

This new regulatory framework should be fully implemented in the years to come, leading thus to the passage from a traditionally conceived microcredit sector to a microfinance system designed and managed through the collaboration of national and international actors, allowing microcredit associations to engage also in other financial and management services (besides their traditional microcredit activity).

These initial reflections on the regulatory framework of the microcredit industry in Tunisia highlight the following: microcredit is limited to associations whose legal form, governance and auditing methods, funding sources and operational areas are strictly regulated by the reference legislation and dependent on the government policies on the sector. Microcredit associations cannot exercise traditional banking activities, such as receiving money from the general public on current deposits or savings, but they can operate as agents of insurance companies.

Microcredit in Tunisia is subject to the control and monitoring carried out by a number of subjects having different functions and responsibilities (Ministry of Finance, 2011, p. 42): the Central Bank (with inspection, information and sanction powers), the Ministry of Finance (with powers to regulate the industry, issue authorisations to operate, approve by-laws/charters and their modifications, and so on), the microcredit supervisory authority (with advisory, supervisory, sanctioning, and informational powers on the sector). Finally, the microcredit trade association ensures compliance to the regulatory framework by its members and informs the Ministry of Finance of any violations.

2.3 Regulatory Framework and Supervisory Authorities in Egypt

Microcredit in Egypt developed in the late 1980s[2] with the objective of ensuring access to credit to those micro and small enterprises (MSEs, Micro and Small enterprises) excluded from the traditional financial system. Since then, and even today, no substantial regulatory framework has been issued for the microfinance industry, in general, and, specifically, for microcredit. The regulations followed by the operators in the sector, mainly NGOs and banks, are constituted by a group of primary (and secondary) pieces of legislation that regulate the single categories of subjects falling under certain legal-institutional forms rather than specifically focusing on microcredit. The Table 2.3 shows the reference legislation for each type of operators in the industry, namely banks, NGOs and Microfinance Enterprise Service Companies.

Just five banks provide microcredit in Egypt; they are mainly government-owned, and microcredit is not their core business but only provided

Table 2.3 Type of MFIs and reference normative in Egypt

Typology of Active MFIs in Egypt	MFIs' Legal-institutional Forms	Reference Normative
Banks	Commercial banks and Specialised Banks	Law No. 88/2003, so-called Bank Law, and its Executive Regulations
NGOs	Foundations and Associations	Law No. 84/2002, so-called NGO Law, and its Executive Regulations
Microfinance Enterprise Service Companies	Commercial companies	Law No. 159/1981, so-called Companies Law, and its Executive Regulations

as a secondary activity. From a regulatory standpoint, they are subject to the so-called Bank Law (No. 88/2003 as subsequently amended) as well as other secondary regulations, which never expressly refer to microcredit in any way. Despite the multiple criticisms (see Abdel-Baki et al., 2010; EFSA, 2010; PlaNet Finance, 2008) about the scarce activity of these banks in the provision of microcredit, there is a lack of incentives for developing this business, given the small returns it offers; only recently, the Central Bank of Egypt (CBE) has sought to stimulate the provision of loans to SMEs, by exempting bank loans granted to them from the loan loss reserve requirement (14%) and reducing the funding cost of 1.5%;[3] however, these measures, de facto, do not cover loans granted to micro-businesses (micro-enterprises and individuals) and as a result, they're ineffective for encouraging banks to extend their activities in the microfinance sector.

Instead, NGOs are more active in the microcredit industry; framework Law No. 84/2002, the so-called NGO Law, regulates the activity of organisations providing community development services; there is, therefore, no differentiation between NGOs operating in the microcredit business and NGOs operating in other sectors. Although NGOs generally enjoy some privileges, such as tax exemptions (including custom duties), they face a number of tight operational restrictions that limit their development in the microcredit sector[4] (see Chemonics International Inc. and CGAP, 2009).

Finally, since 2007, two service companies were established to offer microcredit in cooperation with private sector banks; these companies act as agents for banks and other financial institutions (e.g., insurance companies) to provide microfinance services.

The same kind of fragmentation can be observed with regard to the supervisory authorities in the industry: as there is no specific legislation dedicated to the microcredit industry, the supervisory authorities are those established by the law for each type of institution, as shown by Table 2.4.

The result of such fragmentation is that different types of MFIs operate following different rules, without an adequate level-playing field; this does not favour a sufficient degree of competition between microcredit providers that might result in real benefits for the micro-borrowers.

Table 2.4 MFIs and supervisory authorities in Egypt

Typology of Active MFIs in Egypt	Supervisory Authority
Banks	Central Bank of Egypt (CBE)
NGOs	Ministry of Social Solidarity (MSS)

Operators, in fact, according to their legal "form", enjoy totally different and profoundly uneven benefits – including tax breaks – and operating costs.

The picture of the sector in Egypt highlighted so far is evidence of a lag in defining a regulatory framework that may contribute to the development of microfinance and microcredit in the country; it should also be noted that the last years saw the start of a process of reform and improvement of the microcredit sector, partly delayed by the civil unrest, which began in spring 2010. This process was driven by the impulse of a number of international agencies (UNDP, USAID and KfW) that, through CBE (involved through its affiliate, the Egyptian Banking Institute) and the Social Fund of Development,[5] contributed to define *The National Strategy for Microfinance*[6] for Egypt in December 2005. It is a roadmap that policymakers can use to reform the industry, by trying to encourage institutions to adopt management models more apt to market logics, abandoning the traditional system relying on national and foreign aid. This strategy includes a number of specific proposals, structured on three levels, aimed at removing obstacles and criticalities detected in the microcredit sector (see Table 2.5).

Table 2.5 The National Strategy for Microfinance development in Egypt: Objectives by levels

Level	Focus	Objectives
Micro Level	The micro level aims to improve the institutional capacity of the MFIs to reach out to more clients	To promote the development of a diverse range of sustainable MFIs that may compete and offer various effective financial services to micro-enterprises and the poor and cater to evolving market demand
Meso Level	The meso level, engaged in the creation of a supporting information infrastructure, technical assistance and funding mechanisms	To support sound functioning of existing apex institutions and National Guarantee Mechanisms
Macro Level	The macro level, focusing on the policy and regulatory interventions needed to create a fertile environment for MFIs' growth	To develop a policy and regulatory environment leading to an inclusive financial system that encourages microfinance growth and development

Some of the proposals advanced under this strategy have been adopted by policymakers and a number of government agencies (for instance, the Social Development Fund; see EBI and SFD 2005, p. 16.), but much remains to be done. Despite the suggestions to improve the regulatory framework (macro level), few of them have been actually implemented. One of the measures worth mentioning, under the broader programme of modernisation of Egypt, is the reform of the bank system supervisors. Law No. 10/2009, in fact, permanently assigned regulation and supervision of the banking system to the *Central Bank of Egypt* (CBE), while the entire non-banking financial Sector falls under the regulatory powers of the Egyptian Financial Supervisory Authority (EFSA), which originated from the union of the Insurance Supervisory Authority, the Capital Market Authority and the Mortgage Finance Authority.

Law 10/2009 also entrusted the EFSA with the task of drafting a set of executive rules[7] to license and regulate all non-banking financial activities, including microfinance providers.

In 2010, as a matter of fact, the EFSA issued the General Rules for Microfinance Companies; it is the first actual attempt to provide a definitive regulatory framework to the sector. However, probably because of Egyptian political disorder, these rules are still at a "proposal" stage; therefore, all the above comments on their content may be subject to changes and modifications when the rules are finally approved.

The regulatory proposals at issue were advanced with the aim of:

- Developing professional performance standards in the microfinance sector in Egypt in line with international standards;[8]
- Attracting an increasing number of service providers in the industry as well as international companies interested in improving access to funding for micro-enterprises;
- Helping fill the gap in the supply of financial services and products for micro-enterprises and low-income individuals;
- Increasing access to financial services and instruments specifically dedicated to low-income individuals.

The starting point of such proposal revolves around the definition of the scope and activity of the so-called microfinance companies (MFC): with the exception of collecting deposits from the general public, foreign exchange transactions and remittance services, the proposed regulations allow MFCs "to provide credit, directly or indirectly through agents, to single individuals, with or without collaterals" (art. 2); in addition, these subjects may also provide banking services other than microcredit, provided they comply with regulations and requirements established for the single activities (for instance, *insurance law* in case of micro-insurance, *leasing law* in case of micro-leasing).

For such purpose, these rules provide for a number of specific requirements aimed at ensuring sound and prudent management practices for microcredit operators, in line with the best international practices; in particular, such requirements are to be applied to credit risk management throughout its life cycle. When assessing creditworthiness, for example, in addition to the requirements in terms of transparency and compliance with the Consumer Protection Law (Law No. 67 of 2006), the above rules also impose the use of the Credit Bureau database; as we can read in the recommendations, such a provision is aimed not just at facilitating the assessment of customer creditworthiness, but also at avoiding customers reaching inadequate levels of debt (known as "over-indebtedness").[9]

As for the loans, the rules provide for limits for the concentration of credit risk: a maximum of 5% of the equity for single financial position and a maximum amount no greater than 500,000 EGP for individual loans.

At the preliminary stage, these regulations set a time frame and methods for adequate credit assessment as well as all necessary financial provisions to preserve the soundness of the MFCs. From an examination of the draft rules (Annex V), it can also be observed:

- Great attention is dedicated to methods for determining profits, in order to avoid paying dividends before providing adequate coverage to expected losses;
- A particular focus is put on accounting methods and procedures for expected and effective losses and other credit dysfunctions, by explicitly indicating deduction percentages of the values entered in the balance sheet as well as the amount of the provisions needed in the accounts according to the days of delayed payment (Annex V).

In addition, the legislation establishes that the supervisory authority must assess credit management policies and the relevant procedures in place at the associations as well as the organisation of their internal bodies in charge of it.

In terms of capital requirements, no mention is made of minimum capital required to operate or other requirements against the risk assumed; there is, instead, a specific reference to the necessity of avoiding that employees may assume the role of lenders; at the same time, cross-shareholding between MFCs is strongly discouraged, or at least strictly monitored.[10]

In general, the MFCs must have an adequate management and control system following international standards and their balance sheets, and external auditors must also audit accounting documents. Among the auditing certification requirements are:

* Assessment of business risk exposure, with specific reference to credit risk, liquidity risk, fraud and exchange rates;
* Verification of the functionality of the internal control system;
* Verification of capital allocation policies and their adequacy for protection against losses.

In order to improve the accountability of the operations, and favouring the EFSA effective supervision, the legislation at issue provides for a number of strict disclosure requirements, in terms of content and timing of information (including calculation methods of the indicators required) to be provided to third parties. It is clear here that the regulator has appropriately taken into account the best practices already followed by the major NGOs, which conversely follow the best accounting standards established by CGAP[11] best practice.

The proposed regulations undoubtedly represent a step forward in the consolidation process of the microcredit industry, yet delays in their implementation do not allow obtaining a clear and definite picture of the operators in the industry, especially of NGOs. At the time of publication of the draft, the NGOs, especially the big ones, are involved in an assessment process aimed at changing their legal form into MFCs in order to:

* Diversify the services offered in the microfinance sector, in addition to microcredit;
* Increase their funding sources using both equity and borrowing also on international markets;[12]
* Overcome the strict requirements on governance and management of the NGOs operating in the industry.[13]

According to the Draft General Rules for Microfinance Companies, there are no provisions that seem to prevent such transformation process, mainly because no specific legal form is established for the creation of the MCFs. Yet, we think that within the adoption of the guidelines set forth by this proposal, it is necessary to set a number of regulatory measures that clearly define the NGOs' transformation process into MCFs, including their obligations and requirements as entities subject to the EFSA supervisory authority.

The proposed regulations still do not provide a univocal definition of microcredit: to date, they generally refer to lending granted to low-income subjects, the poor, micro-enterprises and SMEs, but they do not set a quantity parameter that clearly defines the size of the micro-loans.

Since 2004, the Small Enterprise Development Law (Law 141/2004, so-called MSE Law) has provided a specific definition of micro-enterprises, among the main beneficiaries of the micro-loans; the MSE law, in fact, makes a distinction between micro-enterprises, with a paid-up share capital of less than 50,000 EGP (around 5,500 EUR) and small enterprises, with a paid-up share capital between 50,000 and 1,000,000 EGP (around 110,000 EUR) and fewer than 50 employees.

Such distinction was necessary to identify the so-called MSEs enjoying different forms of public incentives, including microcredit lines. Among the privileges granted to the MSEs by the law, the following are relevant for our purposes:

- Local funds: to be established at governorate level by using multiple sources of financing[14] to extend financial services through NGOs to MSEs (SME aw, art. 5);
- Credit guarantees: SFD's credit guarantees facilitating MSEs' access to funding (SME Law, art. 9).

With specific regard to guarantee funds, it should be noted that Egypt has not completed yet the compliance process with the standards under the Basel II[15] agreement started in 2009; therefore, to this day, the guarantee requirements that banks must follow to obtain savings in terms of capital assume a more limited weight if compared to other countries. The examination of the normative does not reveal any specific or explicit provisions regulating such guarantees.

2.4   A comparative analysis of Morocco, Tunisia and Egypt

The analysis carried out so far shows several similarities between the microcredit regulatory frameworks in Morocco and Tunisia, while Egypt is characterised by different features if compared to the other two. In Egypt, as seen above, there is no univocal legislative framework regulating microfinance in general, and, specifically, microcredit; there are only some regulations governing the activity of a variety of subjects, which are entitled to provide micro-loans under different conditions and requirements. This regulatory fragmentation can be found also in the monitoring and control system of the sector: in the absence of specific regulations for microcredit, the supervisory authorities too are those provided for each type of institution.

However, a profound reform of the microcredit industry in Egypt is currently under way, mainly thanks to the impulse of a number of international agencies (UNDP, USAID and KfW), partly delayed by the civil disorders of the 2010 spring. There is a proposal for microcredit regulation that is undoubtedly a step forward in the industry consolidation process, yet the delays in adopting such regulations prevent us from having a clear and definite picture on the future of the institutions operating in the microcredit business.

As seen above, Morocco and Tunisia have instead similar regulatory frameworks of the sector. Both countries introduced microcredit with specific laws with the aim of creating a new microcredit sector serving low-income population segments.

For both the above North African countries, we can say that their legislators chose a structural approach to regulate the whole sector, as they provided a great detail of provisions on the sector operational structure and established strict limits for the provision of microcredit as well as the minimum size of assets and liabilities of the MFIs. Finally, their microcredit is controlled and monitored by several subjects having different functions and responsibilities.

An initial comparative analysis between their regulatory frameworks (Table 2.6) seems to highlight the following:

- In neither of these two countries is there a clear distinction between social microcredit and microcredit aimed at promoting micro-entrepreneurship (the two purposes, on a normative level but also within the executive programmes, are often confused and overlapping);
- The microcredit sector features a "pyramidal" structure, with supervisory bodies at the top, followed by trade associations and, finally, microcredit associations/institutions;
- In both countries, microcredit activity is strictly regulated (even in a similar way): the legislation defines scope and activities of the intermediaries operating in the industry; their organisational structure and operations are specifically determined too; a number of authorities supervise and control the sector, although they overlap each other and are dispersed between various ministries and departments.

Table 2.6 Regulatory framework and supervisory authorities: Comparative analysis of Tunisia, Morocco and Egypt

	Morocco	Tunisia	Egypt
Specific microcredit regulations	**Dahir No. 1–58–376 15 November 1958** regulates the associative right **Law No. 19–97** (published in the Official Gazette of 01 April 1999) regulates microcredit **Law No. 58–03** (Dahir No. 1–04–12 of 21 April 2004) modifies art. 2 of Law No. 18–97 (Official Gazette of 2004–05–06, No. 5210, p. 667) **Law No. 04–07 of 30 November 2007** (Dahir No. 1–07–166 of 30 November 2007, (Official Gazette of 2007–12–06, No. 5584, p. 1368) modifies art. 2 and 3 of Law No. 18–97) **Project of Law N53–10 approved by the Cabinet of Ministers on 06 December 2011 modifying article 1 of Law No. 18–97** **Banking Law 34/03 of 14 February 2006** (art. 13 title I chap. 1) (art. 53, title 4) subjects and microcredit associations under the control of the central bank	**Law No. 99–67** defines the general conditions for the exercise of microcredit. **Ministerial Decree of 29 September 2010** abolishes the limit of 5% on interests applied to micro-loans **Legislative Decree No. 117/2011** introduces a series of reforms for the microcredit sector: governance system, control system, supervisory authority and relevant powers, and so on	The **Draft General Rules for Microfinance Companies** (2010)
Principal contents of regulation	**Law No. 19–97:** Chap. 1: definition of microcredit Chap. 2: conditions for the exercise of microcredit Chap. 3: the resources of microcredit associations Chap. 4: control and supervision of microcredit associations Chap. 5: the tax regime of the microcredit associations Chap. 6: the Microcredit Advisory Committee Chap. 7: the Federation of Microcredit Associations Chap. 8: sanctions **Law No. 58–03** extends the application of these regulations to mortgages for social housing and the financing of works to connect to the water and electricity networks	**Law No. 99–67** defines the general conditions for the exercise of microcredit: Art. 1: definition of microcredit Art. 2: beneficiaries Art. 3: microcredit providers (microcredit associations pursuant Law No. 59–154) **Ministerial Decree of 29 September 2010** abolishes the limit of 5% (2.5% flat rate) on interests applied to micro-loans (with the exception of loans granted under the BTS financing)	Main issues of **Draft General Rules for Microfinance Companies:** Art. 1: Institutionalization of Microfinance Companies Chap. 1: Permitted Financial Services and Operational Activities Chap. 2: Ownership and Governance

	Law No. 04-07 introduces micro-insurance The project of Law No. N53–10: Microcredit may be carried out directly by microcredit associations as well as indirectly through holdings into other credit institutions, new provisions regulating mergers between microcredit associations	Legislative Decree No. 117/2011 introduces the following reforms: 1) Anonymous companies with capital of more than 3 million TND may provide microcredit 2) Definition of governance standards, and so on 3) Creation of a specific supervisory authority 4) Increase of the maximum amount of micro-loans from 5,000 TND to 20,000 TND 5) Authorisation granted to microcredit associations to operate as insurance company agents	Chap. 3: Capital Requirements Chap. 4: Operational Limits Chap. 5: Reporting, Disclosure Requirements and Supervision Chap. 6: Registration
Specific supervisory authorities for MFIs	Central Bank has inspection, information and sanction powers The Ministry of Finances has the power to regulate the sector, issue authorisations to operate, approve by-laws/charters and their modifications, create and regulate the Federation of Microcredit Associations as well as relevant amendments, suspend managers of the microcredit associations for gross misconduct, appoint liquidating commissioners, and so on The Federation of Microcredit Associations ensures compliance with the regulatory framework by its associates and notifies the Ministry of Finance in case of any violations The Microcredit Advisory Committee has consulting-only functions; it provides support activities to the regulatory and supervisory activities performed by the Ministry of Finance on the sector	The Ministry of Finance, entrusted with supervisory powers on the sector Central Bank, which, under the new "concerted vision", performs control/supervisory activities Supervisory authority (Legislative Decree No. 117 2011 created a specific regulatory and supervisory authority, with advisory, information, supervisory and sanctionatory powers)	Egyptian Financial Supervisory authority – EFSA (established by Law No. 10 of 2009 for Regulation and Supervision of Non-Banking Financial Markets and Instruments) will be responsible for regulation, supervision for new microfinance companies
Regulation of guarantee funds	There is no general regulatory framework, only regulations related to specific guarantee funds	There is no general regulation, only regulatory provisions dedicated to specific guarantee funds	There is no specific regulation

- The strong centralisation and control of the sector by the government has led, in particular in Tunisia, to a fragmentation of the industry, a characteristic which clashes with the purpose of achieving its economic and financial balance; it also resulted in total dependence of microcredit providers on government support. Currently, at least in Tunisia, there is a profound and radical rethinking of strategies and actions for the microfinance sector, driven by new regulations that are seriously aimed at removing existing issues and criticalities;
- The regulatory frameworks at issue established some limits to the application of interest rates, which limits sustainability of MFIs, whose operative costs erode a large part of their profits and, therefore, the margins attainable within the microcredit business;
- There is no general legislation on microcredit guarantees, only regulatory prescriptions that define the operative methods of the single guarantee funds.

2.5   Regulatory Framework and Supervisory Authorities in Italy

In Italy, microfinance has recently been granted the status of "privileged institute" within Italy's economic development strategy, as highlighted by the regulations passed by the Italian government to tackle the effects of the economic and financial crisis on human capital (Decree-Law No. 185 of 29 November 2008 and Decree-Law No. 78 of 1 July 2009). In particular, the regulations at issue regard microcredit as a useful tool to start entrepreneurial activities, micro-businesses, and self-employment initiatives (art. 1 of the aforementioned Decree-Law No. 78/2009). Hence, the vision of the Italian policymakers is clear: microcredit is regarded as a welfare tool, finding its place both within policies aimed at stimulating micro-entrepreneurship and the creation of jobs as well as those promoting social inclusion.

In recent years, Italian policymakers have shown several encouraging signs directed at promoting effective policies and measures to support low-income individuals/families and poor segments of the population, especially through the creation of a Permanent National Committee for Microcredit[16] in 2006. This is a public entity entrusted with coordinating at a national level and whose objectives are to promote, direct, facilitate, assess and monitor the microfinance instruments promoted by the European Union as well as microfinance programmes financed through EU funds (Law No. 106 of 12 July 2011, art. 8, para. 4-bis section b). The committee supports initiatives aimed at fighting poverty and facilitating access to credit by social groups that are traditionally excluded from the financial and banking system, in Italy (domestic microfinance), in developing countries and in transition economies (microfinance for international cooperation). It operates to promote and monitor the microfinance instruments and products promoted by the EU as well as the microfinance programmes financed through EU funds.

A regulatory framework on microcredit has only recently been issued. An initial legislative decree was passed in August 2010 (Legislative Decree No. 141/2010) for the execution of Directive 2008/48/EC; this was followed by Legislative Decree No. 169/2012, still awaiting its executive decree. Said regulatory framework establishes a clear distinction between microcredit for social purposes and microcredit aimed at supporting micro-enterprises.

Article 111, first paragraph of Legislative Decree No. 385/1993, as amended by article 7 of Legislative Decree 141/2010, modified by article 3 of Legislative Decree No. 169/2012, establishes that microcredit can only be exercised by those subjects who are regularly registered in a specific roll regulated by article 113 of the Consolidated Law on Banking, which was also amended by the aforementioned Legislative Decree No. 141/2010 and then by article 3 of Legislative Decree No. 169/2012. The recent Legislative Decree No. 169/2012 replaced the registration requirement with the mandatory inclusion in the register of financial intermediaries under the supervision of the Bank of Italy, pursuant to the first paragraph of article 106 of the Consolidated Law on Banking. Microcredit providers must also be included in another specific register; these subjects may grant micro-loans to individuals, legal entities, simplified limited liability companies under article 2463-*bis* of the Civil Code (in accordance with Legislative Decree No. 169/2012), associations and cooperatives.

At present, also in light of the recently introduced regulations, these organisations seem to have been excluded from the group of potential micro-borrowers (Table 2.7):

Table 2.7 Potential microcredit recipients according to Italian regulation

	Included	Not Included
Microcredit for enterprises	Private partnerships Simplified limited liability companies Associations Cooperatives	Individuals
Microcredit for social purposes		Particularly vulnerable individuals

- Foundations, probably because these are basically regarded as "assets" dedicated to achieving a given purpose;
- Committees, probably because they are regarded as associative entities having a limited duration and pursuing specific objectives;
- Limited liability companies with reduced capital introduced by article 44 of Decree-Law No. 83 of 2012 (created by under-35 entrepreneurs and with a minimum share capital which can also be just one EUR), similar to the simplified limited liability companies reserved instead to over-35 members.

Paragraph No. 2 of article 111 of the Consolidated Law on Banking provides registration requirements for microcredit operators (Table 2.8):

- Legal form of joint-stock companies (joint-stock companies, limited liability companies, companies with unlimited responsibility) or cooperatives (originally this form was not included and was introduced by article 3 of Legislative Decree No. 169/2012);
- Paid-up capital no lower than the amount established by the Ministry of Economic Affairs, after consulting the Bank of Italy;
- Integrity requirements for the controlling or relevant shareholders and professional requirements for company managers according to the provisions set forth by the executive decrees that shall be issued by the Ministry of Economic Affairs after consulting the Bank of Italy;

Table 2.8 Registration requirements for Italian microcredit operators

Business purpose	Microcredit along with ancillary and instrumental activities
Legal form	Joint-stock companies, limited liability companies, companies with unlimited responsibility and cooperatives
Minimum paid-up share capital	Minimum capital requirement for joint-stock companies x 5 (600,000 EUR)
Possession of specific integrity and professional requirements for shareholders and managers	
Programme of activities must indicate the following	Characteristics of loans (economic conditions and terms, purposes, customers) Methods of payment and monitoring of the loans granted Subjects providing ancillary and instrumental activities and monitoring methods

- Business purpose limited to the provision of microcredit along with ancillary and instrumental activities;
- A programme of activities must be submitted. Article 111 of the Consolidated Law on Banking does not specify whether such programme must be presented just once, when the activity is started, or if it is a periodic programme; this aspect will be likely clarified by the executive regulations to be issued by the Ministry of Economic Affairs pursuant to paragraph 5 of the above article.

The first paragraph of article 111 of the Consolidated Law on Banking specifies that microcredit may be granted to support self-employment initiatives or micro-enterprises, namely entrepreneurial activities, and also, presumably (as the wording of the provision speaks of "self-employment") professions carried out in the form of sole companies, private partnerships or cooperatives, provided that the loans granted have the following characteristics:

- The amount of the micro-loans must be no greater than 25,000 EUR and they must not be secured by collaterals (pledges or mortgages). However, section b) of the fifth paragraph of article 111 of the Consolidated Law on Banking establishes that the executive regulations, which shall be issued by the Ministry for the Economy and Finance after consulting the Bank of Italy, may allow also for loans in amounts greater than 25,000 EUR in particular cases, where economic conditions and terms may be different from ordinary micro-loans. The bottom line is that there might be loans that will exceed the "micro" size;
- Loans must be granted to support the development of entrepreneurial activities or promote inclusion into the labour market. The latter seems to contrast with the provision, set by the first part of the article, according to which loans should be granted for "starting or exercising self-employed activities or micro-enterprises". Probably here the law refers to inclusion into the labour market as related to self-employed activities or professions, without including any kind of employment relationships, as it would appear from a first reading.
- Loans must be accompanied by ancillary, instrumental and monitoring activities of the borrowers.

The third paragraph of article 111 of the Consolidated Law on Banking establishes that all subjects operating in the microcredit sector may also grant, but only as a secondary activity compared to ordinary microcredit under the first paragraph of article 111 of the Consolidated Law on Banking, loans to individuals affected by particular conditions of social and economic vulnerability, provided that the loans do not exceed the maximum amount of 10,000 EUR. Also, loans must not be secured by collaterals (pledges or mortgages); they must be accompanied by the provision of ancillary and instrumental services to support family budgets. Loans are aimed at facilitating social and financial inclusion of the beneficiaries and are granted on conditions and terms that are more advantageous than those on the market, meaning average market conditions. Such loans must not exceed the number of ordinary loans, and their volume is calculated on the total amount of the sums lent through all micro-loans rather than the total number of loans provided. In any case, this aspect of microcredit should be regulated in detail by the executive regulations to be issued pursuant the fifth paragraph of the above article. Another grey area regards the reference to conditions and terms that are more advantageous than the average market standards; this aspect too should be clarified and specified by the executive provisions.

In this context, it should be emphasised that article 3 of Legislative Decree No. 169/2012 introduced the paragraph 3-*bis* into article 111 of the Consolidated Law on Banking, which reaffirmed the concept, already implicit in paragraph 3, that lending with the objective of supporting start-ups, self-employment initiatives or micro-enterprises and lending to individuals affected by particularly vulnerable conditions should be simultaneously carried out. This necessary implies that micro-loan providers cannot, therefore, specialise in only one of these activities. The same provision of Legislative Decree No. 169/2012 introduced also the fifth paragraph in article 111 of the Consolidated Banking Act, which specified that the use of the word 'microcredit' by operators (in their business name, signs and banners, business documents, web pages, and so on) is subject to the fact that operators carry out both activities while providing micro-loans: microcredit destined to micro-enterprises and self-employment initiatives and microcredit dedicated to social inclusion.

In addition, the amended fourth paragraph of article 111 of the Consolidated Banking Act provides that non-profit legal entities having the characteristics identified by the executive regulations to be issued by the Ministry for the Economy and Finance pursuant to paragraph 5 of the same article, may engage in microcredit provided to individuals affected by particularly vulnerable social or economic conditions by applying "adequate interest rates that allow just the recovery of the expenses met by the lender" (fourth paragraph of article 111 of the Consolidated Law on Banking as amended by article 3 of Legislative Decree No. 169/2012).

Micro-loans granted by non-profit entities, just like those granted by other microcredit providers, must not be secured by collaterals, should aim to facilitate social and financial inclusion of the borrowers and must be granted on more favourable terms and conditions than the average market conditions.

The wording – "non-profit legal entities" – applies first of all to all non-profit organisations, namely: associations (registered or non-registered), foundations and committees. The "content" of the aforementioned new provision would seem to include in the group of potential microcredit providers also cooperative societies (including, obviously, cooperatives pursuing social purposes) for, as it is known, they are non-profit organisations whose mutual purpose is to generate one or more economic benefits for their members other than profit: that is, the generation of dividends to be divided among the members or made available to single entrepreneurs. Nevertheless, this specific point should be clarified by the executive regulations still to come.

Mandatory requirement for exercising microcredit is the inclusion of the non-profit legal entities in the register/roll of microcredit providers according to the first paragraph of article 111 of the Consolidated Law on Banking and governed by the provisions of article 113 of the Consolidated Law on Banking, as integrated by article 3 of Legislative Decree No. 169/2012. The characteristics of these subjects shall be identified by the executive regulations to be issued by the Ministry of Economic Affairs pursuant paragraph 5 of the Consolidated Law on Banking, but in any case they must comply with the requirements of integrity and professionalism of their members and managers, as established always by the upcoming executive provisions.

The regulatory framework on microcredit also provides a specific definition of microcredit, including its objectives and the key operational features of the intermediaries/operators who are willing to associate the name "microcredit" with their operations. Moreover, the regulators have also differentiated and limited the scope of microcredit activities to lending with social purposes and lending dedicated to micro-enterprises.

Today, in the absence of executive decrees of the regulatory framework on microcredit, operators that qualify or call themselves, often improperly, "microcredit institutions", fall under different legal forms in the Italian legal system, with different social purposes and missions;

the lack of a precise framework for microcredit has so far resulted in the proliferation of a variety of entities/institutions that are often difficult to map.

The recent regulatory interventions seem to mark a moment of discontinuity from a recent past where the word 'microcredit' was used (and possibly abused) by a variety of financial intermediaries, and where such operators, which operate as intermediaries in the credit circuit, were not subject to any form of control and/or supervision.

When regulating the microcredit market, the regulators filled this, gap too; in fact, they created a supervisory system specifically dedicated to the microcredit industry, recognising its nature as a full intermediation system. In fact, the microcredit providers registry is kept by the Bank of Italy, in accordance with the provisions of article 113 of the Consolidated Law on Banking, as amended in section u) of article 3 of Legislative Decree No. 169/2012.

According to this article, the Bank of Italy manages the register under article 111 and supervises compliance with the law by all registered subjects, pursuant to article 111, paragraph 5. For such purpose, the Bank of Italy may:

- Require registered members to provide any necessary data and information as well as documents and resolutions, establish deadlines and carry out inspections;
- Remove registered subjects from the registry in the event that they do not follow registration requirements, or in case of serious violations of laws or regulations, including executive regulations, or when members have remained inactive for at least one year;
- In the event of violations of law or administrative provisions, impose a ban on the activity of the registered microcredit operators, preventing them from carrying out new operations or ordering them to scale down their business (paragraphs 2 and 3) (Table 2.9).

Furthermore, when the number of registered subjects is sufficient (although the provision does not specify the number), the Ministry for the Economy and Finance shall create with its own decree, after consulting the Bank of Italy, an authority entrusted with managing the register of microcredit providers as well as supervisory powers on the sector. The very same decree creating the above authority shall appoint its members.

The supervisory authority shall carry out any activity needed to manage the above register and be financed through the contributions

Table 2.9 Powers and functions of the Microcredit Supervisory Authority in Italy

---

Collection of contributions and other sums due for registration purposes

Monitoring compliance of its members to the regulatory provisions, also pursuant article 111, paragraph 5

Information functions and power to conduct inspections at the premises of the registered parties

Cancellation of the registered members from the registry in case of:
- Failure to comply with registration requirements
- Serious violations of the law and executive regulations of article 111 of the Consolidated Banking Act
- Failure to pay the contributions
- Prolonged inactivity of over a year

In case of serious violations of legal or administrative provisions, power to ban the registered subjects from carrying out new operations or impose a reduction of the volume of micro-loans granted (para. 4)

---

of its members not exceeding five per thousand of the amount of the micro-loans granted. In order to carry out its activities, the authority is entrusted with powers under paragraphs 1, 2 and 3, effective from the commencement of its operations.

The Bank of Italy will monitor the activity of this authority and, in case of inaction or malfunctioning of the same, it may recommend its dissolution to the Ministry for the Economy and Finance. The ministry, after consulting the Bank of Italy, will establish the authority's structure, powers and operational methods as well as the integrity and professionalism requirements for its members and criteria and methods for their appointment and replacement (para. 5).

At present, we are still waiting for the executive regulations to be issued by the Ministry for the Economy and Finance, after consulting the Bank of Italy, pursuant to paragraph 5 of article 111 of the Consolidated Law on Banking. The executive provisions will likely focus on (1) requirements for loan beneficiaries and technical forms of financing; (2) integrity requirements for the controlling or relevant shareholders of the microcredit providers as well as professional requirements for their managers; (3) minimum capital requirements for microcredit operators (amounts too high could discourage the creation of microcredit organisations, which might instead start as small associations or cooperatives); (4) clarifications of the methods and terms to be followed by microcredit providers in presenting their programme of activity; (5) objective limits of the volume of activity, economic terms and conditions applied to the single loans, including modifications to the limits of 25,000 and 10,000 EUR for each loan set forth by paragraph 1 section a, and paragraph 3; (6) key characteristics of non-profit subjects entitled to provide micro-loans pursuant to paragraph 4 of article 111; (7) structure, powers and operational methods of the supervisory authority and integrity and professionalism requirements of its members as well as criteria and methods for their appointment and replacement; (8) information to be provided to customers.

With regard to the guarantee funds operating in Italy (used in the microcredit industry, too), their regulation can be found within the legislation on prudential supervision of banks, *Credit Risk Mitigation, Bank of Italy Circular No 263* of 27 December 2006, Title II, chapter 2. In particular, the provisions of Title II, in determining the general and specific requirements of the credit risk mitigation instruments in order to be used for the capital loss absorption of banks, determine the operational and technical characteristics that guarantee funds (including those dedicated to microcredit) must possess in order to be more appealing for the banking sector. It should be noted that while all guarantee funds can provide access to credit to individuals affected by adverse socioeconomic conditions and/ or micro-enterprises, only some of them are eligible to be subject to the prudential regulations for banks and, therefore, suitable to provide the latter with savings in terms of capital against the micro-loans granted.

The *eligibility* of the guarantees must be assessed according to their legal-technical forms (direct/secondary, collateral/personal guarantees) and the approach used by the banks for calculating the mandatory capital absorption requirements for the credit risk related to micro-loans, in accordance with the legal provisions on *Credit Risk Mitigation*.

2.6   Regulatory Framework and Supervisory Authorities in Spain

In Spain, until 2009 the most important institutional supplier of microcredit to small firms was the banking system itself, with savings, commercial and microcredit banks being by far the main providers. Following the crisis of the savings bank, a limited number of banks are currently active in the microcredit market. These institutions cooperate with social and public entities as well as use their own networks or branches in the provision of loans, which enables the institutions to gain scale in their micro-lending activities.

From a regulatory standpoint, banks providing microcredit must meet all requirements under the Spanish banking legislation (regulation and supervision): transparency, minimum capital require-ments, reporting duties to banking authorities and other supervisory bodies, and so on (Law No. 9/2009). Such requirements find their justi-fication in two main objectives: ensure the soundness of the finan-cial market and protect the banks' clients and investors. Savings banks were an exception, as they used to provide microcredit through their foundations.

By referring to other entities providing microcredit, the Spanish legis-lature did not adopt a legal framework for the organisation, operations and development of the "microfinance commercial companies", hence-forth microcredit financial institutions (MFIs). Historically, there have been limited efforts at strengthening the microfinance sector, creating an adequate regulatory framework and including microfinance in the national political agenda, as well as raising awareness within the public sector. On the one hand, this has not allowed for the development of a sufficient number of MFIs to support the sector and, on the other hand, has failed to promote their sustainability over time, mainly due to the scarcity of financial resources available and the need to promote differ-entiation of the funding channels supporting microcredit. These circum-stances have led to the MFIs being strongly dependent on the banking system and public financing, which clearly affect their operations. The need to create a work group for the Legislacion Microfinanziera (micro-finance legislation) has emerged since 2003 within the first Spanish Microfinance Forum, followed by a collaboration agreement with the Fundacion Namtik Lum, the Universidad Pontificia Comillas and the Universidad Autonoma de Madrid.

In 2010, the Microfinance Forum, attended by representatives of universities, NGOs, foundations, financial brokers and public adminis-trations, started a constructive discussion on the reforms needed by the sector, and specifically:

- Regulations to improve the effectiveness of the microcredit sector;
- Legislation aimed at promoting the creation of micro-enterprises.

In light of these targets, a work group[17] was formed, constituted by repre-sentatives of the European Social Fund and European legislation group, European Microfinance Network, which advocated the preparation of a regulatory system (Navarro et al., 2013, pp. 6–12), to set a definition of microcredit, the purposes pursued by operators in the industry, and the definition of activities falling under microcredit aimed at supporting entrepreneurship.

In particular, the draft regulatory proposal stated that microcredit should be aimed at:

- Developing entrepreneurial activities;
- Improving the quality of living of individuals affected by particularly vulnerable economic and social conditions;
- Providing loans in amounts no greater than 25,000 EUR accompanied by ancillary and instrumental services to those subjects who are excluded from traditional financial channels.

Interest rates applied to loans might be higher than average market rates, in order to allow microcredit providers to pursue the economic sustainability of their business.

Microcredit providers must be non-profit organisations complying with a number of requirements for the exercise of microcredit, regardless of their legal form. They must pursue a number of social objectives, such as promoting entrepreneurship, creating jobs, favouring social inclusion and reducing poverty.

For the proper functioning of the sector, the regulations proposed provide for the activation of a specific supervisory authority: this entity, constituted by representatives of the Ministry of Labour, the Ministry of Industry, the Ministry of Health, the Ministry of Social Economic Policies and Entrepreneurship as well as by experts in the field, is responsible for the registration, renovation and revocation of licenses to microcredit providers.

Chapter 3 was dedicated to the legal nature of the microcredit providers. For such purposes, a specific committee was created within the work group itself in February 2012. The committee highlighted that such subjects cannot be assimilated to bank intermediaries, for their activity, exclusively limited to micro-loans and financed through resources from external investors, does not include the collection of money from the general public on current deposits or savings or the provision of payment and remittance services. Therefore, they are not subject to the regulatory provisions on the supervision of bank intermediaries pursuant Law No. 9/2009.

The issue of the nature of the above institutions is related to the broader debate on the new legal forms for non-profit organisations engaged in the provision of services/products for social purposes, which integrate and strengthen the welfare system, in particular pursuing collective interests. These are enterprises engaged in the production of services/products on an ongoing and professional basis, assuming all related economic risks, and they should have a higher degree of independence as for their creation and operations. Their social purpose is achieved through the provision of benefits to the community rather than to their shareholders, generating multiple advantages for different types of stakeholders.

Under many aspects, social enterprises are moved by the original spirit of the cooperative movement; this is why many of them actually choose to adopt the legal form of cooperatives. In the MFIs' specific case, with regard to the three legal forms adopted by these intermediaries (cooperatives, associations and foundations), the above committee regarded the cooperative model as being overly prescriptive in terms of operations and requirements to carry out their activities, which are, de facto, very similar to those imposed on banks.

The prevalent orientation of the committee is to apply the legal form of the foundation (Navarro et al., 2013, pp. 12–21) to microcredit providers, as they are non-profit organisations according to Law No. 50/2002, and pursue objectives of general interest through their organisation and assets. In other words, foundations are created only for public interest purposes (cultural, educational, religious, social or scientific purposes) and are liable for obligations entered with third parties within the limits of their assets. Foundations are registered in a specific register and subject to the supervisory activity of the *Protectorado de Fundationes*, made of three members, which verifies compliance of the foundations' activities with their statutory missions. In particular, the *Protectorado de Fundationes* ensures that foundations comply with the laws and regulations they are subject to and provides useful information on the use of their assets, methods to modify by-laws, and prescriptions to be followed in case of merger or liquidation.

2.7 Regulatory Framework and Supervisory Authorities in France

The legislative framework for the development of microcredit in France has significantly evolved and is considered one of the earliest and most articulated systems in Europe. The concept of microcredit in France was already introduced in 1988; since then, the regulatory framework has evolved through various regulatory interventions concluded with the adoption of the latest modifications introduced in 2013 by article L. 518–61 of the Monetary and Financial Code (Decree-law of 9 May 1990) which regulates the whole sector. According to the above, microcredit is defined as the provision of credit with the aim of supporting economic and social integration of individuals and micro-enterprises, provided that the loans, whenever they are granted by the MFIs, bear the following characteristics:

• Must be granted for pecuniary interest;
• must be granted to entrepreneurs engaged in an economic activity for a period no longer than five years and with three or fewer employees;
• must be aimed at starting or developing projects whose objective is to promote social inclusion or inclusion into the labour market;
• are repayable within a period no longer than five years;
• are not to be granted to microcredit providers;
• must be of an amount no greater than 10,000 EUR for micro-enterprises and 3,000 EUR for individuals;
• must be secured by guarantee funds, cash deposits or credit intermediaries.

In 2010, the reform of the consumer credit sector (Law No. 2010–737 of 1 July 2010 introduced a reform of consumer credit), determined the potential recipients of microcredit and divided microcredit between two types: social or personal microcredit and professional microcredit.

More specifically, personal microcredit indicates micro-loans granted to individuals and aimed at social and economic inclusion (Table 2.10), while professional microcredit consists of loans granted to micro-enterprises throughout their business cycle, from project design to development. Despite having different targets, both microcredit types share the provision of ancillary and instrumental services as well as the objectives of social and economic inclusion.

The French National Committee of statistical information further classifies professional microcredit as follows:

• Microcredit *"classique"* (classic microcredit): These are micro-loans granted for pecuniary interest whose amount is lower than 25,000 EUR, provided by banks or authorised associations to enterprises that have operated for a period of no longer than five years, with less than 10 employees and a turnover of less than 2,000,000 EUR;
• Microcredit *"a caracter des fonds propres"*: These consist of micro-loans free of charge (honourable loans) always of amounts no greater than 25,000 EUR, granted to enterprises that have operated for a period of no longer than five years, with less than 10 employees and a turnover of less than 2,000,000 EUR. Free-of-charge microcredit must necessarily be accompanied by a complementary bank loan.

Table 2.10   Personal microcredit in France: Main characteristics

Definition	Microcredit is an instrument to facilitate access to credit for subjects excluded from the traditional banking system but who are able to repay loans granted for personal or entrepreneurial projects
Amount	Generally, loans are in amounts between 300 and 3,000 EUR and are granted with fixed interest rates (between 2.5% and 8%). They can be refunded in 3 years. In particular cases, the amount might be raised to 12,000 EUR and the loans are refundable in 60 months
Access fees	Not applicable
Provision time frame	Loans are provided between 2 weeks and 2 months from the requests, and there is the possibility of early repayment
Support instruments	Personal microcredit enjoys the guarantees of the Social Cohesion Fund (financed by the government) provided by the networks and associations that operate in collaboration with the banks
Non-financial services	Ancillary and instrumental services to personal microcredit are aimed at assessing the sustainability of the projects to be financed and the adequacy of the micro-loans, through a preventive assessment of the personal and financial position of the borrowers

These technical forms are intended to pursue the objective of creating or supporting professions, trades or commercial enterprises.

A significant, primitive impulse to the identification of subjects entitled to operate in the microcredit industry occurred in 2001 with the introduction of paragraph 5 of article L. 511–6 of the CMF, following the modifications introduced by the article 19 of the Banking Act 2001–420, section "New Economic Regulations" (*Nouvelles Régulations Economiques*), "Modify Monetary and Financial Code" (*Modifie Code monétaire et financier*).

In particular, article L. 511–5 reserves the disbursement of loans to banks only, and only the adoption of article L. 511–6, paragraph 5, of the CMF, following the modifications introduced by Banking Act No. 2001–420, section New economic regulations, article 19 (Modify Monetary and Financial Code – article L. 511–6 [M]), allowed non-profit organisations to engage in lending with the objective of creating and supporting enterprises started by unemployed individuals or beneficiaries of loans of amounts no greater than 10,000 EUR. A binding condition is that loans must be destined to fund start-ups or support entrepreneurial activities and self-employed activities, trades and professions.

This measure helped overcome the strict requirements and limits set forth by the previous legislation, which limited lending only to bank intermediaries, by allowing the MFIs to raise funds not just through donations but also loans from banks and other financial institutions.

Executive Decrees No. 2002–652 of 30 April, Monetary and Financial Code concerning associations authorised to do certain lending, (*Code monétaire et financier relatif aux associations habilitées à faire certaines opérations de prêts*), established the requirements[18] MFIs must comply with in order to engage in microcredit, specifically:

- A minimum operating period of at least 18 months in the provision of ancillary and instrumental services for non-profit organisations providing loans with their own means or the exercise of banking activity;
- Existence of internal monitoring and risk management systems;
- Presence of guarantees on loans granted by authorised subjects;
- Integrity, competence and experience requirements for members of the governing bodies of the microcredit institutions.

Only in 2010, the reform of the consumer credit agreements (Law No. 2010–737 of 1 July 2010 introducing reforms for the consumer credit) completed the framework by introducing a number of provisions on the registration requirements for non-profit associations into the register of microcredit intermediaries.

With regard to supervision of the credit sector, the decree of 3 July 2002, implementing Executive Decrees No. 2002–652 of 30 April 2002, excluded the microcredit associations from banking supervision and created instead a special supervisory authority by the name of the Multi-disciplinary and Inter-Ministerial Committee for the authorisation and monitoring of the activities of authorised microcredit associations.[19]

The committee is composed of three representatives of the Ministry of Economic Affairs, including a member of the General Inspectorate of Finance; two representatives of the Ministry of Labour, including a member of the General Inspectorate of Social Affairs; a representative of the Ministry of SMEs; a representative of the Ministry of Economic Solidarity; two representatives of the banks and two additional experts (art. 2).

According to article 8, this authority is entrusted with the following functions and powers:

- Monitoring the activities carried out by authorised microcredit associations, without prejudice to the controls non-profit associations are subject to;
- Verifications and checks on their balance sheet, income statement, annual activity report and audit report;
- Information powers on the volumes of microcredit activity and non-performing loans.

These powers became effective when they were transferred from the Ministry of Economic Affairs to the Prudential Monitoring Authority (*Autorité de contrôle prudentiel et de résolution*) (ACPR)[20] following decree No. 2012–471 of 11 April 2012[21] on the creation and monitoring of organisations (associations, foundations, and so on) authorised to carry out microcredit operations.

From these summary considerations on the regulation of the sector, we can observe that the normative production and the impulse to change driven by the microcredit operators led to significant legislative developments that had a profound impact on the scope of these associations, with positive effects on the whole microcredit industry in France, which has undergone a deep restructuring phase.

In this regard, Adie[22] (*Association pour le droit à l'initiative économique*) carried out a number of effective actions; this association is still the main actor offering support to subjects excluded from the traditional banking and financial circuits in France, as it advocated the adoption of regulations aimed at establishing some key principles underlying the microcredit industry.

In 2001, Adie obtained an amendment to the French banking law, which now allows a number of microcredit providers to borrow for on-lending to unemployed or low-income individuals during the first five years of activity of newly established enterprises. The Law for the Modernization of the Economy extended this faculty to all kinds of micro-entrepreneurs, regardless of them being on welfare or not. In addition, the SME Law of 2005 abolished the usury rate for loans provided to individual entrepreneurs. The law included the drafting of a report from Banque de France evaluating the impact of the usury rate abolition. This document points out that the abolition of the usury rate has improved the funding mechanisms for MSMEs globally, without, conversely, producing the perverse effects feared by many. Moreover, in 2005, the government introduced also the *Loi de programmation pour la Cohésion Sociale* (Law for Social Cohesion), which created the Social Cohesion Fund (FCS), an entity providing guarantees to financial institutions that disburse microcredit for business purposes.

With the aim of supporting the development of microcredit, the French government passed Law No. 2005/32, the so-called 'Borloo Law', in 2005, which, emphasizing the advantages of self-employment, has facilitated access to a number of support services for the creation of companies and especially recognised self-employment as a means for to enter, or go back to, the labour market. Within the above regulatory framework, an important position is occupied by the newly created FCS, managed by the *Caisse des Dépôts et Consignation* (CDC), whose mission is to promote social[23] and professional microcredit through the provision of guarantees on loans granted by banks and MFIs to unemployed individuals willing to start a business. Mandatory requirement for accessing this fund is the provision of support and coaching activities to the micro-enterprises to be carried out by the major support networks/operators in France.

2.8   A comparative analysis of Italy, Spain and France

In the European countries analysed, the various regulatory frameworks show a number of similarities, also due to a relatively homogeneous concept of microcredit between them, strictly related to the issue of financial inclusion, yet microcredit was born in Europe not only to tackle social exclusion and poverty but also to promote innovation and economic development, by providing opportunities to access financing to subjects willing to unleash their entrepreneurial energies and spirit but excluded from the financial system. This is still a relatively recent and widely unexplored area, the only exception being France, where microcredit benefits from a long-standing regulatory framework.

Such similarities between the regulatory frameworks in the European countries examined are also related to the fact that a sole "director", represented by the European Commission, oversees the sector in Europe.

France, as mentioned, boasts a long-standing legislation on microcredit, as the latter has long been regarded as one of the priorities by the national economic policies.

Italy, as we have seen, only recently introduced new and specific regulations dedicated to the microcredit industry within the Consolidated Law on Banking. Spain, finally, is still in the process of implementing

a specific regulatory framework for the sector. All the above frameworks provide for a definition of microcredit (albeit a general one), MFIs (including their purposes), and supervisory authority or, at least, a control and monitoring system.

Some years ago, the European Commission advanced a proposal for an EU-wide framework for banking and non-banking MFIs. According to such proposal, the non-banking MFIs' framework should include:

- A clear definition of microcredit providers, providing that they do not take deposits, and, therefore, do not constitute financial institutions falling under the capital requirement directive (CRD);
- Credit-only activities conducted by providers;
- The ability to on-lend; and enjoy;
- Harmonised, risk-based rules with regard to authorisation, registration, reporting requirements and prudential supervision (European Parliament, 2009).

A successful European initiative on microcredit could give a substantial contribution to the achievement of the objectives of the Revised Lisbon Strategy in terms of growth, employment and the creation of an innovative, creative and dynamic European economy.[24]

The EU Commission communication

"A European initiative for the development of microcredit in support of growth and employment", published in November 2007 (COM (2007) 0708), encourages all member countries to adopt appropriate national, institutional, legal and commercial frameworks needed to promote a more favourable environment for the development of microcredit. In addition, a new European-level facility, JASMINE, was launched with the intent of supporting the development of non-banking MFIs in the member countries. Even though the elements contained in this initiative are promising, the drawback is that they largely lie in the hands of the member states, instead of establishing a truly European framework.

The commission defines microcredit as any loan in the amount of 25,000 EUR or less, granted to a micro-enterprise (for example enterprises with fewer than 10 employees whose annual turnover and/or annual balance sheet does not exceed 2,000,000 EUR). This limit has been adopted by several regulatory frameworks in Europe, as highlighted by the analysis of the microcredit regulatory frameworks in the European countries examined.

Table 2.11 Regulatory framework: Comparative analysis of Italy, Spain and France

	Italy	Spain	France
Specific microcredit regulation	Legislative Decree No. 385/1993, Legislative Decree No. 141/2010 Legislative Decree No. 169/2012	Microfinance draft law	Law No. 511–6, para. 5 CMF Executive Decree No. 2002–652 of 30 April Law No. 518–61 CMF Law No. 2010–737
Principal content of regulations	Legislative Decree No. 385/1993, Art. 3 **Legislative Decree No. 169/2012**: Individuals entitled to exercise microcredit **Consolidated Law on Banking:** Art. 111. Registration requirements for the registry/roll of microcredit operators. Definition of microcredit Art. 113 (art. 3 Legislative Decree No. 169/2012). Creation of a microcredit Supervisory Body Art. 111 (paragraphs No. 1 and No. 3). Purposes and amount of micro-loans granted to enterprises or for social purposes	Key points of the microfinance draft law: **Objective:** Loans less than 25,000 EUR to individuals excluded from traditional funding channels in Spain, provided to start or strengthen business activities, and/or improve the quality of life of the borrowers **Subjects:** Microcredit providers must all be non-profit organisations, regardless of their legal form. All entities, regardless of their legal form, must meet certain requirements in order to be able to provide microcredit. **Technical, accounting and administrative requirements Incentives Supervisory Body Functions:** Granting, renewing and revoking microfinance licenses; organising an annual meeting of its members **Composition of MFIs:** a. Representatives of different ministries: labour, industry, health, social policies and equality, economic affairs and finance, rural and marine environment and ICO; b. microfinance experts	**Law No. 518–61 CMF:** Definition of microcredit; purposes and amount of micro-loans granted for business and social purposes **Law No. 511–6, para. 5 CMF:** Intermediaries entitled to exercise microcredit **Executive Decree No. 2002–652 of 30 April:** Requirements or the exercise of microcredit; institution of an supervisory body for microcredit **Low No. 2010–737:** Potential beneficiaries
Specific supervisory authorities MFIs	**Ministry of Finance** Bank of Italy Supervisory body (to be constituted)	**Banco de España** Supervisory Body	**ACPR** Multi-disciplinary and Inter-Ministerial Committee
Regulation of the guarantee funds	Present within the regulatory framework on capital requirements (**Bank of Italy, Circular No. 263/2006**), whose compliance is mandatory for banks	**Memorandum No. 5/2008** of 3 October established the principle of equivalent supervision for SGR (*Sociedades de Garanzia Recíproca*)	**Law No. 2005/32**, so-called "Borloo Law"

Nevertheless, it should be noted that regulations on capital require- ments do not seem to pose direct obstacles to the disbursement of microcredit by licensed financial institutions. Generally, traditional banks are not willing to serve "non-bankable" people and, there- fore, non-banking MFIs seem better positioned to cover this target group. Yet, a more favourable treatment of those CRD for micro-loans indicated as less risky by their historical records (the experience of several microcredit providers has shown that repayment rates are, in general, remarkably high) is highly recommended. Introducing the term "microcredit" in the CRD would also contribute to its broader recognition.

Notes

* Although the chapter has been prepared by the authors jointly, sections 2.1, 2.2, and 2.5 were written by Pasqualina Porretta, section 2.3 was written by Ida C. Panetta, section 2.6 was written by Paola Leone, and 2.7 was written by Fabiomassimo Mango; sections 2.4 and 2.8 were written by Paola Leone and Pasqualina Porretta.

1. The maximum amount is 5,000 TND for associations and 20,000 TND for anonymous companies.
2. Actually the first microcredit programmes (subsidised government-led credit programs) were for the agricultural sector and date back to late-1950.
3. CBE's Board Decree No. 2408/2008 with regards to Encouraging Banks Financing of Small and Medium Enterprises.
4. In particular limitations regard:

    NGOs' Governance: The template of the associations and foundations by laws (annexed to the NGO law) requires the NGO's treasurer to sign any check issued by an NGO, which is not a practical system for the NGO-MFIs; the treasurer may delegate this power to other staff members of the NGO through an official request to MSS, provided that the treasurer remains personally liable for all transactions. According to the law, the Board of Directors' tenure is six years, however the number of an individual director's tenure is not limited (i.e., a board member can maintain his post in the board for an unlimited period of time).

    The absence of specific Financial Reporting and Audit Requirements: The NGO law requires simple reporting on NGO operations limited to a manual book for the keeping of expenses and revenues. Such require- ments are not compliant with the internationally recognised reporting standards required for MFIs, and do not enable the MSS staff to appro- priately supervise and regulate the NGO-MFIs sector. Furthermore, the supervisory framework of NGOs is silent on any MFI-specific audit and control requirements for NGO-MFIs.
5. A government agency instituted in 1981.

6. The strategy was released in the form of a report, funded by the United Nations Development Programme (UNDP), the United States Agency for International Development (USAID) and Germany's government-owned German Development Bank (KfW). The Central Bank of Egypt (CBE) was involved through its affiliate, the Egyptian Banking Institute (EBI). The SFD was also represented in the steering committee, in recognition of its active participation in the development of the strategy and its role as the entity designated for national coordination of all SME-related activities.

7. These rules lie below laws in the legislation hierarchy, thus they can easily be amended and do not need the Parliament's ratification, which is a lengthy procedure.

8. Although MFCs are not allowed to accept deposits from the public, the justification behind this prudential regulation, according to the MOI, is to protect the interests of the MFCs' creditors and shareholders (Interview with MoI and GAFI).

9. Currently, besides the Credit Bureau of the Central Bank of Egypt, there is a service provided by a private entity, which is subject to supervision: it is called I-Score, formerly Estealam. It was created in 2005 (though it has been fully operational only since 2008) by 25 banks and the Social Fund for Development. It should be noted that only in 2011 did the MFIs decide to join I-Score as effective members and data providers, and it was not without issues: a specific and comprehensive database dedicated to microfinance, created through the collaboration of three important MFIs, has not been fully implemented yet.

10. In fact, a MCF that intends to acquire a majority interest (49%) in another MFC, both directly and indirectly, must be authorised by the EFSA.

11. CGAP, Disclosure Guidelines for Financial Reporting by MFIs, July 2003. The Consulting Group to Assist the Poor works for the creation of a world in which everyone is able to have access to the financial services they need to improve their lives. CGAP develops innovative solutions for financial inclusion through practical researches and active engagement with financial service providers, policymakers, and funders. Established in 1995 and headquartered at the World Bank, CGAP combines a pragmatic approach to market development with an evidence-based advocacy platform to promote access to financial services by poor people. In particular, the Annex III of the proposed regulations refers to the following types of reports/information to be provided (following the SEEP framework for reporting):

    Type of products offered (on a monthly basis), indicating contractual characteristics (in terms of duration, nominal and actual rates applied, commissions and fees, and so on);

    Active customers (on a monthly basis), indicating products, outstanding portfolios, loan size and their distribution in the various geographic areas;

    Financial reporting (on a monthly basis): balance sheet, income statement and cash flow statement, portfolios at risk, reports on loans according to their size and type;

    Funding sources (on a semi-annual basis);

    Annual report and external audit report (on an annual basis);

Quality portfolio indicators (every four months) in terms of: (i) scale and outreach; (ii) efficiency; (iii) productivity; (iv) risk;

MFC performance report (every four months) for the following areas: (i) financial structure; (ii) profitability/sustainability; (iii) revenues; (iv) expenses; v) liquidity.

12. NGOs are required to get the approval of the MSS before accepting any funding from foreign channels.
13. The NGO law requires all NGOs to use and keep financial and administrative records (hard copies) officially stamped by the MSS.
14. SFD's own resources, donors' grants, donations, state budget, and popular councils.
15. As part of the banking reform program, the CBE has completed the second phase in March 2012. Implementation of that phase started in January 2009. Its main concern was the application of the Basel II standards in the banking sector. The application of the executive prescriptions of Basel II standards was scheduled to commence in 2012.
16. Law No. 81, of 11 March 2006, art. 4-bis, paragraph 8, which created the Permanent National Committee on Microcredit, is the direct implementation of the ethical objectives indicated in the aforementioned UN resolutions.
17. At present, the work group is constituted by 120 organisations sharing a common objective: fight poverty and revive the entrepreneurial spirit in Spain. The work group was joined also by a number of European institutions, such as the FSE and European fund de Inversiones. 10 meetings have been held so far and the following key objectives have been identified:

    Promotion of the development of the Entitad Sociales supporting microcredit, such as ESAM;

    creation of specialised microcredit intermediaries/brokers;

    use of the experience in the sector of the savings and loans banks;

    improvement of microcredit's positive impact on borrowers.
18. As a registration requirement of the legal entities, the legislation established that they must have a consolidated experience in supporting start-ups, specific prudential provisions, and conditions and terms.
19. According to article 8, the committee shall supervise the activities of the authorised associations, without prejudice to the controls non-profit associations are subject to. It shall control their balance sheet, income statement, annual activity report and audit report. Particular attention is given to the production and loan reimbursement report.
20. Created by the Order of 21 January 2010 and set up in March 2010, the ACP become ACPR by the law of separation and regulation of banking activities resulted from the merger between approval authorities (CEA [Committee of Firms Insurance] and CECEI [Committee of Credit Institutions and Investment Firms]) and control authorities (ACAM [Banking and Insurance Supervisory authority and Mutual]) of the banking sector. With Law No. 2013–672 of 26 July 2013, ACPR has become a prudential monitoring body, chaired by the governor of the Bank of France and constituted by 19 members.
21. Law-decree No 2012–471 of 11 April 2012 on the approval and control of associations, foundations and companies authorised to provide credit.

22. Since it was created, Adie's mission has always been unchanged, namely financing micro-entrepreneurs who cannot access the banking system, in particular unemployed individuals and individuals on social welfare, through microcredit; supporting entrepreneurs prior to, during and after the creation of their businesses in order to ensure their sustainability; contributing to improve the institutional conditions for microfinance and micro-entrepreneurship.

23. Actually, social microcredit can be assimilated to credit provided to low-income subjects, with amounts between 500 and 2,300 EUR.

24. In particular, microcredit can support one of the four priorities of the Lisbon strategy, namely the unlocking of business potential, by helping socially and economically (re-)integrate people through self- employment. In fact, the Lisbon strategy should be regarded as successful only if the level of employment is significantly raised.

3
Mapping Microcredit Institutions/ Operators: A Comparative Analysis

*Paola Leone, Sabrina Leo, Ida C. Panetta and Pasqualina Porretta**

3.1 Microcredit institutions/operators in Morocco

The microcredit sector developed in the early 1990s under the impulse of the national legislator and the international aid programme.[1] The existence of Apex organizations for centralizing international aid and redistributing funds has probably improved international donors' participation (Allaire et al., 2009). In fact, financial contributions by international agencies EIB and USAID[2] were the key for the growth of the microcredit industry in Morocco.

Today, Morocco's microcredit market represents over 70% of the whole of North Africa (Algeria, Tunisia, Libya and Egypt). The success of microfinance is generally related to population density, the small geographical size of the country, low literacy rates, the degree of indus- trialization, lack of postal services, poverty and the amount of interna- tional donor funds countries receive. The availability of oil exports as a source of revenue may lead to a delay in developing the microfinance sector. Establishing a specific legal framework for the industry, such as in Morocco, may help foster the growth of the sector. Conversely, in coun- tries such as Algeria and Libya, profits from net exports of petroleum may have discouraged the development of microcredit as a weapon to fight poverty (in alternative to state subsidies). Nevertheless, whereas Morocco and Tunisia have specific laws regulating microfinance institu- tions, Egyptian and Algerian NGOs are only regulated by the general law on NGOs (Reille and Lyman, 2005).

Moroccan banks have set up microcredit associations or foundations, rather than provide micro-loans directly themselves.

Today, Morocco boasts two of the top fifty MFIs in the world, even if, overall, there are eleven microcredit institutions operating in the country for a total loan portfolio (in 2013) of approximately 1983 million dollars;[3] their legal status is that of associations (the main five MFIs are seeking to transform themselves into financial institutions) or foundations. Among the Moroccan MFIs, three of them cover the whole national territory (Al Amana, Zakoura and FONDEP), three have a regional focus and, finally, five are officially proximity associations.

The MFIs are predominantly NGO-MFIs or state-owned, and they are heavily subsidised by the state. In all Maghreb countries, the state seems to play a major role in the banking and postal systems, and this is true for the microcredit sector too.

The size of the first five Moroccan MFIs varies from ARDI, with 90 employees, to Al Amana with 1,845 employees.[4] The Moroccan MFIs contribute 10%–15% of the gross internal product.

Al Amana is the largest Moroccan MFI in terms of outstanding loans. It was set up in 1997 with a sizeable financial contribution and support from USAID. Its operations currently cover almost all of the national territory and serve over 315,000 borrowers, mostly organised in groups. Al Amana carved a niche market in rural areas: 134 branches opened in 2004 alone.

FONDEP was established in 1996 and now counts about 129,000 borrowers. It is a MFI targeting low-income earners, especially in rural areas, and offers credit in the form of joint liability loans.

The Zakoura Microcredit Foundation is the industry leader in terms of number of active clients; it counts, in fact, on a base of 455,000 borrowers. It benefited largely from bank funding last year. It has grown rapidly while keeping its initial target group: disadvantaged people in urban, semi-urban and rural areas.

The microcredit industry in Morocco is thus heavily concentrated, with only 4 MFIs accounting for more than 95% of the country's gross loan portfolio[5] (Table 3.1).

In Morocco, MFI federations contribute to strengthen the negotiating capacity of the whole sector, raise awareness of the industry and support the development of know-how, skills and instruments, thus creating scale economies and allowing small MFIs to survive.

Records indicate that not only does Morocco have the largest microfinance sector, but also the highest repayment rate. It would almost seem that the poor in Morocco are more honest than the poor in other North African countries. Yet, it must be noted that whenever microfinance enjoys increasing amounts of donor aid (and Morocco has largely benefited from it), it is easy to disguise loan defaults by granting new loans to repay the old ones (Allaire et al., 2009, p. 16).

The exuberant growth of the microcredit sector in Morocco was driven, for several years, by four leading MFIs — Zakoura, Al Amana, Fondation des Banques Populaires (today named ATTAWFIQ MICRO-FINANCE), and Fondep. This success could not have happened without the constant support of the Moroccan Government. The Microfinance Law of 1999 provided a clear framework for the development of the industry, and the Moroccan Government supported it through the government fund – *Le Fonds Hassan II* – that helped create the first MFIs. The Ministry of Finance ensured close monitoring over the industry at the beginning, then the Central Bank, Bank Al-Maghrib (BAM) took over this supervisory role in 2007. The sector benefited also from consistent support provided by the international donor community.

A unique characteristic of the Moroccan microcredit sector is the role played by local banks into it: commercial banks indeed are important backers of the industry, having created two of the largest MFIs and currently funding an extremely large percentage of the sector's assets.

MFIs operate mainly in large urban areas such as Rabat and Casablanca and target mainly urban or semi-urban customers (compared to the rural population, which is more scattered), mostly in the retail and fishing sectors. Retail business and the fishing industry represent the main sectors supported by the MFIs, as they traditionally have a poor record of accessing traditional credit, mainly because banks, with the exception of Credit Agricole, did not developed specific knowledge to finance such sectors, which benefit from a minimal percentage of their credit portfolio. On the other hand, in rural areas, where poverty levels are particularly high, MFIs are not very active, mainly due to high micro-lending costs and risks, which could seriously harm their financial self-sufficiency. Difficulties accessing many rural areas and the risks traditionally associated with agriculture are two additional reasons why the microcredit associations chose not to focus their activity there. The microcredit legislation, in fact, establishes that MFIs must reach their full financial sustainability within the first five years of operation.

In Morocco, besides the traditional instruments such as personal loans and loans for the creation of businesses, a range of new products is becoming increasingly popular in the microcredit sector, such as micro-lending for social housing and micro-insurance policies.

Access to credit is quite problematic for small enterprises in Morocco, mainly due to the high value of the guarantees requested by banks and financial institutions, which prevents many micro and small entrepreneurs from obtaining the necessary funds.[6] In order to facilitate access to credit for enterprises, the Moroccan Government implemented, among other measures, a guarantee system supported by a major public entity: the Caisse Centrale de Garantie (CCG).[7] The CCG is a nonprofit, financial public institution, treated as a bank and, therefore, subject to the supervisory authority of the Central Moroccan Bank. It is a government "arm" aimed at promoting the creation, development (including social development, in particular, through guarantees for social housing loans) and modernisation of enterprises. The CCG supports the economic development by providing guarantees to facilitate loans for investments, debt restructuring and venture capital as well as by co-financing investment and innovation programmes along with other banks; it also supports social development by securing loans for social housing purposes. In line with its mission, the CCG offers also other instrumental and ancillary services for the whole maturity of the loans. Each of these products targets different beneficiaries and sectors and has its own peculiarities, although the operating mechanisms are quite similar.[8]

Although the CCG is a public guarantee institute, its board members include representatives from the private sector, such as the bank association – Groupement Professionnel de Banques du Maroc (GPBM) – the federations of the Chambers of Commerce (commerce, industry and services, craft, agriculture) and the general federation of Moroccan enterprises. The CCG operations do not fall under the microcredit regulatory framework as defined by Law No. 18/97. The CCG, in fact, does not pursue the social objectives under the microcredit legislation, as its core activity is not directed to support individuals affected by economically and socially disadvantaged conditions; in addition, the maximum amount of loans it guarantees is higher than the cap imposed by the microcredit law. The CCG, within its mission, focuses on financing and providing guarantees to micro-enterprises; 80% of the operations implemented by this institute were, in fact, aimed at facilitating access to credit for this type of enterprises.

In the period 2009–12, the CCG underwent a phase of strategic restructuring, aimed at modifying its traditional operating and functional structure. Until 2009, when this transformation process started, the activities carried out by CCG showed, in fact, more weaknesses than strengths: excessive bureaucratisation, procedural complexity, lack of proximity to local areas, management of an excessive number of guarantee funds created[9] for different business sectors (textile, export, tourism, and so on) accompanied by procedural complexity and confusion of tasks, responsibilities and sub-normal use of available resources for the guarantee activity. The revision process of the national guarantee system sought to correct this situation, aiming at a rationalisation of the CCG operating structure in order to strengthen its capacity of intervention in local areas through new types of guarantees adjusted to the life cycle of enterprises; optimisation of the guarantee delivery process; and increased contact with local enterprises and banks through the creation of new branches.

The numerous modifications introduced to the CCG operating mechanisms were accompanied by government measures aimed at improving risk management and information processes related to the provision of loans, in order to improve effectiveness and sustainability of the guarantee mechanism. In 2009, to achieve such objectives, the Central Moroccan Bank promoted the creation of a modern risk management entity not owned by the state (FNAM), where all bank customer data could be collected, from large companies to micro-enterprises, in order to provide a comprehensive and updated database that might offer a higher degree of precision to assess borrowers' creditworthiness and risk profile. Moroccan MFIs also contribute to this entity, as they provide and receive information on their customers. The future objective of this data centre is to involve all other MFIs, so that they provide information on their customers in order to improve the screening and monitoring process of potential microcredit beneficiaries.

In recent years, the Moroccan Government prioritised financial access alongside stability in its ongoing program of financial reforms, and introduced measures to extend access to credit through microcredit associations, banks, and a new postal bank. In 2008, banks were invited to develop financial inclusion strategies, and, more recently, the central bank signalled its openness to banking product innovations and delivery mechanisms.

As a consequence, the Postal Service has improved its financial operations with the assistance of consultants (IT systems, branches, back offices, audit), including improvements in internal controls required by the Central Bank during a two-year licensing process. The separation of postal and financial activities should improve the quality of services, while outreach should be improved too, with the specialisation of branches and staff, as well as the opening of new branches (550 new branches are expected by 2018) and distribution channels (100 mobile branches and 50 cash points planned by 2018). The Postal Bank will be subject to the supervision of the Central Bank, like all other public commercial banks (Douglas, 2011).

Limits of microcredit sector in Morocco

The exuberant growth of microcredit in Morocco turned out to be a critical factor for the microcredit industry. Some signs of stress had already started to emerge in 2007, most notably loan delinquency and multiple lending (clients with loans from two to five different MFIs). The number of non-performing loans – one of the lowest levels in the world – started to rise significantly.[10] The cause of the crisis is represented by unsustainable growth. The global financial crisis is not to be blamed. This is primarily a crisis of the MFIs themselves. The previous unprecedented growth, in fact, overstretched the MFIs' capacity, resulting in lenient credit policies, obsolete management information systems (MIS), lack of internal controls and substandard governance. Multiple lending to the same clients was also an aggravating factor, though not the origin of the crisis (CGAP, 2009).

The roots of the credit crisis should be researched in the institutional capacity of the microcredit associations. The unprecedented growth of the sector overstretched their capacity, resulting into lenient credit policies, obsolete management information systems (MIS), lack of internal controls and substandard governance.

Multiple lending to the same clients was an aggravating factor. A study conducted by the central bank estimated that 40% of microcredit beneficiaries have been granted multiple loans. The problem is particularly acute in urban areas.

Microcredit associations have put in place recovery plans, including management shake-ups and freezing of new disbursements. Associations are tightening their credit processes, putting in place teams focusing on loan recovery, and taking judicial actions against delinquent borrowers. They are also exchanging credit information on a weekly basis to monitor over-indebtedness. Smaller microcredit associations are planning to share resources, such as back office systems, or to merge. These efforts are slowly paying off. However, some associations have been severely hit by the crisis and will have to be wholly restructured; others are emerging stronger than before and are well positioned for another phase of growth.

The response of the Moroccan microfinance sector has been swift and timely. The government organised the acquisition of some MFIs, in an effort to consolidate and strengthen the sector, improve transparency, control multiple lending, prevent over-indebtedness and secure liquidity to the industry by encouraging relationships and links between MFIs and banks (Douglas, 2011).

At the same time, the MFIs have considerably slowed down their activity and reduced the size of their balance sheets; they have implemented aggressive recovery plans, including, in some cases, senior management changes; they have been tightening their credit processes, putting together specialised teams dedicated to loan recovery, and are taking judicial actions against delinquent borrowers. Finally, small- and medium-size MFIs are planning to cut costs and share resources by merging or sharing their back office systems. These efforts are slowly paying off, and a recovery of the sector is expected in the first semester of 2010.

In the last years, the Réseau de Microfinance Solidaire (RMS), an association of small Moroccan MFIs, forged stronger ties, though it has not yet consolidated, with its partners. It recently advanced a number of proposals to allow the Moroccan MFIs to merge or acquire each other. The proposed actions by the RMS (shared best practices, shared MIS, and reduced borrowing costs from Credit Agricole) demonstrate that the small Moroccan MFIs want to remain independent, opposing mergers with any of the big three players in the market (Al Amana, FBPMC, and FONDEP).[11]

3.2 Microcredit institutions/operators in Tunisia

Tunisia was the first North African country to start microfinance; the first microcredit activities were spin-offs of development programmes set up by NGOs in rural regions in the 1980s, with the objective of alleviating youth unemployment, the paucity of micro-enterprises and poverty. In particular, the first microcredit programme attempts involved the agricultural sector; in the period 1962–69, Tunisia saw the introduction of the first savings banks, which started to allocate small loans to agricultural cooperatives. The experience did not last long and ended with the failure of the cooperative experiment in 1969.

The emergence of specialised MFIs and microcredit activity in urban regions is a more recent phenomenon, which started in the mid-1990s (Ziadi, 2005). Microcredit started to be incorporated in operating procedures more consistently from 1995 onwards. Just a few years later, in 1999, as highlighted in the previous chapter, the government authorised and regulated microcredit institutions with a specific law. Currently, the microfinance market in Tunisia counts approximately 270,000 clients, for a total micro-loans volume of 220 million TND – approximately 105 million EUR (Ministère des Finances, 2011, p. 32).

Table 3.1 Main MFIs in Morocco

MFIs	Type	Start date	Mission	Legal Status	Property	Territorial penetration	Target Group	Gross Loan Portfolio (USD)	Number of active borrowers (2013)
AIMC (Association Ismailia pour le microcredit)	NGO	n/a	n/a	Association	Mainly public		n/a	374,177	1,329
Al Amana (Association Al Amana for the Promotion of Micro-Enterprises Morocco)	NGO	1997	Enterprise microcredit	Association	Mainly public	National	Rural Population Urban Population Women	237,182,257	314,878
Al Karama (Association Al Karama de Microcredit)	NGO	1999	Social microcredit Enterprise microcredit	Association	Mainly public		Rural Population	4,050,300	15,845
AMOS (Association Microfinance Oued Srou)	NGO	2000	Social microcredit Enterprise microcredit	Association	Mainly public		Rural Population Women Low-income earners	783,195	2,653
ARDI (Fondation ARDI)	NGO	2001	Social microcredit Enterprise microcredit	Foundation	Mainly public		Youth, Rural Population Women	25,461,490	105,708

Name	Type	Year	Services	Legal Form	Ownership	Scope	Target Population		
ATIL (Association Tétouanaise des Iniziative Sociaux Professionelles)	NGO	2001	Social microcredit Enterprise microcredit	Association	Mainly public		Rural Population Urban Population	653,485	1,376
Attadamoune (Attadamoune Ex AMSSF/MC)	NGO	1999	Social microcredit Enterprise microcredit	Association	Mainly public		Rural Population	5,933,359	13,549
ATTAWFIQ MICRO-FINANCE (Fondation Banque Populaire pour le Microcredit)	NGO	1991	Enterprise microcredit	Foundation	Mainly public		Rural Population Urban Population Women Other	208,232,217	224,22
FONDEP (Fondation pour le Développment locale et le Partenariat)	NGO	1996	Social microcredit Enterprise microcredit	Foundation	Mainly public	National	Youth, Women, Low-income earners	81,599,046	128,62
INMAA (Institution Marocaine d'Appui a la Micro-entreprise)	NGO	1999	Enterprise microcredit	Association	Mainly public	National	Rural Population Urban Population Low-income earners	2,669,939	6,201
Zakoura (Fondation ZaKoura pour le Microcrèdit)	NGO	1995	Social microcredit Enterprise microcredit	Foundation	Mainly public	National	Rural Population Women	171,458	455

The Tunisian microcredit sector is founded on two main pillars (Table 3.2): public loans allocated by the Banque Tunisienne de Solidarieté (BTS, founded in 1997) and distribution throughout the territory ensured by the microcredit associations (MCAs) and the NGO Enda Inter Arab.[12] These two institutions are highly complementary in terms of clientele and geographical coverage, albeit with different missions, operating methods and organisational structure. The BTS, which operates following a national policy that advocates extreme centralization of the microcredit business, provides subsidised loans, both directly and indirectly, largely charged to the state; Enda's operations instead follow market-based logic and international standards.

Most Tunisian MCAs were created before the BTS and usually offer other services as well (professional training, assistance and counselling services). They operate thanks to subsidies provided by the BTS itself or funds from various donors. Currently, there are 270 MCAs operating in Tunisia; in 1999, there were only six (Ministère des Finances, 2011, p. 35). MCAs are non-profit associations that enjoy a very "light" regulatory framework; their only obligation is to maintain a minimum refund rate of 80% in order to benefit from the BTS's re-financing. Microfinance territorial penetration was thus achieved almost all over the country thanks to the MCAs themselves, but also due to the availability of a number of services snubbed by the traditional financial system, as they were deemed to be pertaining to micro-financing (by banks and the postal network). In carrying out their activity, MCAs can also take advantage of guarantees provided by the FNG (Fond National de Garantie), which helps cover between 50% and 90% of the loans granted, in exchange for a contribution of 1% of the loan value. The MCA sector is not transparent; little information can be obtained about it.

The BTS is a deposit bank that facilitates access to microcredit for projects that are able to generate income and create employment in different business sectors all over the national territory. It is the first Tunisian bank that specialises in financing small-size projects; it is a governmental body that provides interest-free capital to 227 NGO-MFIs to on-lend. The government and other public bodies hold a 54% share of its capital. The BTS focuses on lending to university graduates and people with professional qualifications or crafts, who do not have sufficient collaterals required by banks (Belgaroui, 2005). It also finances micro-enterprises and self-employment initiatives in urban, suburban and rural areas, especially in the Family Support Network intervention areas. Finally, the BTS encourage any entrepreneurial initiatives and opportunities deemed to create income and revenues. In fact, in addition to granting microcredit directly, the BTS does so indirectly, via

Table 3.2 Main MFIs in Tunisia

MFIs	Type	Start date	Mission	Legal Status	Property	Territorial penetration	Target Group	Gross Loan Portfolio (USD)	Number of active borrowers (2013)
Enda Inter-Arabe	International non-profit NGO	1990	Social microcredit Enterprise microcredit	International non-profit NGO	Private	Regional	Women Urban Population Rural Population Unemployed	91,055,803	226,625
Banque Tunisienne de Solidarieté	Bank	1997	Enterprise microcredit	SA	Mainly public	National	Rural Population Urban Population	n/a	70
MCAs	Other (non-profit association);		Enterprise microcredit	Associations	Private property, Public control	Provincial (270)	Rural Population Urban Population	n/a	n/a

the MCA network. In particular, the latter is the only bank involved in financing micro and small business projects through two channels:

- An indirect channel consisting of the re-financing of the MCAs, with loans up to 5000 TND[13];
- A direct channel consisting of medium-term loans of amounts equal to 100,000 TND.

As of December 2011, the BTS had approximately 70,000 active clients. It is funded through state-owned assets, mainly national solidarity funds. From an organisational point of view, the BTS operates through two agencies and a network of 23 "cellules".

ENDA, an international NGO,[14] was created in 1990 with a focus on environment and urban development. As an international company, it is not subject to the limitations established by the 1999 law and is free to apply market interest rates. Since 1995, it has focused its activity on the development of microcredit through loans, partnerships and training programmes in the regions of Etthadhamen, M'nihla, Omrane, Séjoumi, Sidi Hassine and Douar Hicher. This entity boasts a series of national and international partners (European Union, EIB, Oikocredit, Agence Française de Développement). Today, it is largely oriented to providing access to credit to women,[15] with the awareness that they constitute the poorest part of the population, despite the fundamental role that they play in satisfying families' vital needs. With this focus in mind, Enda Inter-Arabe chose to implement microfinance programmes favouring women, regarding this as a powerful tool to tackle poverty.

Although Enda-ia recently developed other programmes, it has maintained its focus on microfinance. Enda tries to strengthen the micro-entrepreneurs' capacities by offering different types of non-financial services: training programmes in simple accounting, management and marketing, counselling services (health, legal regulations), marketing, networking (discussion groups, excursions, trade fairs, get-togethers), and technical support (most clients are self-taught).

Approximately 80% of the loans granted by Enda-ia have been financed by the Tunisian banking system;[16] for the remaining 20%, Enda-ia depends on funds raised through a vast network of international partners (government development agencies, foundations, investment funds specialised in microfinance, and so on). From an organisational point of view, Enda-ia's network consists of 65 agencies operating through 206 delegations. Each branch covers a 15 km radius, thus providing services within customer reach and helping reduce transportation costs and time. Enda-ia contributes to the improvement of the living conditions of low-income Tunisians through local lending institutions that are socially responsible and committed to the environment.

Besides the traditional micro-loans aimed at creating new micro-enterprises, Enda-ia provides loans targeting specific objectives (for instance, to Tunisian nationals coming back to their country from Libya or individuals willing to start a business from home) for a maximum amount of 5,000 TND.[17]

Most of the activities financed by Enda-ia belong to the informal sector, especially in the trade business. Since 2007, Enda-ia has divided its clients into two groups. The first segment (30%) sees a larger proportion of male micro-entrepreneurs and includes activities run in premises that are separate from their home, with a more substantial share in services, employing more salaried workers and producing higher incomes. The second segment (around 70% of the total) is made up of clients working from home, mostly unregistered, low-income, seasonal workers with limited education and experience.[18]

Enda-ia is the only entity in Tunisia dedicated to microcredit. It is currently focusing on the development of micro-enterprises in rural areas and is also taking measures to target manufacture/handicrafts and services more accurately. This has reduced the share of commercial activities financed. In parallel, there has been a substantial increase in the financing of livestock rearing businesses in recent years. Its operating methods are based on rapid and flexible procedures, with guarantees from solidarity groups or existing clients who have access to progressive lines of credit.

Limits of microcredit sector in Tunisia

One of the major criticalities of the Tunisian microcredit sector is the poor transparency and communication with regard to detailed information on microcredit products and the technical terms and conditions of their provision (access methods, commissions and fees charged, timing, beneficiaries, business sectors involved, and so on). It certainly represents a limit to the diffusion of microcredit products and services in the country, as developing a communication culture and dedicated detailed information could help widespread a sustainable microfinance model all over the country.

The word-of-mouth system often replaces traditional communication channels (advertising, brochures, and so on), with the result that illiterate segments of the population or individuals living in remote areas gain little or no knowledge at all of microcredit programmes, the existence of the MFIs and the range of products offered.

In some cases, the price complexity of microcredit programmes (entry fees, management fees, and so on) further hinders the diffusion of microcredit products and services (Ministère de Finance, 2011).

The central role played by the BTS, which is entrusted with the task of facilitating access to credit for different kinds of beneficiaries, certainly provides microfinance operators with a constant reference point for communication and assistance, in terms of IT infrastructure, training programmes and skills. On the other side, though, the presence of a sole institution (the BTS) monopolising a large part of the microcredit industry does not facilitate the expansion of the business and makes the complex microcredit activity overly bureaucratic.

Another criticality of the microfinance sector in Tunisia is represented by its sheer dependence on government subsidies, which is, de facto, a threat to the long-term profitability and sustainability of the industry itself. Such dependence often discourages donors and other national or international institutions from investing in the sector.

Nevertheless, it should be also noted that the microcredit legislation in Tunisia does not allow applying interest rates higher than 5%; this cap hinders a sustainable development of the microfinance sector, as it often prevents the MFIs, especially the small ones, from covering their operating costs. This regulatory provision and the international financial crisis add further risks to the survival of many MFIs as well as jeopardize the implementation of microcredit policies.

Our brief analysis indicates that the success of microfinance in Morocco is related to population density, small geographical size and poverty levels as well as the amount of international donor funds received in the last year and a tendency towards the evolution of credit management processes (such as the use of the credit bureau), yet much remains to be done to modernize the MFIs' sector.

3.3 Microcredit institutions/operators in Egypt

Microcredit started to develop in Egypt in the second half of the 1980s, with the kickoff of the first programmes of the National Bank for Development and the Alexandria Businessman Association (ABA). Since then, the number of various institutions operating in microcredit, mainly banks and NGOs, as well as the volume of loans granted, have considerably increased. According to EFSA data (2010), we can see that over 400 MFIs provide microcredit services in Egypt; most of them have quite small client portfolios, with a total number of 50,000 active customers. Three types of MFIs provide microfinance in Egypt:

- NGOs
- Commercial banks
- Service Companies

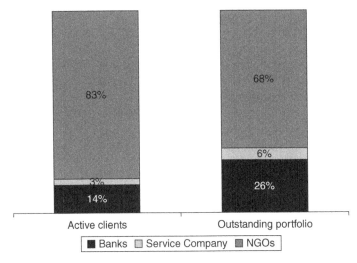

Figure 3.1   Structure of the microcredit offered in Egypt: distribution per number of clients and portfolio managed (as of 2009)

Source: Own elaboration on EFSA data.

Figure 3.1, though based on 2009 data, shows the preponderance of NGOs in the sector.

These NGOs have a market share of 83% in terms of active customers and manage almost 68% of the total microcredit portfolio at a national level (EFSA, 2010); these results are obtained through different operating dimensions and models (see Box 3.1). According to EFSA, two main groups of NGOs can be identified in this monopolised, yet extremely fragmented, market:

• A first group is characterised by a variety of small operators operating at a local/village level through community development associations, which hold a market share of just 23% (in terms of active customers) and over 24% of the total portfolio (EFSA, 2010). These are mainly entities enjoying technical and financial support from the Social Development Fund (SFD) – over 390 NGOs – and other national lenders (Data reported by EFSA as of 31 December 2009);
• A second group, made of the six largest NGOs, operates according to the model Specialised NGO (Box 3.1), with a 56% market share (Figure 3.2), and holding almost 44% of the active loan portfolio (Figure 3.3); these are associations and foundations created thanks to

the support of international agencies and donors, still mainly bank-rolled by USAID.

Although, as previously mentioned, NGOs are subject to registration, at present it is impossible to access such register, and therefore we cannot provide a comprehensive mapping of all the operators in the

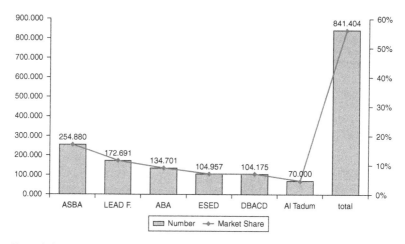

Figure 3.2   Largest NGOs' active clients: number and market share (as of 2009)
Source: Own elaboration on EFSA data.

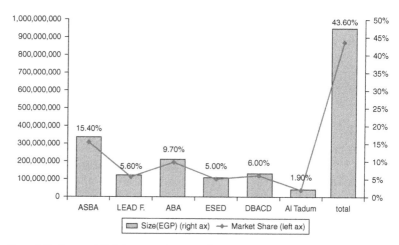

Figure 3.3   Largest NGOs' outstanding portfolio market share and size (as of 2009)
Source: Own elaboration on EFSA data.

market. In this research, then, we thought it more appropriate to map the data related to the six largest NGOs (Table 3.3).

Box 3.1 Types of NGOs operating in Egypt

Four types of NGOs operate in the microcredit sector in Egypt:

- Specialised NGOs are business associations generally managed by trained professionals, specialised in the provision of microcredit, which constitutes their core business; these are NGOs created thanks to contributions and support of donor Agencies, such as USAID. These are the largest NGOs, also boasting the best performance in terms of outreach.
- Social Development NGOs are organisations aiming to offer a wide range of services to support local communities, where microcredit constitutes just a part of their business. In this regard, compared to the Specialised NGOs, the Social Development NGOs pursue a broader mission, although they have a more limited experience and knowledge of the microcredit sector. This is reflected by their modest results in terms of outreach and sustainability.
- Umbrella NGOs are nationwide networks of local organisations (community-based organisations), mainly government-owned. Like the Social Development NGOs, their profiles are quite modest in terms of results and knowledge.
- Community Development Associations (CDAs) are small, voluntary, local organisations playing a role of "credit retailer" on behalf of the Umbrella Social Development NGOs. Mostly volunteers carry out their activities.

All NGOs – the six large ones and the small organisations – share a common issue: the difficulty of financing their microcredit activity. Their legal status (foundations or associations) and the NGO legal model do not enable them to raise funds through the collection of deposits; moreover, other legal provisions (see section 2.3) prevent them from accessing bank financing. On the one hand, in fact, NGOs cannot collateralize their assets; on the other hand, there are restrictions to bank loans secured by collaterals.

Their main funding source, therefore, is constituted by the contributions provided, in their various capacities, by the so-called donor agencies, mostly international donors. Besides providing capital contributions, the donor agencies provide also the guarantees needed to access bank loans. This is the case of USAID, which supports some NGOs with deposits in US dollars, used as collaterals, against which the NGOs can take advantage of a 0.95x leverage to provide micro-loans. Currently, thanks to a combination of technical support and guarantees offered by Grameen Iameel, DBACD and Al Tadamun, the NGOs have successfully

Table 3.3 Main MFIs in Egypt

MFIs	Type	Start date	Mission	Legal Status	Property	Territorial penetration	Target Group	Gross Loan Portfolio (USD, 2012)	Number of active borrowers (2012)
The National Bank for Development (NBD)	Bank	1987	Social microcredit Enterprise microcredit	Joint-stock company[19]	Private	Governorates (18)	Micro and Small enterprises	n/a	n/a
Principal Bank for Development and agricultural Credit (PBDAC)	Bank	1993	Social microcredit Enterprise microcredit	Joint-stock company	Public	National	Rural Micro-enterprises	n/a	n/a
Banque Du Caire	Bank	2001	Enterprise microcredit	Joint-stock company	Public	National	Micro and Small enterprises	11,077,662 ***	99,000*
Bank of Alexandria (BoA or AlexBank)	Bank	n/a	Enterprise microcredit	Joint-stock company	Private	National	Micro and Small enterprises	n/a	n/a
Banque Misr	Bank	1993	Social microcredit Enterprise microcredit	Joint-stock company	Public	National	Small and medium enterprises	n/a	n/a
Dakahlya Businessmen' Association for Community Development (DBACD)	NGO	1995 Operative since 1997	Enterprise microcredit	Association	Private	Governorates (1)	Micro-enterprises	26,589,887	107,608

Name	Type	Year	Focus	Legal form	Ownership	Governorates	Target	Loan portfolio	Clients
Lead Foundation	NGO	2003	Social microcredit, Enterprise microcredit	Foundation	Private	Governorates (7)	Micro-enterprises, Women, Low-income earners	21,659,657	141,299
Alexandria Business Association (ABA)	NGO	1983	Enterprise microcredit	Association	Private	Governorates (5)	Micro-enterprises, Women	50,929,049	234,371
Assiut Businessmen Association (ASBA)	NGO	1994	Enterprise microcredit	Association	Private	Governorates (7)	Micro-enterprises, Unemployed	51,854,750	225,289
Al Tadamun	NGO	1996	Social microcredit	Foundation	Private	Governorates (1)	Women	5,206,214	40,823
Egyptian Small Enterprise Development Association (ESED)	NGO	1988	Social microcredit	Association	Private	n/a	n/a	6,300,861	70,640
Tanmeyah	Other (Microfinance service company)	2009	Enterprise microcredit	Joint-stock company	Private[20]	Governorates (13)	Lower-income tier individuals and small businesses	13,554,064**	30,175**
Reefy	Other (Microfinance service company)	2007	n/a	Joint-stock company	Private[21]	Governorates (11)	n/a	9,578,116**	26,691**

*2009;** 2010; ***2011.

increased borrowing from commercial banks, reaching a 2x (leverage ratio), or 50% coverage.

More recently, the Specialised NGOs started to use the Credit Guarantee Company (CGC), which secures the NGO portfolio for a pre-negotiated fee, as will be explained in section 4.3.

It is also worth mentioning that the NGOs benefiting from the support of donor agencies are also those that perform better, due partly to the availability of resources, but mostly to the stringent requirements that NGOs must meet in order to be eligible for financial support.

Another interesting aspect of the largest NGOs' operations is the use of the so-called *step lending methodology* in the provision of credit (clients receive a higher loan amount at each "step"); following such approach, borrowers may access to microcredit programmes that offer increasingly higher loan amounts only when the borrowers have proven to be good payers.

The second type of microcredit providers is constituted by commercial banks; as highlighted in Figure 3.1, banks hold quite a small market share in the business. As a matter of fact, only five banks are engaged in the provision of microcredit, which anyway does not represent their core business:

- Three state-owned banks: Banque Du Caire, Banque Misr, and Principal Bank for Development and agricultural Credit (PBDAC);
- Two private banks: the National Bank for Development (NBD or ADIB) and the recent Bank of Alexandria (BoA).

With the exception of a number of programmes implemented by PBDAC in the agricultural sector, the other banks provide short-term micro-loans mainly to enterprises involved in the trade and service industry. Although the lending methods vary from bank to bank, generally all of them seem to adopt the step lending methodology, following the NGOs' practice.

In general, banks boast a relative poor presence in the microcredit business, except for the aforementioned cases. This is because, firstly, the banks' territorial expansion through branches historically followed other logics and is not suitable to reach potential microcredit beneficiaries. Secondly, they lack a specific knowledge to assess and manage microcredit customers, who are often perceived as high-risk customers and, therefore, are shunned by the traditional banking institutions. In fact, also in the case of loans provided by commercial banks, most microcredit programmes started with the support of international development agencies, donors or other forms of incentives implemented at a national level.

To overcome the above criticalities, two banks decided to invest in the microcredit sector by creating so-called *microfinance service companies* (MSCs). There are two current MSCs, founded in 2007 and 2009 respectively, created as bank service companies with the legal status of joint-stock companies; this model was used by Reefy, in cooperation with Commercial International Bank (CIB) and by Tanmeyah in collaboration with Egyptian Gulf Bank (EGB). Jointly, the two MSCs hold (as of 2009) 5.8% of the total outstanding loan portfolio and around 3% of active clients (see Figure 3.1). Tanmeyah, the most recently created company, offers two types of micro-loans with different amounts and maturity according to the size of the borrowers' activity as well as some payment services (ATMs, bill payment points to be used mainly for payment of utility bills).

Two forms of microcredit exist in Egypt (Table 3.4):

- Solidarity group lending – A group of three to five borrowers receives a loan that is equally divided among them and then they guarantee each other for repaying the loan. The loan is used to finance income-generating activities mostly in the informal sector;
- Individual lending – Owners of small or micro-enterprises operating for more than a year receive loans to finance their business, provided they present a personal guarantor.

By analysing the different kinds of products offered by the banks, within the limits of available information, it is clear that the only form of microcredit provided is individual loans, whose amounts tend to be higher than those provided by the NGOs. It is also evident that the intervention of donor agencies, such as USAID, resulted in quite similar characteristics of the products offered, especially in terms of eligibility requirements, maturity, conditions and terms applied.

Territorial penetration (Figure 3.4) is instead diversified; although banks operate at a national level and the larger NGOs cover more than one governorate, microcredit is more concentrated in the Upper Egypt regions (43% of customers) and urban areas. The poorest areas seem to be affected by a scarcity of services. As for the business sectors (Figure 3.4), most of the micro-loans provided benefit the trade industry (71% of customers); this figure must be related to the nature of the micro-loans, which generally involve reduced repayment periods, not allowing for investments with a longer return on investments.

Table 3.4   Main microcredit characteristics by type of loan in Egypt

Main loan terms	Solidarity group lending	Individual lending
Loan size	50–1,500 EGP (per group member)	500–100,000 EGP
Repayment period	10–40 weeks	4–24 months
Annual Interest Rate	24%–28%	13.5%–16%
Instalment Repayment Frequency	Weekly/bi-weekly	Monthly
Collaterals	None (checks or promissory notes are signed by clients)	None (checks or promissory notes are signed by clients)
Guarantor	Mutual Guarantee of Group Members	Personal Guarantor (usually a first-degree relative)
Required Documents	ID* card / birth certificate / marriage certificate	Minimum: ID card* / rental ownership contract of business and residence
Number of Group Members	3–5 members	n/a
Eligibility Criteria	Gender: Female/Male (majority of programmes target females) Age Range: 18–60 Existing or start-up businesses (mostly informal/home-based) Good reputation	Gender: Male/Female Age Range: 18–60 Existing businesses for more than one year Good reputation
Providers	NGOs	NGOs – Banks

Notes: * *National Identification Number.*
Sources: Based on EFSA (2010).

A variety of organisations and associations contribute to the organic development of microcredit in Egypt, providing technical assistance, specific services and, more frequently, financial instruments for the MFIs providing microcredit.   ·

At a national level, we must mention the oft-recalled Social Fund for Development (SDF), a public body created for other purposes[22] in 1991; since 2004, it has played a reference role in all supporting and facilitating measures for the MSMEs. Its specific role in the microcredit industry is to provide financial resources, in addition to technical support, to the MFIs.[23] In particular, about 1,062 million EGP have been spent since

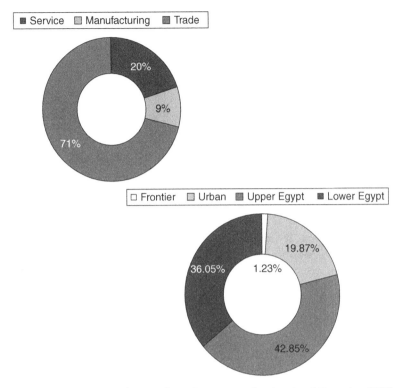

Figure 3.4 Breakdown of active clients by sector and region (as of December 2009)
Source: Own elaboration on EFSA data.

1991, through subsidies and provision of working capital, in order to allow MFIs to provide microcredit.[24]

Always at a national level, particularly significant is the role played by the Environmental Quality International (EQI), an institution born in 1985, which developed specific skills and know-how in microcredit programme management. This allowed the provision of standardised technical support to NGOs and banks for the delivery and management of microcredit, including the necessary IT infrastructure.[25] Since 2001, EQI has been working also with two banks engaged in the provision of microcredit services, Banque Du Caire and Banque Misr, by offering support to micro-loan management as well as traditional loans.

Moreover, the MFIs can rely on two national networks: The Egyptian Microfinance Network and Sanabel. The former was founded by SDF and 12 MFIs in 2006 to implement the guidelines of the National Strategy for Microfinance; it currently counts 20 members, yet it does not look particularly active, except for the organisation of conferences and analysis on microcredit projects. On the other hand, instead, Sanabel is a highly active network in Arab countries, including around 17 MFIs in Egypt; it processes and examines data on the sector performance in the region and offers training programmes to its members.

Limits of microcredit sector in Egypt

Egypt is often referred as one of the African countries boasting one of the most developed microfinance sectors. Yet, the sector, despite its high growth rate and general positive performance, still shows several limits. It is true that the industry grew rapidly, with an average annual growth rate of around 28% (at least until 2008) in terms of number of customers and 29% of the credit portfolio (Abdel-Baki et al., 2010). But despite such encouraging figures, which may look important, much needs to be done to develop the industry: this is an area where a large part of the potential microcredit demand is still unmet. If we consider the data of the Global Financial Inclusion Database (Global Findex), Egypt still shows the lowest level of financial inclusion,[26] with percentages that put it behind several other lower-middle income countries and/or belonging to the MENA area.[27]

Additional considerations should be made about the use of microcredit by its beneficiaries. According to a study by I-Score and IFC,[28] a sample of microcredit operations in 2011 highlighted the following:

- Over 14% of the NGOs customers examined (around 50,000) had also obtained loans (1.2 or more) from banks, corresponding to approximately 500 million EGP (three times the total active loans of NGOs);
- Around 13,000 NGOs customers had been granted loans by other NGOs (one, two or more), for amounts totalling approximately 14 million EGP.

These figures highlight a distorted use (or maybe misuse) of the microcredit provided by NGOs, which often adds to, rather than replaces, the microcredit or traditional loans provided by banks; in addition, NGOs show overlapping lending and, as a result, the high number of active NGOs does not match a higher number of borrowers, as they end up serving, in this case, the same population segments.

As for the microcredit providers, the market is highly fragmented in term of number of provides (over 400 MFIs) but also concentrated: 69.9% of the microcredit portfolio is provided by five banks and six

NGOs. The latter are MFIs suffering, as mentioned in section 2.3, from a lack of clear regulatory framework governing the sector. The regulations provided for the NGOs do not allow them to further expand their activity, as their funding options are limited (in local currency); this is aggravated by the complex bureaucratic procedures NGOs are subject to, which are not calibrated to the peculiar productive process of microcredit. All this results in a complicated and inefficient credit delivery process. As for funding, although most institutions are privately owned, they still largely rely on donations and contributions from donors, mainly international agencies, and public entities promoting social and economic development; this is true for NGOs and banks alike, as the latter also benefit from financial support of agencies such as USAID. The adoption of the new regulatory framework (see section 2.3) could definitely contribute to solve such issues, especially for NGOs, as well as indicate a clear path for sustainable development of microcredit, by (likely) rationalising the number of operators and introducing a few basic notions of healthy and prudent management.

To the delays in adopting new regulations for the MFIs, we must add the political instability that characterised the last three years. The "Arab Spring" in Egypt has, in fact, resulted in further slow-downs for the whole sector, and the ongoing disorders do not help the economic recovery: the MFIs, regardless of their type, highlighted a number of operating problems already in 2011.[29] In fact, a number of special financing measures were proposed to tackle the crisis and help the MFIs – mainly NGOs – continue their activity. Response by government and regulators now must be timely and effective in order to avoid losing many of the benefits acquired by the sector in the last 20 years.

3.4 Mapping microcredit institutions/operators: A comparative analysis of Morocco, Tunisia and Egypt

The brief examination of the MFI systems in the North African countries so far has shown that their respective microcredit sectors are highly dependent on public subsidies and international support provided by international donor agencies.

Moreover, the MFI sectors in Morocco, Tunisia and Egypt seem to be highly concentrated.

- The exuberant growth of the microcredit sector in Morocco was driven, for several years, by four leading MFISs;
- The microcredit sector in Tunisia revolves around two main institutions: BTS and Enda-ia.

NGOs are widespread in all three North African countries analysed, although their performances, according to our study, seem to be more effective and pervasive. Egyptian NGOs hold most of the active customers and the largest chunk of the total microcredit portfolio at a national level. Unlike Morocco and Tunisia, the MFI sector in Egypt is characterised by a lot of institutions, and at present it is impossible to obtain a comprehensive mapping of the NGOs operating on the whole national territory.

On the other hand, the MFI industry in Tunisia is definitely the most concentrated and also driven by a more centralised model if compared to Morocco. More specifically, the two main Tunisian MFIs operate following two different models: Banque Tunisienne de Solidarieté is the result of an extremely centralised national policy, while Enda-ia operates following market-based logic and international standards.

The MFI industry in Morocco, instead, appears to be less concentrated and is inspired by market-driven logics; in the last years, the Tunisian government itself encouraged banks and other financial intermediaries to assume a more active role in the microfinance sector.

The exceptional development of microfinance in Morocco, compared to the other two countries, can be ascribed not only to sociocultural factors, but also to economic, political and institutional differences (among them, governance, financial and regulatory system) and to the activation of a credit risk management model, albeit at an embryonic state.

In fact, the MFI system in Morocco seems inspired by modern operating principles and attentive creditworthiness assessment of the microcredit beneficiaries and, consequently, also by a more adequate credit risk assessment compared to the systems in place in Tunisia and Egypt. In the latter, the banks' presence in the microcredit sector is scarce, as the territorial distribution of their branches is not suitable to reach an adequate number of microcredit borrowers; in addition, they lack the specific knowledge and skills to perform risk assessment and management of a population segment which is generally deemed to be high-risk.

Properly functioning credit reporting systems help reduce adverse selection and moral hazard, and can contribute to both an expansion of microcredit and a reduction in lending costs by facilitating the adoption of credit-scoring lending technologies. The development of credit registries and offices in Morocco, implemented in recent years, is particularly important for the development of the microfinance system. Their role is crucial indeed, as they support banking supervision, allow implementing an embryonic credit risk management model, and thus help mitigate risks for the MFIs. Supervisors can make use of the credit reporting systems to predict MFIs portfolio performance. Conversely, the MFIs can make use of the credit reporting systems to screen potential borrowers and monitor their performance. In the absence of solid credit information, lenders tend to adopt defensive positions, requiring substantial collaterals, increasing their interest rates, or crunching credit altogether, thereby hindering the growth of segments like micro-enterprises.

Generally, as known, access to credit for the small and micro-enterprises in the African countries examined is quite problematic, mainly due to the substantial collaterals requested by banks, which prevent many small and micro-entrepreneurs from obtaining the necessary funds. Among the weaknesses of the credit sector, the most commonly mentioned are a lack of information on solvency of the entrepreneurs and the lack of adequate risk assessment tools.

The above deficiencies in the microcredit industry prompted several government interventions aimed at expanding the microfinance sector in the last few years. In particular, the governments of the countries examined:

- in some cases, invited banks/other intermediaries to develop financial inclusion strategies and introduce innovations in products and delivery mechanisms. This is particularly true in Morocco, where the microcredit sector is strongly brokered by banks: commercial banks are important backers of the industry, having created two of the largest MFIs and funding an extremely large percentage of the sector's assets. Banks operating in the industry often offer innovative microfinance products, such as social housing loans and micro-insurance policies. In Egypt, instead, banks hold a negligible market share of microcredit; only five banks are engaged in the provision of microcredit services, and it does not constitute their core business;
- create a number of instruments to support access to credit for micro-enterprises. In some countries, public guarantee schemes were implemented (such as the Moroccan Caisse Centrale de Garantie or the Egyptian Credit Guarantee Company), which provide guarantees to support access to credit for micro-enterprises (generally unable to provide personal or collateral guarantees) or for NGOs active in the microcredit sector.

In general, the MFIs analysed enjoy tax exemptions in the early phase of their activity (or in the case of NGOs) in order to stabilize their operations, as well as a sustained source of financing for their subsequent growth; it is a further easing instrument of public policy.

The state's presence in MFIs in the North Africa countries seems inevitable for the development of sustainable microfinance. However, it seems that it is not always easy to pursue a balance between the support of the policymakers and the necessary operating independence that these MFIs should have in order to carry out their mission efficiently.

From this perspective, it is important to note that, in addition to the traditional role of ensuring the stability and efficiency of the MFI sector with different type of financial support (guarantee, MFIs capitalization, and so on), governments should ensure a greater access to finance by promoting a favourable legal and regulatory environment.

The legal and regulatory framework should be complemented by a sound financial infrastructure, which improves the efficiency and effectiveness of MFI intermediation.

A well-functioning microfinance/microcredit information framework and a sound regulatory framework are two essential elements of any efficient financial infrastructure (in microfinance, too). They are crucial for the efficient functioning of the whole system.

In this regard, our brief analysis highlighted that one of the main criticalities affecting the three MFI sectors examined is represented by the scarce transparency and communication of detailed information on the different types of MFIs operating in the territory, their products, terms and conditions, and their credit delivery methods (access methods, commissions and fees applied, timing, beneficiaries, business sectors involved, and so on). The preferred information channel is the word-of-mouth model between MFI customers, with the result that illiterate segments of the population or individuals living in remote areas have a scarce knowledge, or no knowledge at all, of microcredit programmes, MFIs operating in their areas and the range of products offered.

The above criticalities represent a limit to the diffusion and development of microcredit in all three countries analysed, although Morocco, as previously noted, successfully developed a more advanced MFI system compared to the other two.

3.5   Microcredit institutions/operators in Italy

The Italian microcredit system, aimed at facilitating access to credit, is based on multiple levels and involves different kinds of institutions, both private and public, including social insurance institutions, banks and other financial institutions, non-financial private institutions and

Table 3.5 MFIs in Morocco, Tunisia and Egypt: a comparative analysis

	Morocco	Tunisia	Egypt
Start date	1990s	1990s	1985
Number of microcredit institutions/operators	11	2 MFIs, 270 MCAs	Over 400
Type	NGOs	International non-profit NGOs, Banks, non-profit associations	Over 400 NGOs, 5 banks, 2 MSCs, 2 Support Organisations Banks: Enterprise microcredit
Mission	Social microcredit Enterprise microcredit	Social microcredit Enterprise microcredit	Major NGOs: Social microcredit, Enterprise microcredit Minor NGOs: Social microcredit and Enterprise microcredit (2), Enterprise microcredit (4); Support service (1)
Legal Status	NGOs	SA, Associations	NGOs: Associations and Foundations Banks and Service Companies: joint-stock companies
Property	Mainly public	Private, Mainly public, Public control	Mainly private Public (3)
Territorial penetration	National (3) Regional (3) Local level (5)	National (1) Regional (1) Provincial (270)	Governorates (MFIs) National (Banks)
Users/products /sectors involved	Rural Population Urban Population Women Low-income earners Youth	Women Urban Population Rural Population Unemployed	Women MSMEs Unemployed Lower-income individuals
Microcredit criticalities	Lenient credit policy Exuberant growth of sector Multiple lending NPLs increase	Poor transparency and public communication Microcredit providers strongly dependant on public subsidies Price complexity of microcredit programmes	Measure of micro-loans by clients Limited funding options due to regulatory restrictions Dependant on donor agencies

Table 3.6 Main MFIs in Italy

MFIs	Types	Start date	Mission	Legal Status	Property	Territorial penetration	Target Group
Banca Etica	Bank	1999	Social microcredit Enterprise microcredit	Cooperative Bank	Private	National	No client-specific target
Il Villaggio dei Popoli Etimos	NGO	1990	n/a	Cooperative	Private	Local	No client-specific target
MAG2 Finance	Non-banking financial institution	1999	Social microcredit Enterprise microcredit	Consortium	Private	International	People excluded from mainstream financial services
	Non-banking financial institution	1980	Social microcredit Enterprise microcredit	Cooperative	Private	Local	People excluded from mainstream financial services
MAG4 Piemonte	Non-banking financial institution	1987	Social microcredit Enterprise microcredit	Cooperative	Private	Local	Cooperatives Associations Mutual aid associations
MAG6 Servizi	Non-banking financial institution	1988	Ethical finance and microcredit	Cooperative	Private	Local	Associations and cooperatives in the third sector Culture and biological agriculture
Cresud	Non-banking financial institution	1999	Social microcredit Enterprise microcredit	Joint-stock company	Private	International	MFIs Sustainable and Fair Trade Producers Cooperatives Associations and NGOs in Latin America Latina, Africa and Asia
Chico Mendes	NGO	1990	Social microcredit Enterprise microcredit	Cooperative	Private	Local	Cooperative, in particular to support sustainable and fair trade with developing countries
Cooperativa Pace e Sviluppo	Social Cooperative	1993	Social microcredit Enterprise microcredit	Cooperative	Private	Local	Cooperative, in particular to support sustainable and fair trade with developing countries

Name	Institution type	Year	Service	Legal form	Ownership	Scope	Target/clients
Microfinanza Srl	Non-banking financial institution	2000	n/a	Limited liability company	Private	Local	*Association* / NGOs / Other MFIs
PerMicro	Non-banking financial institution	2007	Social microcredit / Enterprise microcredit	Joint-stock company	Private	National	No client-specific target
MAG Venezia	Non-banking financial institution	1992	n/a	Cooperative non-profit	Private	Local	Social, cultural and environmental projects
MAG Verona	Non-banking financial institution	1978	Social microcredit	Cooperative non-profit	Private	Local	Social, cultural and environmental projects
MAG Roma	Non-banking financial institution		Social microcredit	Cooperative non-profit	Private	Local	Social, cultural and environmental projects
Fondo etico Le Piagge	Citizen association		Ethical finance and microcredit	Association	Private	Local	Cultural initiatives related to ethical finance
Fondazione San Carlo	NGO	1999	Social microcredit	Foundation	Private	Local	People excluded from mainstream financial services
CTM-Altromercato	Consortium	1988	Enterprise microcredit	Cooperative	Private	International	Producers in developing countries (with Banca Etica)
La Bottega Solidale	NGO	1990	Enterprise microcredit	Association	Private	Local	Cooperative, in particular to support sustainable and fair trade with developing countries
Microcredito di solidarietà S.p.A.	Non-banking financial institution	2006	Enterprise microcredit	Joint-stock company	Private	Local	People excluded from mainstream financial services
Micro.BO	NGO (Support organization)	2004	Social microcredit / Enterprise microcredit	Association	Private	Local	No client-specific target
Banca Prossima	Bank	2007	Enterprise microcredit	Joint-stock company	Private	National	Third sector
Ente Nazionale per il Microcredito	Governmental body	2010	Social microcredit / Enterprise microcredit	Governmental Body	Public	National	Promore microcredit programmes / Manage microcredit project and funds / Research in the field of microcredit
Eticredito	Bank		Social microcredit / Enterprise microcredit	Joint-stock company	Private	Local	Third sector operators

national, regional and local funds. The government plays a key role in supporting the system, by supplying resources to social insurance funds and supporting government-sponsored programmes.

Until very recently, the lack of specific legislation on microcredit led to different institutions engaging in microcredit initiatives/ programmes. This fragmentation makes it particularly difficult to map all microcredit operators, which include regions and regional financial entities, religious entities, third sector organisations, non-banking foundations and public-institutional subjects. Among the latter, the first place is occupied by the regions and regional financial entities, also thanks to EU prescriptions and the financing provided through EU funds for intervention in the microcredit industry, but there are also provinces and municipalities, which promoted (in 2011) 11% of the total microcredit projects (*Ente Nazionale per il Microcredito-Italian National Public Agency for Microcredit*, 2012). The picture of the microcredit institutions in Italy is, therefore, quite diversified; it includes also a broad network of microcredit promoters that often assume the form of non-profit entities. In addition to this variety of subjects operating in the microcredit sector, there are also a number of banks and financial intermediaries that, de facto, provide microcredit and/or other microfinance products.

However, according to a stricter definition of microcredit (art. 111 of the Consolidated Law on Banking as modified by Legislative Decree No. 141 of 2010, as subsequently amended and modified), we can narrow down the field and restrict the list of MFIs to the subjects included in Table 3.6. We would like to remind that, at present, the register of microcredit providers has not been established; therefore, there is no official mapping to which we can refer. Although the Italian MFIs mapped are quite different as to their mission, legal status, and core business (Table 3.6), it seems that they boast quite a consolidated operating experience, taking into account that half of them were created in the 1980s and 1990s and the other half after the year 2000. As for their territorial range of operations, there is prevalence for a model based on "territorial proximity", which coincides with the size of the municipalities or provinces they operate into, rather than a regional or national size.

The Italian MFIs often operate in synergy with other public or private partners in the industry. Most microcredit initiatives are, in fact, promoted through articulated partnerships that involve the simultaneous presence of different actors, both public and private entities belonging to the third sector and actively collaborating to implement microcredit programmes/projects. The partnerships creating microcredit projects are participated, in 85% of cases, firstly by private subjects (including banks), secondly by third sector organisations in 77% of cases, and thirdly by public entities in 60% of the cases (*Ente Nazionale per il Microcredito*, Italian National public agency for Microcredit 2012). Purely public or private initiatives are not frequent; microcredit initiatives, in fact, often require the concomitant presence of both public and private subjects.

Microcredit projects usually involve/cover provincial territories (in some cases the whole region), evidence of the fact that microcredit is a typical operating configuration of local banking, which takes place in relatively small areas where, in order to optimise the whole microcredit chain, it would be appropriate to improve the network of relationships with local associations, policymakers, microcredit promoters and other subjects that interface, in their respective capacities, with the borrowers' financial needs.

In 2012, 32% of the microcredit programmes activated in Italy were focused on support of enterprises, and 38% of them were aimed at social purposes (Table 3.7); 50% of the former were activated by the convergence regions (Puglia, Calabria, Campania, Sicily).

In Italy, there are numerous subjects promoting microcredit programmes/projects; many of them also provide their customers with other instrumental and complementary services, such as tutoring, business monitoring, coaching, and so on. They often play a fundamental supporting role in the microcredit chain. The Table 3.8 shows some of the main and most active microcredit promoters in Italy.

Within this vast pool of existing microcredit operators/institutions/promoters in the country, a further selection will likely follow the implementation of Legislative Decree No. 141/2010, which expressly requires these subjects also to provide instrumental and ancillary services, such as assistance and monitoring of the subjects financed, in order to qualify themselves as microcredit providers.

Table 3.7 Microcredit programmes activated in Italy by beneficiaries

	Italy	Convergence Regions
Beneficiaries of microcredit for enterprise development	32%	50%
Beneficiaries of social microcredit	38%	22%
Beneficiaries of mixed microcredit	30%	28%

Source: Own elaboration on Ente Nazionale per il Microcredito (2012).

Table 3.8   Main promoters operating in Italy

Classification of promoters	Names
1) Promoters exclusively operating in the microcredit sector to support enterprises created by migrants	• Fondazione di Venezia – Venice • Ass. Trentina Accoglienza Stranieri ATAS – Trento • Province of Turin – Turin • Ass. Amb. Democrazia Locale – ADL – Brescia
2) Promoters operating in the microcredit sector to support the creation of enterprises, regardless of the entrepreneurs' nationality	• Foundation San Carlo Onlus – Milan • Regional Administration of Marche – Ancona • Caritas Diocesi Andria – Minervino Murge (BT) • SMOAT (Fidi Toscana SpA) – Florence
3) Promoters exclusively operating in the social microcredit sector ("other purposes")	• Foundation La Casa Onlus – Padua • Foundation Ethnoland – Milan • Foundation Antiusura Interesse Uomo – Potenza • Caritas Diocesana Bergamasca – Bergamo • Caritas Diocesana Pisa – Pisa
4) Promoters involved in mixed microcredit: to support micro-enterprises (including those created by migrants and social microcredit)	• Foundation CR Carpi – Carpi (MO) • Foundation Risorsa Donna – Rome • Micro Progress Onlus – Rome

Limits of microcredit sector in Italy

Our analysis has so far highlighted a highly fragmented picture of the MFI sector in Italy, also due, as mentioned above, to the lack of a specific legislation, a problem that affected the industry for many years. Now, following full implementation of the new regulatory framework, we are looking forward to strong development and growth of the MFI sector.

Particularly populated is the area of non-banking institutions engaged in the provision of support services, many of them from the third sector. This often translates into a relative lack of professional skills and knowledge to properly support the microcredit beneficiaries with adequate non-financial services.

We also noticed that, in the absence of an official register or roll of microfinance operators, it is impossible to provide a comprehensive mapping of the sector; moreover, the absence of a certification body that is able to attest to the professional quality and skills of the several operators/intermediaries that qualify themselves as MFIs does not help, either.

3.6 Microcredit institutions/operators in Spain

Origins of microcredit in Spain

The microcredit market in Spain appears highly fragmented, and given the lack of specific regulations, a comprehensive mapping of the microcredit operators is rather difficult; therefore, it is also hard to calculate the size of the market. However, the following main categories can be identified (Rico Garrido et al., 2005):

1. Financial Institutions:
   - Commercial banks (BBVA, Citibank Spain)
   - Specialised (MicroBank de la Caixa)
   - Exresponsable del programa de microcreditos de Fundacion CajaSol
2. Social microcredit financial institutions (SMFIs) (Entidadeds Sociales de Apoyo al Microcrédito):
   - Public and private non-profit organisations and foundations (Fundaciòn CajaSol, Fundaciòn CPAC, Fundaciòn Mujeres Progresistas, Fundaciòn Tomillo).
3. Public entities (Fundación Instituto de Crédito Oficial-ICO, Direcciò General d'Economia Social i Cooperativa i Treball Autònom, Istitut Balear de Joventut, Madrid Emprende).

According to a recent survey carried out at European level (Bendig et al., 2012), participated in by the main players in the market – over 50% of which is represented by SMFIs and foundations and only 8% by banks – the size of the microcredit business can be summarised (as of 2011) in Table 3.9. It is surely an expanding market as indicated in the table, but one that underwent profound changes in 2009 following the crisis of the savings banks.

For over a decade, the savings banks played a key role as actors and landmark in the microcredit industry. They contributed decisively to the provision of micro-loans to small and micro-enterprises in the period

Table 3.9 Microcredit in Spain by size (2010–11)

Number of clients	75,191
Number of operators	36,188
Portfolio amount in Euros	232,497,046

Source: Based on EMN data.

Table 3.10 Microcredit in Spain by number of operators

	Year	Number of operations	Value (€000,000,000)
Saving Banks and ICO Line	2001	4,106	1.1
	2002		3.7
	2003		6
	2004		26.5
	2005		33.2
	2006	1,319	46.9
	2007	3,348	85
	2008	7,132	153.7
	2009	5,172	200.3
MicroBank and NGOs	2010	n/a	212.9
	2011	n/a	232.4
	2012	n/a	232.4

Source: Based on Calderòn and Rico (2012).

2001–09 as highlighted in the Table 3.10. If we subtract the ICO line volumes from the total volumes of the period 2001–09, we can observe that the savings banks easily represent the main microcredit providers (out of a total amount of 22,149 million Euros, such intermediaries granted 21,077 million Euros, that is over 90%); vice versa, following the severe crisis,[30] their operations were greatly reduced in 2011–12.

The business model

The prevalent business model among the financial institutions is characterised by the presence of partnerships with the SMFIs, which serve as a liaison between banks and micro-entrepreneurs. SMFIs are recognised for their close contact with vulnerable groups and their experience in social/labour integration through the promotion of self-employment initiatives.

As shown by Figure 3.5, following the Spanish model, micro-loans are usually granted as follows: (1) the micro-entrepreneur contacts an SMFI for information; (2) the SMFI identifies the potential beneficiary, provides the necessary help to complete a microcredit application, and forwards the application to the financial institution; (3) the financial institution then makes a credit rating based on the project's feasibility, and if the assessment is positive, formalises the microcredit agreement. This agreement is signed directly by the financial institution and the micro-entrepreneur. (4) In addition to the above, the SMFIs are also responsible for follow-up work, providing the necessary support to micro-entrepreneurs throughout the maturity of the loan.

From this collaboration, credit intermediaries benefit by:

- providing first-hand knowledge to the customers applying for micro-credit, helping ensure a better evaluation of the transaction;
- counselling on the preparation of business projects and carrying out a prior assessment of their viability and rationale.

An evolution of this model occurred when banks, in particular the Caixa de Catalunya, started to outsource the whole credit process (preliminary assessment, monitoring and supervision) to the SMFIs, although the operating risks remained on the banks' balance sheets.[31]

The severe crisis affecting Spain had a further impact on the evolution of this business model,[32] (Figure 3.6) calling for a greater involvement of all actors in the microcredit chain in order to make it more efficient and sustainable, with regard both to public and private subjects already

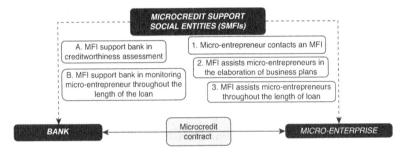

Figure 3.5 Credit granting model in Spain through the SMFIs' intervention

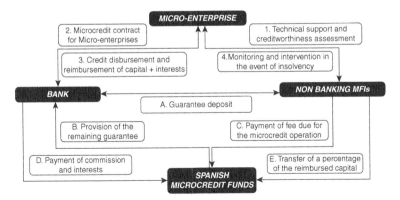

Figure 3.6 Microcredit model in Spain

Source: Based on CP'AC (www.microfinanz.net).

operating at local levels. The objective here is not just the involvement of the above parties but also sharing the credit risks in proportion to the activity carried out within the chain, where a relevant role is played by the Spanish Microcredit Fund, participated in by the Spain government through the del Ministero de Empleo y Securidad Social, the European Social Fund and ICO (Instituto de Credito Oficial).

A special mention is deserved for the business model developed by MicroBank, which has grown as one of the most important stakeholders in the Spanish market. Its capacity to substantially contribute to the success of this particular type of credit is shown by the efficiency of the microcredit chain, whose main stakeholders are the sole MicroBank shareholder, CaixaBank, and over 500 *collaborating entities* (SMFIs, foundation and so on). The major shareholder plays a supporting role in the development of the microcredit by facilitating the sale, on one side, of MicroBank products through its commercial network that covers all national territory and, on the other, of commercial and credit monitoring services provided by the bank itself against a fee which is paid according to terms and conditions indicated in the agency agreement. The collaborating entities act as a link between entrepreneurs and MicroBank, basically offering professional support to entrepreneurs in drawing up business plans and monitoring their implementation, allowing MicroBank to offer its services to a greater number of beneficiaries.

Microcredit operators: main characteristics

In order to identify the main characteristics of the operators in the microcredit market in Spain, we carried out an investigation of a sample of microcredit operators, analysing their websites. (Table 3.11) More specifically:

- 3 financial intermediaries providing credit: 1 public and 3 private entities;
- 3 public institutions promoting and supporting microcredit programmes; and
- 9 SMFIs specialising in microcredit and promoting microcredit programmes and providing other services: 3 state-owned and 6 private entities.

The Table 3.12 summarizes the main characteristics of the above actors operating in the microcredit chain, with particular attention to their mission, territorial penetration and target group.

Table 3.11   Sample of MFIs analysed

Financial intermediaries	Public entities	SMFIs
1. Microbank	1. Instituto Catalán de Finances (ICF)	1. Fundación Mujeres
2. Fundación Cajasol	2. Associación Madrilena de Empresas de Insercion (AMEI)	2. Fundación Cp'ac
3. Instituto de Crédito y Finanzas Región de Murcia (ICREF)	3. Direcció General d'Economia Social i Cooperativa i Treball Autònom (Generalitat de Catalunya)	3. Cooperativa Creant
	4. Fundacion ICO	4. Fundación Nantik Lum
		5. Servei Solidari per la Inclusió Social
		6. Fundación Privada Trinjove
		7. Barcelona Activa
		8. Madrid Emprende
		9. Fundación Incyde

All the institutions examined offered some information on their respective missions. While analysing the distribution of the missions according to their type, we can observe that support to enterprises and creation of jobs are particularly common among them (Table 3.13).

Generally, microcredit beneficiaries (Table 3.14) are entrepreneurs who intend to start or develop some business, or families seeking to support some of their needs, such as education, healthcare or others; they have a characteristic in common, namely the difficulty to access traditional financing channels, due to their socioeconomic conditions and unemployment.

The products offered vary according to the actors and providers in the microcredit chain; we should also take into account that a limited number of intermediaries directly provide loans and bear directly the risks of their operations. Products and services offered by MFIs cover a broad range of loan types, additional financial services and support services for consumer finance and entrepreneurial activities.

As illustrated in Table 3.15, micro-loans are currently offered by banks and are aimed at both the social sector and micro-enterprises.

From a technical point of view (Table 3.15), the average amount of micro-loans is between 600 and 25,000 Euros, their average maturity varies from 6 months to 6 years, while the average interest rate is comprised between 3.25% and 6%. Generally, other costs, such as

Table 3.12 Main MFIs in Spain

MFIs	Type	Start date	Mission	Legal Status	Property	Territorial penetration	Target Group
MicroBank	Bank	2008	Social Microcredit Enterprise Microcredit	Joint-stock company	Private	National	Entrepreneurs and self-employed professionals; Entrepreneurs in a situation of financial Exclusion; Micro-enterprises; Social enterprises; Families and individuals
Fundaciòn CAJASOL http://www.cajasol.es	Financial Intitution	2010	Social Microcredit Development of regional economy	Foundatión	Private	Regions of Andalusia, Estremadura and Castiglia-La Mancia	No client-specific target
Instituto de Crédito Y Finanzas Región De Murcia (ICREF) http://www.icrefrm.es	Bank	2009	Development of regional economy Enterprise Microcredit	Joint-stock company	Public	Region of Murcia	MSMEs
Institut Catalá de Finances (ICF) http://icf.gencat.cat/ca	Public Entity	1995	Development of regional economy	Public body	Public	Region of Catalunya	Micro-enterprises; Self-employed; Entrepreneurs who invest in Catalunya
Madrid Emprende http://www. madridemprende.com	Other (SMIF)	2005	Development of local economy	Public body	Public	Metropolitan area of Madrid	MSMEs

Name	Type	Year	Focus	Legal entity	Public/Private	Region	Target
Direcció General d'Economia Social i Cooperativa i Treball Autònom http://www14.gencat.cat/sacgencat/AppJava/organisme_fitxa.jsp?codi=4910	Public entity	n/a	Development of local economy	Local Governmental entity (Generalitat de Catalunya)	Public	Region of Catalunya	Individuals MSMEs entrepreneurs excluded from mainstream financial services
Barcelona Activa http://www.barcelonactiva.cat	Other (SMIF)	1986	Development of local economy	Public body	Public	Metropolitan area of Barcellona	MSMEs
Fundación ICO http://www.fundacionico.es/	Public entity	1993	Social Microcredit Enterprise Microcredit	Foundatión	Public	National	Self-employment MSMEs Entrepreneurs and People excluded from mainstream financial and social services
Asociación Madrilena de Empresas de Insercion (AMEI) http://www.ameei.org/	Public entity	1995	Development of local economy	Company established by Law 44/2007	Private	Metropolitan area of Madrid	Cooperatives promoted by associations, foundations and non-profit (law 44/2007)
Fundación Mujeres http://www.fundacionmujeres.es/	Other (SMIF)	1994	Microcredit for women	Foundation	Private	National	Women
CP'AC Fundación (per A la Promoció de l'Autoocupació de Catalunya) http://www.cpac.es/	Other (SMIF)	1986	Development of economy	Foundatión	Private	Catalunya: BarcellonaRegions of Girona, Terrassa, Tarragona e Lleida	Self-employment Entrepreneurs MSMEs

Continued

Table 3.12 Continued

MFIs	Type	Start date	Mission	Legal Status	Property	Territorial penetration	Target Group
CREANT	Other (SMIF)	2005	Social microcredit	Cooperative	Private	National	People excluded from mainstream financial service
Fundación NANTIK LUM http://www.nantiklum.org/	Other (SMIF)	2003	Social microcredit	Foundatión	Private	International (Chiapas-Messico, Republica Dominicana and Haiti)	People excluded from mainstream financial service
Servei Solidari per la Inclusió Social www.serveisolidari.org	Other (SMIF)	2006	Social microcredit	Foundatión	Private	Metropolitan area of Barcellona	People excluded from mainstream financial service Young Immigrants
Fundaciòn INCYDE (Instituto Cameral para la Creación y Desarrollo de la Empresa) www.incyde.org	Other (SMIF)	1999	Enterprise microcredit	Foundatión	Private	National	No client-specific target
Fundación Privada TRINJOVE www.trinijove.org	Other (SMIF)	1985	Social microcredit	Foundatión	Private	National	Women Under 30 Over 50 People excluded from mainstream financial service Immigrants

Table 3.13   Breakdown of MFIs analysed by their mission

Type of Mission	MFIs %
Creation of jobs	29%
Support to enterprises	47%
Financial inclusion	6%
Social inclusion and poverty reduction	24%
Women employment	6%
Youth employment	6%
Others	18%

Table 3.14   Breakdown of MFIs analysed by type of customers

Target group	MFIs %
Micro-enterprises	29.1%
Unemployed	20%
Women	16%
Regular migrants	16%
Individuals under 30 years	9%
Single-parent families	9%
Individuals, over 50 years old of age	0.4%

Table 3.15   Main characteristics of the microcredit programmes

Financial Institution	Requirement	Type of Microcredit	Target	Micro-loan conditions
Bank Foundation MicroBank	(a) To form part of disadvantaged social group with of the target segment particular difficulties in finding employment (b) No access to a formal financial system due to lack of collateral (c) To possess entrepreneurial skills and feasible business initiative	Social microcredits Financial microcredits Family microcredits	Self-employment projects Business ventures that create wealth Temporary difficulties and facilitating personal development	*Loan size:* from 600 to 25,000 *Grace period:* from 0 to 6 months *Repayment term:* from 6 month to 6 years *Current rate of interest:* between 3,25% and 6% No guarantees no fees

Table 3.16   Services provided by the MFIs in the sample

For the micro-entrepreneur	Identification of potential beneficiaries: • Assistance, information and advice for the micro-entrepreneur • Training of the micro-entrepreneur in the preparation of his/her business plan • Revision of the business plan • Presentation of the documentation required by the financial institution for the microcredit. Provision of moral endorsement or guarantee of the beneficiary • Training and technical assistance throughout the term of the microcredit • Control and monitoring of the microenterprise for at least one or two years in order to guarantee its feasibility and the repayment of the credit
For the financial institution	Selection of the micro-entrepreneurs on the basis: • Exclusion from any other type of ordinary credit • Potential for business success due to an enterprising spirit • Evaluation and selection of the projects in terms of economic sustainability • Monitoring and control of the business in order to ensure credit repayment

preliminary investigation expenses, are not expected, nor is collateral required to access credit.

The MFIs are responsible for selecting the beneficiaries and coaching them during the start-up phase and throughout the maturity of the micro-loans. Table 3.16 illustrates the main services provided by MFIs examined, divided according to support to enterprises/families.

Limits of microcredit sector in Spain

In spite of a lack of a specific legislative framework dedicated to the industry, the purposes and mission of the sector clearly emerges within the general economic system: the economic and financial inclusion of marginalised subjects, be they individuals or enterprises. In this sense, the SMFIs and foundations play a relevant role within the economic system.

Yet, the sector inevitably also bears some weaknesses, namely the scarcity of funding, risk- sharing and the low efficiency of the business. These circumstances have prompted a number of changes that are underway and can be observed from the very same microcredit programmes, with the aim of evolving the model itself. The comparative analysis carried out has highlighted that MFIs can be private or public institutions geared towards bolstering the creation of micro-businesses, promoting self-employment and providing incentives for entrepreneurial activities. More specifically, they are public organisations run by regional or local councils (employment agencies, local development agencies, employment enterprise centres, and so on), or, generally, non-profit private organisations.

The increasing predominance of the MFIs in the microcredit-granting model is highly acknowledged. Nonetheless, following the financial crisis, many of their programmes have been shut down, meaning that MFIs are left facing two main problems: (1) offering financing alternatives to those beneficiaries who intend to start up or consolidate small businesses, and (2) their own survival, as they used to receive financial support to run the programmes.

Another issue is the role of public finance supporting micro-enterprises, whose interventions stretched along an articulated path, characterised, on one side, by an increasing integration between local and EU dimensions and, on the other, by the creation and consolidation of the micro-enterprises in their capacity to promote economic development and the creation of jobs through the development of regional policies granting incentives to intermediaries that operate in the sector on a stable basis.

However, the future of microcredit will depend on the capacity of the policymakers to support and implemented a national strategic plan, which should coordinate and be integrated with the skills and know-how developed in the microcredit sector by local players in their respective territorial contexts; mostly, though, it will depend on the definition of a regulatory framework where objectives, actors, products and a supervisory authority are clearly indicated.

3.7   Microcredit institutions/operators in France

The market

Professional microcredit in industrialised countries aims to facilitate access to credit (private and bank credit) for financially excluded subjects (Brana and Jégourel, 2011). The main reasons underlying financial exclusion of some groups of subjects are identified by the European Commission (2003) as high costs faced by banks, lack of/insufficient guarantees and loans perceived as too risky.

Looking at the European contest, the French experience is particularly interesting, as it offers a highly developed microcredit system in terms of organisation, instruments and operators.

In terms of supply, the professional microcredit in France can be divided into:

• Micro-loans provided by banks (mainly cooperative or mutual banks);
• Non-banking microcredit, provided by non-profit associations;
• 'Mixed' credit, provided through platforms where honour loans are provided by the banking system with the support of private (private donors, local communities) or public resources. These are a particular form of loans promoted by local initiatives (Banque de France, 2008).

In 2012, 147,315 microcredit operations were negotiated in total (Table 3.17), for an amount of 874.8 million Euros and average loans lower than 10,000 Euros; among these micro-loans, those labelled as "Classiques" by the Banque de France were 45,275 for 417.6 million Euros, while those called "À caractère de fonds propres"[33] were 102,040 for a total of 457.2 million Euros (Banque de France, 2013). Major beneficiaries were individual enterprises [34] operating in the third sector. Compared to 2011 (Banque de France, 2012), professional credit recorded a significant increase, both in terms of capital and interest amount 45.36%, and micro-loans provided 14.95%.

From available data of the Observatory of Banque de France, we cannot trace information on microcredit performance before 2011; therefore, although we are aware that data shown are not

Table 3.17   Professional microcredit in France

	Capital and interest amount		
	2011	2012	Variation %
Classiques	185.4	417.6	125.24%
À caractère de fonds propres	416.4	457.2	9.80%
Total	601.8	874.8	45.36%
	Micro-loans provided		
	2011	2012	Variation %
Classiques	39,640	45,275	14.22%
À caractère de fonds propres	88,521	102,040	15.27%
Total	128,161	147,315	14.95%

Source: Own elaboration on Banque de France data, years 2012–013.

Table 3.18 Professional microcredit in France (2008–11)

	2008/2009	2010/2011	Variation %
Number of operations	28,863	28,690	–0.60%
Number of active customers	70,252	52,074	–25.88%
Portfolio volume	152,600,000	165,250,309	8.29%

Source: Own elaboration on EMN data.

homogeneous, we referred to the work by Bendig et al. (2012),[35] to present an overview of the microcredit sector in the years following the crisis (Table 3.18).

The data shown reveal that the professional microcredit sector in France declined in terms of number of active customers, around 26% (it should be noted that it is not possible to attribute the decline to a shrinking supply or demand) while portfolio volume is increase of 8.29%. We can assume that, in the face of a reduction of the number of active customers, the average amounts disbursed increased; this assumption is confirmed by the fact that the number of operations activated remained essentially unchanged (-0.6%). In light of the economic-financial crisis, the above decrease could be attributed to customer self-exclusion or to an increased selectivity of the projects to be financed operated by microcredit operators, in particular banks.

The microcredit in France developed thanks to the intense activity carried out by the MFIs, in particular by Adie (now the largest MFI in France), which constituted a stimulus for the national legislator. The MFIs in France support disadvantaged subjects

- Directly, through economic/financial support and other instrumental activities[36];
- Indirectly, by ensuring that the provision of microcredit is the first step to access traditional banking loans.

The microcredit sector and the activity of MFIs in France cannot be fully understood without a reference to the legal system that regulates lending and microfinance institutions. In particular, two crucial moments marked a watershed for the French microcredit industry:

- The amendment to the banking law in 2001;
- The possibility granted to the NGOs to change their legal status into MFIs.

In particular, the amendment to the banking law allowed non-profit associations to grant micro-loans for the creation of micro-enterprises with a maximum amount of 10,000 Euros, through their own funds, bank loans or similar, or through entities/services under article L 518–1 of the Code Monétaire et Financier (CMF). The expansion of the funding sources has certainly contributed to increase the activities carried out by MFIs, which, by accessing financing sources at subsidised rates, and not just subsidies and donations, were able to significantly grow while continuing to operate and pursue their mission.

On the other hand, the ceiling imposed to micro-loans contributed to define the range and type of subjects who can access this form of financing. Prior to the introduction of the above limit, the MFIs, within the limits of their capital, could finance any project independently without any intervention by banks (Figure 3.7).

Currently, however, microcredit projects follow two different schemes: those below 10,000 Euros continue to be entirely financed by the MFIs, while those above such amount follow a different procedure and involve

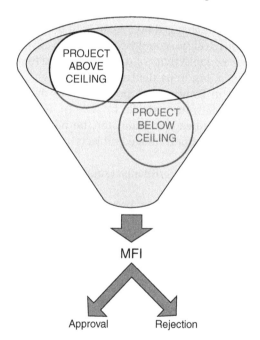

Figure 3.7   Loan allocation without ceiling
Source: Own elaboration.

the intervention of banks. More specifically, micro-entrepreneurs whose projects have a budget greater than 10,000 Euros must firstly contact a bank to apply for a loan for the part exceeding the limit imposed; only then, following the approval of the loan by the bank, they can contact the MFI to start the procedure for the disbursement of the micro-loan (Figure 3.8).

The MFI lending process in France is similar to that carried out by banks: investigation, through the examination of the loans application performed by loan officers; approval or rejection of the applications by the credit committee; determination of loan terms and conditions – amount, maturity, interest rates, reimbursement methods and subsidies (Cuzarenco and Szafarz, 2013). The operating model is characterised by the presence of public guarantees (see section 4.7) and a convergence of actions carried out by different agents: the main MFIs are deeply rooted in the territory thanks to their support networks and contact points (known as "antennae"), which constitute the reference

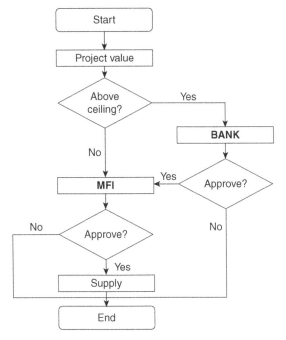

Figure 3.8 Loan allocation with ceiling
Source: Own elaboration.

points for customers. Therefore, the microcredit chain includes the following:

- Associations providing microcredit;
- Associations facilitating access to bank credit; and
- Support networks

that differentiate themselves according to their target, products, funding methods and internal organisation.

Operating experiences and models

Among the microcredit providers, a particularly significant role is played by Adie (Table 3.19). It was created in 1988 thanks to an initiative by Maria Nowak and is now recognised as a public utility association.

The goal of this association, in the belief that self-employment is a powerful tool to achieve social and economic inclusion, is to fight unemployment and social exclusion, by granting funds and support services for start-ups to those subjects who do not have the guarantees needed to access traditional bank loans.

The initial model adopted by Adie is the same that led to the success of Grameen Bank in Bangladesh, which, anyway, soon proved to be incompatible with the French context and, therefore, led to the subsequent adoption of a model based on special agreements with the banks that used to grant loans to enterprises supported by the association.

Today, Adie operates through as follows:

- It lends using its own funds, thanks to the authorization to receive[37] donations, or through access to financing sources and collaborations with banks.
- It provides micro-loans by activating microcredit programmes (The main ones are indicated in Table 3.20).
- It provides customers (unemployed and minimum-income subjects, who represent 48% and 39% of the target respectively) with support services before and after the creation of the micro-enterprises (Banque de France, 2012).

Box 3.2 below shows Adie's operating model. Given the points in common, the same model can be applied, with regard to the initial contact and assessment stages, to the other MFIs examined hereafter.

Table 3.19 Main MFIs in France

MFIs	Type	Date	Mission	Legal Status	Property	Territorial penetration	Target Group
Adie	Other (non-profit association)	1988	Social microcredit Enterprise microcredit	Association of public utility	Private	National	Unemployed people or people on welfare; People excluded from mainstream financial services Micro-enterprises
France Initiative	Other (Associative network)	1985	Enterprise microcredit	Association of public utility	Private	National	Micro-enterprises
France Active	Non-banking financial institution	1988	Enterprise microcredit	Association	Private	National	Micro-enterprises
Nef	Non-banking financial institution	1988	Enterprise microcredit	Cooperative	Private	National	Micro-enterprises
Parcours Confiance	Other (Associative network)	2006	Social microcredit Enterprise microcredit	Association	Private	National	People excluded from mainstream financial services Micro-enterprises
OSEO	Non-banking financial institution	2005	Enterprise microcredit	Joint-stock company	Private	National	Micro-enterprises
BGE	Other (Support organisation)	1980	Support service	Association	n/a	National	Micro-enterprises

Box 3.2   Adie's operating model

Contact	The first contact made by potential customers is free of charge and informal, by telephone or email. The project ideas are screened, and if positively assessed, appointments are made to discuss them at the closest contact point/office. If the projects are not sufficiently developed, the association offers the opportunity to attend a free training programme; after that, applications for funding can be submitted
Assessment	Projects are assessed according to the following criteria: Motivation, expertise, experience Potential customers, business volume expected, and so on Purpose: business creation or development Loan reimbursement capacity according to current/ expected annual incomes
Financial terms and conditions	Limit amount: 10,000 Euros Maximum maturity: 48 months Interest rate: 7.76% up to 6000 Euros; 6.76% from 6000 to 10,000 Euros Solidarity contribution: 5% of the loan amount

Source: based on www.adie.org

Since its creation, Adie has disbursed 120,000 micro-loans and supported 85,000 micro-enterprises through its territorial network, which consists of 15 regional offices, 120 local branches and 246 direct lines[38] throughout the country.

Eighty-two percent of the association's credit activity consists of micro-credit for social purposes, which, due to the high cost of the tutoring service, the risk profile of the target customers and the scarce profitability on small loans, involves the application of higher interest rates[39] than those charged by banks (Lammermann, 2010) and an additional fee. Moreover, Adie requires one or more than one person in the customer's entourage[40] to cover 50% of the loan in order to mitigate credit risk and encourage people close to entrepreneurs to support their efforts. For the aforementioned purposes, as of the end of 2011, the association supported 10,311 projects that resulted in the creation or keeping of 61,802 jobs. The business survival rate of the enterprises supported by Aide after three years amounts to 59% (Table 3.20).

Table 3.20 Main Adie operating programmes

Programme	Objectives
CréaJeunes	Start: 2007 Purposes: free training programme, loan maturity 2–4 months Beneficiaries: young people between 18 and 32 years of age Implementation methods: individual support to formalize the projects and possibility to access microcredit funds through unsecured, no-interest loans; support also in the start-up and development phases of the micro-enterprises Entities/institutions involved and their role within the programme: Le Cabinet Andante, PAI Human Capital, La Fondation Bettencourt Schueller, My Company Files, Conseil Supérieur du Notariat, Turenne Capital, La Française des Jeux, L'Association Française des Investisseurs en Capital (AFIC) Monitoring: No Website: www.adie.org
Projet Banlieues	Start: 2006 Purposes: creation of jobs and social cohesion in disadvantaged neighbourhoods Beneficiaries: projects sponsored by non-profit associations supporting education, professional training, social development and focused on specific needs related to environment and local residents Entities/institutions involved and their role within the programme: BNP Paribas Monitoring: No Website: www.adie.org
Programme ISOMIR (Industrialisation solidaire en milieu rural)	Start: 2010 Purposes: training and economic support for the purchase of agricultural equipment Beneficiaries: agricultural workers Monitoring: No Website: www.adie.org

Source: based on www.adie.org

France Initiative (Table 3.18) is another microcredit association offering financial services with the objectives of tutoring customers and promoting the creation of local businesses. Created in 1985 thanks to a government and quasi-government initiative that reunited 20 programmes supporting local businesses, it now comprises 240 independent local platforms (Banque de France, 2012) under "France

Initiative's platforms", spread throughout the national territory and with offices at the local Chambers of Commerce or Business Trade Associations. Each branch focuses on the peculiar economic needs of its local area, which are met through the creation of local partnerships and funds. The financial instrument used is honourable loans – personal, interest-free and refundable loans – which target subjects with no experience but who are "nearly bankable", and whose projects aim to create three to ten jobs. As of the end of 2011, the association, supported by 14,200 volunteers and 882 employees (of which 624 are full-time workers), financed 15,953 projects through 14,815 honourable loans, 5,734 Nacre loans,[41] and 1,060 loans for the creation of new enterprises, resulting in the creation or keeping of 167,751 jobs. The survival rate of enterprises supported by France Initiative still in the business after three years is 85% (Banque de France, 2012; see Table 3.21).

Following France Initiative, promoted by Fondation de France, Caisse des Dépôts et Consignations (CDC), French National Agency for Enterprise Start-up (APCE) and Crédit Coopératif, there is France Active (Table 3.19), which includes a network of 38 local funds (Fonds territoriaux France Active), created in 1988. This association grants micro-loans by providing financial support through equity measures without collaterals and facilitates access to bank credit through guarantee systems. Lending essentially consists of unsecured, interest-free government loans, including advances for the micro-enterprises financed, mainly dedicated to social associations and enterprises, with a particular focus on those businesses employing individuals coming from depressed areas and/or affected by disabilities. As for credit guarantees, France Active operates through its own guarantee system called France Active Garantie (FAG), which, since 2002, manages four public guarantee schemes that

Table 3.21   Comparison of Adie, France Initiative and France Active (as of 2011)

				Loan terms and conditions			
	Project funded	Survival rate after 3 years	Jobs created / kept	Amount	Loan maturity (months)	Interest rate	Commissions / Fees
Adie	10,311	59%	61,802	€10,000 (max)	48	6.8%-7.8%	5% of the loan
France Initiative	14,815	85%	167,751	€8340 (av.)	24–60	0%	n/a
France Active	5,300	78%	28,404	€10,000 (max)	12–60	0%	n/a

Source: Own elaboration from Banque de France (2012).

will be examined in Section 4.7. The guarantees provided by the association allow accessing to bank loans at favourable rates (94% of the loans obtained through France Active in 2011 had interest rates lower than 5%) and limit the use of joint guarantees (79% of the loans granted 2011 did not require any personal guarantees by entrepreneurs or their entourages). Besides lending, France Active coaches and supports enterprises throughout their business projects and development. As of the end of 2011, the association supported 5,300 projects and raised almost 158 million Euros, allowing for the creation or keeping of 28,404 jobs. The survival rate of the enterprises financed after three years is 78% (Table 3.21), against a national average of 65.9% (Banque de France, 2012). Today, France Active is the main guarantee provider to SMEs and micro-enterprises in France, mainly thanks to funds provided by the CDC.

In the list of MFIs supporting professional microcredit in France, we find also two quasi-banking providers: Nouvelle Economie Fraternelle (Nef) and Parcours Confiance. Nef (Table 3.19), founded in 1988, is a solidarity finance cooperative that supports social, cultural or environmental projects by raising funds and providing credit. Following the approval of Banque de France, it provides medium- and long-term loans in amounts between 10,000 and 125,000 Euros with interest rates calculated according to market rates adjusted to the individual loans' characteristics (amount, maturity, risk, and so on).

On the other hand, the associations Parcours Confiance (Table 3.19) were created by the French savings banks in 2006 to provide microcredit to workers and for social purposes. These associations are tightly linked to bank groups but maintain their independence. Their core business is represented by the provision of microcredit aimed at the creation of enterprises, with unsecured loans in amounts lower than 30,000 Euros (limits vary according to different regions) granted to subjects excluded from the traditional bank system at subsidised rates. The savings banks provide the loans and partly ensure coverage to the credit risk, while France Active guarantees up to a maximum of 70% of their amount.

Among the operators facilitating access to bank credit, there is OSEO (Table 3.19), founded in 2005 as public development bank (it operates under the supervision of the Ministry of Economic Affairs, Finance and Industry); it mainly provides guarantees but also micro-loans to SMEs and micro-enterprises involved in the technology innovation and export business.

OSEO operates in the microcredit sector through partnerships with the major MFIs, support and bank networks, granting *prêts à la création d'entreprise* (PCE, enterprise loans). PCE loans consist of a disbursement with variable interest rate between 2,000 and 7,000 Euros, fully refundable in five years with the payment of the first instalment postponed by six months. PCE loans are granted to support start-ups (operating in all business sectors, except for real estate and agriculture) or those activities with less than three years and whose projects' budgets are lower than 45,000 Euros. PCE loans do not prevent borrowers from accessing other type of financing provided by the MFIs, which must, in any case, be supported by bank loans with loan maturity of less than two years and amounts at least double that of the PCE loans (some variations are allowed for disadvantaged areas). Bank loans are freely approved by banks according to the information provided by OSEO on a specific dedicated network, and enjoy guarantees provided by OSEO itself up to 70%. In 2011, 16,000 PCE loans were granted to individuals or legal entities, with an average amount of 5000 Euros. Since its foundation, PCE loans helped the creation of 200,000 jobs and financed 150,000 entrepreneurs (Banque de France, 2012).

As previously indicated, along with financial services for micro-enterprises, the MFIs provide also other ancillary and instrumental services to support entrepreneurs in administrative procedures, implementation of accounting and management systems, relations with banks and identification of new business opportunities. Along with Adie (which provides support before and after the disbursement of loans), France Initiative (which provides support services for the development of business plans, access to credit and establishment of relationships with the most suitable banks for the projects) and France Active (which provides entrepreneurs also with technical training), the French microcredit market also includes the Boutiques de Gestion (BGE). Unlike the aforementioned MFIs, the BGE (Table 3.19) provide only customised counselling and consulting on business development skills, through a number of training modules in business management for the whole life of the projects. In 2011, this network, which includes 430 branches, 950 employees and 750 volunteer administrative counsellors, allowed the creation or recovery of 17,202 enterprises and created 22,535 jobs. BGE-supported enterprises have a survival rate after three years equal to 72% (Banque de France, 2012).

The above considerations show that in France, like many other countries, commercial banks are the main lenders for SMEs (Berger and Udell, 2002), accompanied by the significant presence and operating volume carried out by the MFIs in the microcredit industry. In this context, the mandatory loan-size ceiling imposed by the French legislator may be seen as a measure to protect the privileges of the banks, which traditionally provide loans in amounts greater than 10,000 Euros (Brabant et al., 2009) to SMEs and micro-enterprises alike. After all, the French legislation led to the creation of a system where microcredit projects are usually co-financed by banks and MFIs. In practice, the imposition of a loan-size cap combined with the co-financing model, built an original model based on "pool microcredit" or "syndicated microcredit", which reveals beneficial to both lenders in terms of soft information sharing.

Both banks and MFIs enjoy several advantages from the co-financed microcredit model (Bennardo et al., 2009):

- Co-financing projects offers the banks the opportunity to enter new market sectors while mitigating credit risk.
- Despite the presence of a loan-size ceiling, the MFIs can continue attracting micro-entrepreneurs applying for loans whose amount is higher than the limit, as they benefit from the screening processes carried out by the banks.

While the literature on the subject shows examples of existing co-financing systems that connect formal and informal institutions in developing countries (Jain, 1999; Andersen and Malchow-Moller, 2006; Degryse et al., 2013), models based on co-financing between banks and MFIs cannot be found in any developed countries (Cuzarenco and Szafarz 2013).

From this standpoint, therefore, the French system is characterised by a number of innovative elements and a more advanced structure when compared to other industrialised countries.

3.8   Mapping microcredit institutions/operators: a comparative analysis of Italy, Spain and France

In the last decades, social and economic changes in the Western countries led to the emergence of new needs, especially in Europe – first of all, financial needs but also new issues related to unemployment. Immigration, transformations in the traditional labour market and the severe economic-financial crisis are all factors that contributed to the above.

Whereas one of the major criticalities in the microcredit sectors of the African countries analysed is represented by the spread of credit intermediaries, the major criticality in the European countries is the development of an efficient capillary networks, in particular between public and private entities. The different institutional models of MFIs in the three European countries examined highlight not only methodological but also substantial differences. On one side, we find regulated financial intermediaries, banks or other financial institutions that operate in the microfinance sector with the aim of expanding the supply of sustainable financial products and services. On the other side, we have specialised institutions, mostly NGOs or non-profit organizations that pursue social objectives such as the reduction of poverty.

In other cases, we have models where the MFIs were originally created as NGOs and then, in order to maximize their objectives of outreach and sustainability, change their legal status into formal financial institutions (e.g., Adie in France).

The substantial difference between these models is related to their ownership and corporate governance structure: normally, institutions that initiate an upscaling process are MFIs operating in the informal or semi-informal sector; a commercial bank that commences a down-scaling process can be identified in a medium/large formal institution that diversifies a small part of its portfolio by investing in a new market, following the indications of its shareholders.

However, the evolution of such models has been affected by the strong perception of considering the credit granted to micro-enterprises as riskier than the "traditional credit" – mainly due to a lack of adequate creditworthiness analysis methods, high fixed costs and, consequently, inadequate operating margins.

We also notice that the public intervention still plays a vital role in the sustainability of the MFIs in European countries analysed.

Spain constitutes a clear example of how the development of the micro-credit sector was negatively affected by the inability to create effective synergies through networks able to combine the efforts of public and private entities, besides having been hit by the crisis of a whole group of banks (savings banks). These circumstances are mostly the consequence of a lack of specific regulatory framework dedicated to microfinance. In Italy, too, the absence of a specific legislation on microcredit until recently, resulted in a plethora of institutions engaged in microcredit programmes. This is why it is impossible to obtain a complete mapping of the microcredit providers operating in the country, as the category includes regional government institutions, regional financial companies, religious organisations, third sector organisations, non-banking foundations and public entities.

France represents an exception: specific legislation on microcredit allowed for an organic development of a sector, where microcredit providers collaborate with associations promoting access to credit and support networks. The evolution of the microcredit sector in Italy and Spain, therefore, will depend on the new regulatory framework and the creation of an official registry/roll of microfinance intermediaries as well as a modern regulatory and supervisory body.

As confirmation of this brief introduction, the comparative analysis between the three European countries highlighted the following (Table 3.22):

• The MFI sector of the countries examined is relatively young and populated also by extremely small organisations and institutions that often struggle to survive. The French sector is different, as it includes MFIs that have been active in the market since the 1980s.
• Most microcredit programmes activated by the MFIs follow an operating model revolving around an extensive network of partnerships between several institutions. Such initiatives are generally promoted by articulated partnerships, where private and public subjects, including third sector organisations, actively collaborate to implement microcredit programmes. The coexistence of different actors in the MFI operating model in the sample is also the result of a risk-sharing policy, which is increasingly popular between the actors involved in the programmes, according to their degree of participation.
• Microcredit programmes often see the relevant participation of public or semi-public MFIs (mostly local MFIs), as they, according to EU guidelines, are the recipients of EU funds specifically provided to promote microcredit.
• The public sector supports MFIs in different ways: through donations, public subsidies and revolving loan funds with the use of EU structural funds (ERDF/ESF).
• Several MFIs are engaged in social and business microcredit indistinctively.
• MFIs range of operations usually covers regional or local areas.
• Several of the activated programmes target beneficiaries affected by financial exclusion rather than poverty.
• Microfinance expertise and know-how developed by the single MFIs are not structured and integrated by a national coordinated strategy. Especially in Italy and Spain, several public and non-profit organisations operate without interacting with each other and/or following a coordinated strategy.
• In Spain, several MFIs activated programmes to support youth; in France, instead, most of them support start-ups (Jayo et al., 2008).

Table 3.22 MFIs in Italy, Spain and France: comparative analysis

	Italy	Spain	France
Start date	A large part of the MFIs were created in the 80s and 90s and the other half after the year 2000.	The first MFIs were created in the 90s and operated mainly within the ethical finance sector; the number of MFIs grew considerably after 2000.	1985
Number of microcredit institutions/ operators	There is no official/unequivocal map	There is no official/unequivocal map.	7
Types	NGOs Financial intermediaries (banks) Religious organisations Third sector organisations and non-banking foundations Public-institutional subjects	Financial institutions: Commercial banks, Savings banks, Specialised MC banks Social Microcredit Support Organisations (*SMIFs*) Public entities	Association of public utility (2) Non-banking financial institution (3) Support organisation (1) Other (1 Association)
Mission	Social microcredit Enterprise microcredit	Social microcredit Enterprise microcredit	Enterprise microcredit (4) Social microcredit and Enterprise microcredit (2) Support service (1)
Legal Status	Joint-stock company Organisation Cooperative Association	Joint-stock company Foundation Associations Cooperative	Association of public utility Association Cooperative Joint-stock company
Property	Public Private	Public Private	Private

Territorial penetration	Provincial Regional or national (rarely)	Regional or national	National
Target groups	All business sectors	Micro-enterprises Unemployed People excluded from mainstream financial services No client-specific targeting Others	Micro-enterprises Unemployed subjects or people on welfare People excluded from mainstream financial services No client-specific targeting Others
Limit of microcredit	Scarce use of EC funds Scarce transparency No impact evaluation of microcredit programmes No centralised monitoring Confusion between purpose and beneficiaries of the activated programmes	Absence of a regulatory framework that governs microfinance and promotes the development of micro-enterprises Lack of SMSOs sustainability Lack of coordination between public initiatives in the public and private sectors and between the subjects operating in the same sector (banks, public sector, SMIFs, micro-enterprises) Lack of information on the sector Scarce development of specific microfinance products and services	Not found

• Institutions belonging to the third sector are generally engaged in the provision of instrumental services. This often translates into a lack of adequate expertise and skills to correctly support microcredit beneficiaries through adequate non-financial non-financial services.

The next biggest challenge for the MFIs is to develop sustainable and flexible business models that are able to sail through periods of recession and economic stagnation such as the current phase. In this perspective, proper use of EU structural funds dedicated to microcredit represents a valid instrument on which, in any case, MFIs have always depended, especially in their start-up phase.

With this regard, we would like to point out that one of the EU's main objectives is promoting the development of its member countries through "more intensive growth and more jobs for all EU regions and cities" (EU regional policy, 2006). In order to speed up the convergence process, the EU provided for the use of structural funds and a policy of cohesion, with the following objectives: economic growth, competitiveness, employment, sustainability, subsidiarity, regionalism and a good level of governance (Allen, 2005, p. 213).

The European policy is original under two aspects. On the one hand, it constitutes the best approximation of a real policy for economic and social development at a European level; it is a common policy based on public investments that represent a consistent part of the EU budget, as well as on its own financial instruments, namely the structural funds. EU funds can be provided through different forms of support. Our research refers to the most common classification, that is, the difference between direct and indirect funds (Figure 3.9). The former are contributions managed by the European commissions or agencies operating at European level or in the member countries.[42] These funds are disbursed in the form of subsidies or non-commercial payments, which must be integrated by the resources of the end beneficiaries. Generally, they are related to EU programmes such as CIP, Seventh Framework Programme, JASMINE, Progress, and JEREMIE.[43] In several of the European programmes activated by the MFIs examined, contributions are made available directly through the use of financial engineering instruments under the EU Structural Funds or through the JEREMIE initiative.

On the other hand, indirect funds are managed by national and/or regional institutions and integrated by the resources of the EU member countries in order to implement the principle of economic and social cohesion within the EU. The relationships between the European Commission and the end beneficiaries are mediated by national, regional or local institutions that deal with planning and management of EU funds. This group includes the Structural Funds, the European Regional Development Fund and the European Social Fund, the Cohesion Fund and other EU instruments.

While EU Structural Funds resources are primarily used for support to enterprises (mainly SMEs), urban development and regeneration, energy efficiency and the use of renewable energy in buildings, EU Structural Funds are used to support self-employment, business start-ups and micro-enterprises. More generally, the EU Structural Funds aim to increase employment, foster entrepreneurship, enhance inclusion and ensure mobility and education in Europe, in line with the revised Lisbon Strategy and the Integrated Guidelines for Growth and Jobs.

For the next financial planning period of the Structural Funds (Europe 2020), the European Commission set the concept of performance as its central theme; in this sense, the MFIs involved in the use of the structural funds will need to assess and report the results achieved in order to show improved use and management of EU resources.

- The microcredit initiatives of the European Commission are funded by the European Investment Fund[45] (EIF). Structurally, they are divided into sections; those specifically dedicated to microfinance programmes are the following:*The Directorate-General for Enterprises*

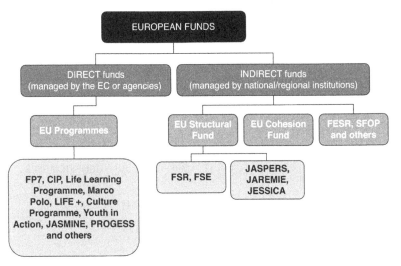

Figure 3.9   Direct and indirect funds in EU[44]
Source: Own elaboration.

and Industry created a framework programme for innovation and entrepreneurship called CIP (Competitiveness and Innovation Framework Programme) in 2007; active from 2007 to 2013, it's now replaced by the programme COSME for the period 2014–20.

- *The Directorate-General for Employment, Social Affairs and Inclusion* in 2010 developed and launched, in collaboration with the Directorate-General for Economic and Financial Affairs, an initiative named "European Progress Microfinance Facility" (within the broader programme PROGRESS). Microcredit operators can benefit from a provision of 200 million Euros, equally funded by EIF and EIB, aimed at increasing the number of loan portfolios instead of re-financing existing portfolios. These credit lines can be provided to the MFIs both as guarantees (25%) and direct loans (75%).
- *The Directorate-General for Regional Policy* launched JASMINE (Joint Action to Support Microfinance Institutions in Europe) for the period 2007–13. Originally, the project provided mainly technical assistance and training to the MFIs, covering topics such as governance, risk management, ICT systems, strategic planning, etc. Admission to its training programme was preceded by an eligibility assessment carried out by a rating agency.
- The same Directorate-General, always for the period 2007–13, launched JEREMIE (Joint European Resources for Micro to Medium Enterprises), whose objective was to improve access to credit for SMEs and micro-enterprises;
- *The Directorate-General for Internal Market and Services* deals with measures supporting social entrepreneurship in EU member countries. Its

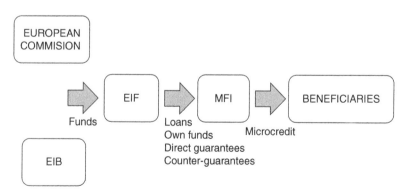

Figure 3.10   Funding of the EC financial instruments
Source: Own elaboration from Banque de France (2010).

"social" approach includes a number of action plans and guidelines for the creation and positive development of this sector.

The funding mechanisms of the financial instruments created by the European Commission to support microcredit are indicated in Figure 3.10.

Notes

* Although the chapter has been prepared by authors jointly, Sections 3.1, 3.2, 3.4, and 3.5 have been written by Pasqualina Porretta, Section 3.3 have been written by Ida C. Panetta, Section 3.6 have been written by Paola Leone, whereas Section 3.7 have been written by Sabrina Leo, Section 3.8 have been written by Paola Leone and Pasqualina Porretta.

1. In 1993, AMOS (*Association pour le Microcédit Oued Srou*) started its microcredit operations catering to 300 clients in the region of EL Kbab.
2. Donor aid and government funding followed the creation of these agencies. The Micro Start program of UNDP (United Nations Development Program) started in 1998, providing financial and technical assistance to six associations with an operating budget of USD 1.7 million. Subsequently, USAID granted more than $16 million, largely to the Al Amana association. In 2000, the funds "Hassan II" bankrolled the sector to the tune of 100 million DH (EUR10 million). This financial contribution allowed for an increase in number and amount of the loans granted, in particular for the three main associations: Al Amana, Zakoura and FBPMC.
3. http://www.mixmarket.org.
4. http://www.mixmarket.org.
5. http://www.mixmarket.org.
6. According to the Africa Competitiveness Report 2009 (WEF, 2009, p. 299), the percentage of collaterals required by banks amounts to 169% of the loan value, compared to an average of 103% in countries similar to Morocco. Moreover, loans granted and secured by collaterals represent 89.7% of the total number of loans.
7. The CCG, created in 1949, is regulated by Law No. 47 of 1995 and executive decree No. 2–95–805 of 14 October 1996. Dar Ad-Damane, a private company, was involved in guarantee funds management, along with CCG, including public funds, until 2009. Later on, following the modifications to the national guarantee system introduced by the government, only CCG was entrusted with the task of managing the national guarantee funds. Dar Ad-Damane was allowed to continue its guarantee funds management activity, albeit limited to private funds.
8. http://www.ccg.ma.
9. CCG e Dar Ad-Damane used to manage up to 14 different guarantee funds (Banque Africaine de Development, 2009).
10. Based on MIX data and MFIs audited reports
11. http://www.mixmarket.org/mfi/country/Morocco/report#ixzz2MlbcaNoo.
12. http://www.bct.gov.tn/bct/siteprod/francais/politique/structures.jsp.
13. Portail Microfinance: profil Pays Tunisie, April 2012, www.lamicrofinance.org.

14. It is also a member of Enda third world family (based in Dakar, Senegal).
15. A specific project, known as CRENDA, was created in 1995, especially dedicated to women in micro-business.
16. www.endarabe.org.
17. http://www.endarabe.org.tn/index.php?option=com_content&view=article &id=46&Itemid=110&lang=en.
18. http://www.endarabe.org.tn/index.php?option=com_content&view=article &id=55&Itemid=117&lang=en.
19. Law No. 43 of 1974.
20. 51% Finance Unlimited, 24.7% EGB, 24.3% Management.
21. 70% Gemini Investment (100% owned by Naguib Sawiras), 20% SFD, 10% Management.
22. SDF was created with the aim of providing a "social safety net", a cushion for the potentially negative impact that the economic and structural reforms in the country could have on the most vulnerable segments of the population.
23. Of the total resources spent by SDF, around 62% is destined to SME development and only 9% was specifically invested in microcredit.
24. These funds were allocated as follows:

    33% to productive family associations

    31% to NGOs

    20% to the Principal Bank for Development and Agricultural Credit

    9% to the so-called village banks

    2% to commercial banks

    5% to other lenders
25. The package allows MFIs to meet some minimum management requirements and become fully functional in a few months, and financially sustainable shortly after.
26. According to estimates by Sanabel (and reported by EFSA, 2010), if we assume that all population near and within the poverty line should be considered eligible for microcredit, then the potential demand consists of 6.9 million people; if we include also low-income individuals, then the figure is close to 21 million (World Bank estimates). Conversely, the customers reached by microcredit were estimated in more than 1.4 million, with a total volume of microcredit provided in the amount of 2.2 billion EGP.
27. World Bank, Global Financial Inclusion Database (Global Findex), http://datatopics.worldbank.org/financialinclusion/.
28. The study was aimed at the creation of a specific office dedicated to the MFIs.
29. In particular (MIX and Sanabel, 2012):

    Some branches shut down

    Loan limits lowered: Some banks closed and a limit to the funds provided by CBE was established

    SFD decided to postpone reimbursements to its counter-parties by three months

    Increased risks for loan officers (attacks were reported)

    Disruption to work schedule: sometimes personnel work from home and it is possible to work only in the first part of the day

Absence of police force and malfunctioning of judicial courts with severe impact on payments and litigations

A few new loans provided and with more stringent terms and conditions; loans renewed with increased prudence

Obviously tourism-related sectors experienced severe slow-downs, including activities that benefited from microcredit; the alarm state, curfews and an increase in thefts contributed to weaken all micro-enterprises and businesses, with significant impact on loan reimbursements

30. Microcredit operations, despite being out of the balance sheets of the savings banks, have been influenced by:

Savings banks' strategic choices: these intermediaries gradually abandoned their regional dimension, expanding their range of operations and fiercely competing with commercial banks.

The significant influence of local governments and political parties on savings banks' objectives.An inherent conflict exists between the public sector as regulator and the presence of public stakeholders in the savings banks model.

31. This model was first applied within the social inclusion programme in Catalonia and the Autonomous Community of Madrid, implemented by the Caixa de la Catalunya along with CP'AC.

32. The system works as follows: Loan applications are submitted by micro-enterprises to a specialised microcredit intermediary (MFI) in order to benefit from its assistance. The MFI carries out creditworthiness assessment of the applicants; banks, therefore, are not involved in the credit assessment and granting process, as they simply make available the capital provided to enterprises and collect the repayments that are periodically paid by borrowers. In the event of late payments, banks evaluate their motivations and possible solutions. The credit limit for financing the operations is created: (1) by the MFIs in the form of deposits at the managing banks as percentage of the micro-loan value, in order to cover any capital losses, interests, arrears and incidental costs generated by the loans; (2) by the Spanish Microcredit Fund as for the part exceeding the percentage covered by the MFIs, up to full coverage of the loans. As for the economic profile of the operations, banks periodically transfer to the fund the difference between the repayments made by borrowers and the operating costs met. The fund periodically pays a commission to the MFIs for each transaction to cover costs and risks against the loans as well as the capital amortised and repaid, in order to replenish the capital provisions of the MFIs.

33. The microcredit *à caractère de fonds propres* is defined in the same way as the classic microcredit, except that interests are not necessarily charged (it is mostly provided interest-free) and includes equity contributions.

34. In particular, individual enterprises benefiting from microcredit are EURL, single-member limited companies, and EIRL, individual limited companies.

35. Overview of the Microcredit Sector in the European Union is a survey that puts a special emphasis on collection and analysis of data from the EMN membership base, the most active and visible organizations in the sector. Therefore, a set of key microfinance institutions (MFIs) surveyed in more detail was selected.

36. In this case, the distinction is between MFIs that cover most of the financing, those covering just a small part of it and those that merely facilitate access to credit.
37. The possibility to raise funds through donations has proved to be the main reason for the success of the association, as it allowed it to speed up the disbursement of loans and reach a greater number of customers. On average, 30 days pass between the first contact and the disbursement of the loan.
38. www.adie.org.
39. This is now possible, thanks to the abolition of the usury law in 2005.
40. Specifically, the association requires that someone close to the micro-entrepreneur be available to provide guarantees in case of default of the latter, for three reasons: mitigate credit risk, increase the entrepreneur's responsibility towards his/her entourage and ensure that the network of individual close to the entrepreneur may support the latter in his/her activity.
41. The measure, activated since 1 January 2009, is aimed at supporting unemployed individuals or people in difficult work situations. The government, in collaboration with the CDC, developed it. Its covers three phases: before, during and after the creation or acquisition of enterprises. Nacre relies on the Social Cohesion Fund to secure interest-free loans for the projects. In 2011, FCS activated guarantees for a total amount of EUR 12.4 million, allowing for a total of EUR 62 million in loans actually provided.
42. http://www.fondieuropei.it.
43. JEREMIE funds for microfinance were set up in Greece, Malta and two French regions.
44. The European Bank for Reconstruction and Development (EBRD), is an international developing bank created in 1991 under the European Union, headquartered in London. Its mission is to facilitate the transition of the former Eastern Bloc countries to open market economies. It mainly operates by granting loans or guarantees and investing in private enterprises; the bank is particularly committed to environmentally sound and sustainable development and projects are individually assessed in order to evaluate their environmental impact. The Council of Europe Development Bank (CEB) is a "multilateral bank with social purposes. Originally created in 1956 to provide support to refugees, it later expanded its scope of activities to other sectors, in order to contribute even more effectively to social cohesion in Europe".
45. The EIF was created in 1994 to provide venture capitals to SMEs, in particular start-ups and tech enterprises. The EIF does not provide loans or subsidies to businesses and does not directly invest in private enterprises, but operates through banks and other financial intermediaries, which use these funds to secure the loans granted to micro-enterprises. The EIF is financed through its own funds, those granted by the European Investment Bank or the European Union.

4
The Microcredit Guarantee Funds and Institutions: A Comparative Analysis

*Paola Leone, Sabrina Leo, Ida C. Panetta, and Pasqualina Porretta**

Credit guarantee schemes are one option to facilitate microenterprises and SME's in accessing the credit market. The credit guarantee schemes represent a vast and heterogeneous number of realities worldwide, usually classified into two main categories: *guarantee companies* (or institutions) and *guarantee programmes*.

Guarantee companies pursue their objective through two basic models, both governed by company law framework: corporate commercial companies (companies or institution) and mutual companies, joint initiative of enterprise – or their representative association – which generally provide a collective guarantee for loan granted to their members.

In the guarantee programmes, the guarantee is generally run within the legal or normative framework of a public or administrative institution according to institutional regulations or programmes resulting from an administrative or political (governmental) decision (Douette et al., 2014, p. 13). Under guarantee programmes, public, limited and temporary resources are provided to an entity/body (public agency, public financial institution or ministerial department, and so on) in order to be managed (generally as an autonomous asset, sometimes called a "guarantee fund") in line with a specific purpose.

This chapter will explore the main technical and operating features of microcredit guarantee schemes with reference to the two main models listed in the analysed countries.

Due to the lack of available information for all microcredit guarantee schemes present in the selected countries, we decided to analyse and compare only those guarantee companies and guarantee programmes (guarantee fund) with sufficient detailed and reliable data. The difficulties of finding information about guarantee funds make it impossible to fill the initial analyses scheme in the form presented in Chapter 1; a final comparison is made with only the available information. The lack of information underlines a great problem for guarantee schemes, and funds in particular, (especially the microcredit ones): a lack of monitoring and disclosure activity related to those funds.

4.1   The microcredit guarantee funds and institutions in Morocco: main features

At the end of 2010, investments in the Mediterranean countries to develop microfinance, promoted by the international community (government agencies, donors, private investors, and so on), area amounted to approximately 600 million USD and represented just 2.5% of the total (CGAP Annual Report 2011). Borrowing results the most-widespread funding source (68%) while guarantees are still little used, though they increased by 5% in 2008 and 10% in 2010 (CGAP, 2010).

The oldest guarantee fund in Mediterranean countries was established in Morocco in 1949, while the most recent in Syria started its operations in 2010. The average equity is 50 million USD, ranging from 10 million USD in Syria, to 75 million USD in Morocco. Half of these guarantee funds are state-owned (Morocco, Tunisia, Jordan, Syria, Saudi Arabia, UAE), while the others are mostly owned by banks (Lebanon, Egypt, Iraq) or donors.

Caisse Centrale de Garantie

A lot of guarantee fund in Morocco are managed by Caisse Centrale de Garantie (CCG); the CCG is a state-owned financial intermediary that represents the main public institute allocating guarantees. Over the past few years, it increased partnership relations with the banking intermediaries in order to optimise the whole microcredit-guarantee process. The CCG's partner banks are generally entrusted with the tasks of screening potential clients and funding. The allocation of the guarantees by the CCG is, therefore, subject to the outcome of the creditworthiness analysis carried out by the banks.

Technical-operational features of guarantees vary in accordance with each guarantee fund (and their respective purposes) managed by the CCG as well as the terms and conditions negotiated with the partner banks.

The CCG manages a number of guarantee funds (Table 4.1); some of them are aimed at businesses (for financial restructuring, investment

Table 4.1 Guarantee funds and other products managed by the CCG

	Enterprise		Personal	
Guarantee Funds	Co-financing Products		Housing Microfinance	Student Loans
Damane Express	FOMAN		Damane Assakane (FOGARIM, FOGALOGE)	Enseignement Plus
Damane Crea	FODEP		FOGALEF	
Damane Exploitation	INNOVATION TIC			
Damane Dev	FOPEP			
Damane Istmrar	MOUKAWALATI			
Damane Capital Risque	ENSEIGNE TEXTILE			
Intégra Textile	RENOVOTEL			

Source: http://www.ccg.ma/fr/index.php?option=com_content&view=article&id=45&Itemid=4.

projects, increase of risk capital) while others pursue objectives related to financial inclusion and social cohesion, such as those offering guarantees on loans to purchase housing and land (Damane Assakane, Fogalef) and on student loans (Enseignment Plus).

Some of the guarantee products managed by the CCG, though not specifically and exclusively dedicated to microcredit, are anyway strongly targeting this sector, such as the "Damane Express", "Damane Crea" and "Damane Dev"(Table 4.2) guarantee funds, aimed at guaranteeing medium and long-term loans for investment projects, or the "Moukawalati" self-employment support fund and the "FOGARIM" guarantee fund, part of the "Damane Assakane" fund, which promotes social inclusion by providing guarantees on loans for residential construction for low-income subjects.

The "Moukawalati" self-employment support fund is a particular product offered by the CCG based on a co-financing model; it combines advances supplied by the government with guarantees granted by the CCG on bank loans. This project is aimed at the creation of new businesses and targets young Moroccans between 20 and 45 years of age in order to help them enter the business world. It therefore promotes social cohesion, development of the labour market and creation of micro-enterprises.

The "Damane Express" and "FOGARIM" guarantee funds, while having different purposes and beneficiaries, are based on a similar operating mechanism: the guarantee covers a maximum of 70% of the loan, its maturity is 18 months but can be renewed up to five consecutive times, and the procedures to reply to the requests for guarantees are quick and easy; turnaround time is usually two days from the submission of the application to the CCG.[1] With regard to the guarantee payment to the bank in the event of insolvency of the beneficiary, the CCG pays 50% of the guaranteed amount within a month from the bank's request, while the remainder is refunded once the legal collection procedures for the guarantee supplied by the beneficiary are terminated. However, refunds must be carried out within three years (Saadani et al., 2011, p. 18). In this way, banks are given a guarantee for recovering the loans disbursed, thus mitigating the uncertainty of the repayment.

In order to assess the operations of the economic impact of the above funds, Tables 4.3 and 4.4 show some statistics related to the guarantee activity carried out by CGC, as of 31 December 2012, through guarantee funds dedicated to enterprises and those dedicated to other social purposes.

As shown in Table 4.2, the extent of credit risk mitigation achieved by the above funds is proportional to the risk level of the business projects/ initiatives; it is quite high in the case of start-ups.

Guarantee funds financed by USAID

In Morocco, several microcredit guarantee programmes were started, also thanks to USAID, which release guarantees on individual loans (portable guarantee/loan guarantee) or on the entire loan portfolio (loan portfolio guarantee) for some MFIs. Specifically,

- *Loan guarantees* cover a single loan granted by a financial institution to a specific borrower for a particular activity. This guarantee is used when borrower, lender, and use of the proceeds are known in advance, whereas the loan would not be made available in the absence of the guarantee.
- *Portable guarantees* are similar to loan guarantees, except that the guarantee starts out with the borrower, not the lender. The lender has not yet been identified. A portable guarantee is used when a borrower cannot access credit due to excessively high interest rates, overly burdensome collateral requirements, or high level of risk associated with the requested loan as perceived by the financial institution. If the borrowers' request for a portable guarantee is approved, they receive a commitment letter from USAID to be presented to potential lenders describing USAID's intent to provide the lender, once identified, with a partial guarantee on its loan to the borrower. With the letter, the

Table 4.2 Key features of the main programmes managed by CGC

| Guarantee Funds | Purposes | Beneficiaries | Operating Methods for Implementation | | | | Coverage Ratio | | |
			Business Sectors	Loan Size	% Beneficiary's Own Fund (min)	% Loan (max)	Min	Max	Fee
DAMANE CREA	To stimulate start-ups by supporting the purchase of material goods (buildings, equipment, and so on) or immaterial goods (start-up phase, patents, rights on third party assets)	Start-ups: Created under the Moroccan law and by less than 3 years with potentially profitable investment projects	All except real estate and fishing	Credit < 1 million DH Credit > 1 million DH	10% 20%	90% 80%	80% 70%	85%	1.5% 2%
DAMANE DEV	To stimulate private entrepreneurship by supporting the purchase of material goods the purchase of material goods (buildings, equipment, and so on) or immaterial goods (start-up phase, patents, rights on third party assets)	Enterprises, individuals or legal entities meeting the following requirements: Created under the Moroccan law by less than three years With potentially profitable investment projects Not subject to reorganisation or liquidation	All except real estate and fishing			Up to 100% of the investment	60% on capital account		2%

Continued

Table 4.2 Continued

Guarantee Funds	Purposes	Beneficiaries	Operating Methods for Implementation				Coverage Ratio		Fee
			Business Sectors	Loan Size	% Beneficiary's Own Fund (min)	% Loan (max)	Min	Max	
DAMANE ISTMAR	Loan repayment to banks (loans supporting the financial restructuring) for loans to finance working capital or long-term investments, except those disputed with the banks	Enterprises, individuals or legal entities meeting the following requirements: Created under the Moroccan law by more than three years With potentially profitable investment projects Not subject to reorganisation or liquidation	All except real estate and fishing	Max 10 million DH for enterprise		50% of the consolidated loan			2%
DAMANE CAPITAL RISQUE	Loans for venture capital increase: Company capital investments through equity or similar (stocks or shares, convertible bonds, equities or investment certificates, current account advances) by private equity companies. These investments cannot be guaranteed by other institutions	Enterprises: Created under the Moroccan law No subject to reorganisation or liquidation at the date of disbursement of the capital contributions	All except real estate and fishing	Max 5 million DH for enterprise			50% of equity and quasi-equity contributions (60% for innovative projects)		1.5%

DAMANE EXPLOITATION	Credit for export	Enterprises, individuals or legal entities meeting the following requirements: Created under the Moroccan law; Potentially profitable	All except real estate and fishing	n/a		0.5% for transaction
INTEGRA TEXTILE	Short-term loans for financing operations of the eligible enterprises; medium and long-term loans to finance stocking of the eligible enterprises	Enterprises in the textile sector that: Benefit of the support programme for aggregators, distributors and transformers according to the National Support Contract in the textile sector; Are sub-contractors and distributors benefiting from the support programme, provided that are referred to by the latter according to criteria indicated in the "target contract", under the above agreement; Affiliated with the government according to terms and conditions provided by specific agreements and created under the Moroccan law	Textile	n/a	70% on capital account	1% for short-term loans 2% for medium and long-term loans

Source: http://www.ccg.ma/fr/index.php?option=com_content&view=article&id=45&Itemid=4.

Table 4.4   Guarantee fund for loans social housing (as of 2012)

Guarantee Fund	Start Year	Number of Applications	Investment *	Volume of Loans*
Damane Assakane	2003	97,593	20,468.01	16,386.45
FOGALEF	2003	113,825	47,604.33	19,145.95
Enseignement Plus	2008	545	90.99	43

*Note: * million DH*
Source: http://www.ccg.ma/fr/statistiques.php.

Table 4.3   Guarantee fund for enterprises/micro-enterprises credit (as of 2012)

Type of Loans	Start Year	Number of Applications	Investments*	Volume of Loans*
Credit for investment projects	1998	3,434	24,388.02	13,305
Start-ups/Recently-created enterprises	2003	3,207	1034.45	849.82
Financial restructuring	2006	94	–	379.28
Credit for ordinary business management	2009	569	–	2983.94

*Note: * million DH*
Source: http://www.ccg.ma/fr/statistiques.php.

borrower has greater leverage to access affordable financing. Once a lender is identified, the portable guarantee becomes a loan guarantee covering up to 50% of the lender's risk.

• *Loan portfolio guarantees* cover a pool of new loans granted by a financial institution to multiple borrowers in an area or sector specified by USAID. The latter shares the risk of default on the loan portfolio to those borrowers, to encourage local financial institutions to extend credit to underserviced sectors, activities and/or areas.

Under these programmes, the percentage of coverage ensured by the guarantees on individual loans may reach up to 100% of the loan guarantees, and up to 50% for portfolio guarantees.

Some guarantee funds have broader developmental objectives, such as supporting export capacity; microcredit programmes making use of guarantee funds often lack structured relationships with the banking intermediaries though; moreover, the very few programmes on which public information is available are characterised by a limited territorial range and lack any national coverage.

Yet Morocco's government seems to have activated a number of financial education programmes in the last few years. These are customer training and coaching initiatives that include interactive tutorials and video clips for illiterate individuals; the government produced a number of video clips that can be used not only in Morocco but in other countries as well.

4.2 The microcredit guarantee funds and institutions in Tunisia: main features

As noted before, Tunisia is not open to the creation of a system of independent and private microfinance institutions, except as a government-financed safety net, although it has authorised one NGO on an ad hoc basis.

Hence, guarantee funds are state-owned or controlled/financed by the government. The main public guarantee fund in Tunisia is the *National Guarantee Fund*, created in 1981, and originally aimed at ensuring that banks allocate some types of loans to small and medium businesses or farmers. In July, Law No. 2000–72 extended the fund's guarantee to microcredit granted by the MCAs; in 2003, its mission was directed prevalently towards agriculture, fishing and handcraft.

The National Guarantee Fund covers loans with variable percentages between 50% and 90%, depending on their type and nature (see Table 4.5). Generally, it offers financial guarantees (funded guarantees).

The National Guarantee Fund is compensated by micro-borrowers with the following fees:

- 3% of the amount of the loan to small and medium companies operating in the manufacturing sector;
- 1.5% of the amount of the loan endorsed also by the *Société de Caution Mutuelle*;
- 2% of the amount of the loan for all types of warrantable loan.

The BTS (Banque tunisienne de solidarité) established a funding mechanism that includes the provision of small loans directly to customers and micro-loans provided through the mediation of a non-profit entity. In the second case, the BTS remains associated with the MCA through an agreement and an annual programme. The BTS generally grants

Table 4.5 Percentage of risk taken by the National Guarantee Fund of outstanding credits

Type of Loans	Coverage Ratio
Short-term loans granted to companies associated to the *Société de Caution Mutuelle*	70%
Short-, medium- and long-term loans granted to small and medium farmers, fishermen, cooperatives or healthcare companies which benefit from government aid	90%
Medium-term loans granted to micro-businesses and higher education graduates who benefit from the FONAPRAM assistance	90%
Short-, medium- and long-term loans granted to small and medium companies operating in the manufacturing sector and in other activities eligible for FOPRODI service contributions	2/3 by the fund and 1/3 by the bank in case the guarantees cover projects benefiting from loans supplied through the FOPRODI resources
Short-term loans granted for financing projects which benefit from FITI aid	90%
Credit for exports	50% for pre-financing 70% for discount of bills

Source: Based on ALPHA-CONSEIL data (www.alphatunisie.com).

0%-interest loans that involve the disbursement of the amount in four payments of 25% each. To receive the consecutive payments, the entity must certify a return rate of at least 80%. Loans must also be granted to the more disadvantaged segments of the population, which are usually excluded from the conventional banking system (Jose et al., 2008).

The BTS mainly turn to the guarantees provided by the National Guarantee Fund to mitigate the credit risk of the loans granted; nevertheless, if the National Guarantee Fund covers 90% of the loans granted by the BTS, it could discourage the same from adopting efficient credit risk management processes. The high insolvency rate of the BTS loan portfolio in recent times, however, should prompt the BTS to tackle this issue, both in order to optimise the available resources and to facilitate the actual economic development of the country and the economic emancipation of Tunisian citizens. It should also be noted that the law establishes a 5% cap on interest rates. BTS and Enda-ia implement in-house training courses on financial and micro-financial topics for their employees.

As previously mentioned, as of July 2000, the MCAs can also make use of guarantees provided by the National Guarantee Fund, which cover from 50% to 90% of the loans allocated against a contribution of 1% of the loan value. Currently, it seems that MCAs not only have not yet made use of the above National Guarantee Fund (Ministère des Finances, 2011, p. 42), but also that they have not reserved any provisions in their balance sheets to cover guarantees against non-performing microloans (despite a 27% NPL rate after three months in 2011; Ministère des Finances, 2011, p. 34). All that highlights the lack of a strategy for mitigating/insuring the credit risk linked to this activity, which represents, as a matter of fact, an important aspect to optimise the credit-guarantee supply chain.

In Tunisia, there is also another important public guarantee scheme: SOTUGAR (Société Tunisienne de Garantie) provides guarantees specifically dedicated to enterprises operating in the manufacturing sector (Decree No 94–492, 28 February 1994, Annex 1). Initially funded by the government and EU, SOTUGAR is a public guarantee scheme. In recent years, SOTUGAR launched an export credit guarantee and energy efficiency fund guarantees for SICAR investments.[2] SOTUGAR offers guarantees on medium- and long-terms loans; the percentage of coverage varies from 50% to 75%. The beneficiaries must pay a fee according to the technical terms and conditions of the loans (Table 4.6).

SOTUGAR has now gained acceptance among banks and is steadily expanding its activity. It has also launched a number of training courses. There are no statistics available on the number of guarantees granted, their beneficiaries, average loan amount and other information on its operations. While the importance of information on customer cross-indebtedness and debts towards other credit suppliers is highly recommended and acknowledged, the sharing of information and the participation in credit risk schemes or the creation of a credit bureau are still being debated in Tunisia.

Table 4.6 SOTUGAR: Fees and types of loans

Type of Loans	Fee
Medium- and long-term loans	0.6% a year or a one-time percentage between 0.9% and 2.6% of the loan value
Short-term loans and leasing	A one-time 1%
SICAR participation	A one-time 3%

Source: http://tunisieopportunites.unblog.fr/2013/01/09/tunisie-les-mecanismes-de-garantie-des-credits/

The scarcity of available information on SOTUGAR's guarantee funds highlights the necessity to revise and redesign the approach, restructure the support management and achieve a clear definition of roles and responsibilities of the several actors operating in the credit-guarantee chain in Tunisia.

In Tunisia, the European Union supported a lot of PMI projects (Projet de modernisation industrielle, 50 million EUR, closed in 2009). It was closely integrated with the Tunisian enterprise support organisation; it provided technical support to the "Centres Techniques", enterprises, public financial institutions (BFPME, SOTUGAR) and business support institutions (Industrial Property, Certification). It also financed market studies and research, and provided part of the initial funding (9 million EUR) of the SOTUGAR. The PMI project is to be followed by the PCAM (23 million EUR over four years), which will be assisting enterprises and quality institutions (ECO, 2010, p. 22–68).

Bechri et al. (2001) examined the case of the Tunisian scheme FOPROPI, which became unsustainable and eventually collapsed in 1997 as a result of a major institutional failure.

The few pieces of publicly available information on the issues covered herein do not allow for an adequate preparation of the guarantee fund analysis scheme.

4.3 The microcredit guarantee funds and institutions in Egypt: main features

In Egypt, credit guarantee schemes have been in place since the 1990s. They are provided by a number of private and public institutions not subject to any specific regulations, unlike other countries. As we will see in detail later on, these initiatives were created:

- On the one hand, to facilitate access to unsecured loans for small and micro-enterprises;
- On the other hand, to increase the financial resources of the NGOs operating in the industry.

In Egypt, guarantee funds are funded by international institutions, which have traditionally supported the government in implementing policies and instruments to assist micro and small enterprises and MFIs, in the belief that they could contribute to the general economic development of the country. More specifically, a number of private initiatives were developed between the late 1980s and the early 1990s to facilitate access to credit for SMEs and micro-enterprises through guarantees:

- The *Credit Guarantee Company for Small and Medium Scale Enterprises* (hereinafter CGC), provides guarantees on loans granted to the SMEs.
- The *Cooperative Insurance Society for Small Enterprises* (hereinafter CIS),[3] provides insurance and micro-insurance services on micro-loans granted by NGOs.

To the above, we must add the individual guarantee programmes in place between micro-loan providers and donor agencies. The role played by the CGC and its operating methods will be examined below, while other initiatives and programmes will only be briefly mentioned, given the difficulty of obtaining reliable and updated information on their operations.

The Credit Guarantee Corporation (CGC)

The CGC was created in 1989 (it started its operations in 1991) as a private joint-stock company (under Law No. 159/1981), thanks to an initiative of the Ministry of International Cooperation and USAID, with the initial goal of encouraging financial intermediaries to fund SMEs by providing guarantees on loans; subsequently, the CGC extended its range of operations to micro-enterprises.

The founding members – nine banks and an insurance company – injected an initial share capital of five million EGP and, besides providing financial resources, offered human resources and their professional expertise[4] to enable the new established entity to be fully operational in a short time. Still today, the donor agencies, mainly foreign organisations, play a big role in funding the CGC. Generally, when receiving aid by the donor agencies, often in the form of cash donations in international currencies, the CGC opens interest-bearing accounts wherein deposits are placed with its partner banks and then use them as collaterals to secure the credit provided to SMEs and micro-enterprises; in this way, CGC can profit both from the spread between the interests on the deposits and the funding cost, and also by collecting the fees paid on the collaterals by the banks. Generally, net revenues are used to refinance the guarantee funds managed by the company. Since borrowing is quite onerous, unlike the funds obtained from the donor agencies, CGC does not resort to this form of funding, limiting, at the same time, the use of the financial leverage of the funds managed to provide guarantees; the leverage ratio, in fact, is hardly higher than 2.2 to 1. In general, therefore, the CGC's funding sources are represented by the funds managed and the contributions it receives from the international donors and the government of Egypt (GoE),[5] which cover around 90% (funds represent around 85%) of CGC's total financial resources (371 million EGP, around 51.9 million USD).

From an operating perspective, the CGC manages several guarantee funds, funded by different subjects, namely the government, USAID and some European countries, including Italy.[6] The company manages each fund separately, with specific risk management and investment policies established in the agreements signed between CGC and the financing entities according to the objectives of the latter (whether development-related or financial objectives). These agreements determine the strategic guidelines that CGC must follow as well as the expected results, identifying also the assessment benchmarks to be used for monitoring the funds' performance and their reporting schedule (quarterly and annual reports on funds and portfolio are sent out to donors): each fund has a separate accounting and is managed as an independent entity. The CGC operates, therefore, according to what is known as a "funded scheme" (Deelen and Molenaar, 2004), issuing guarantees on the loans against the mentioned funds.

The subjects eligible to obtain the guarantees, the type of loans they can apply to and the percentages of coverage are also indicated in the agreements signed with the donor agencies. The CGC guarantees for percentages up to 100% (for instance, for projects in collaboration with the NGOs) of the loans value granted by its banks partner (around 30 bank branches[7]). The percentages guaranteed, besides varying depending on the fund, have been subject to adjustments over time; for example, in 2010 some programmes dedicated to SMEs have achieved percentages up to 75%, whereas the initial coverage was not higher than 50% (Roper, 2011, p. 21). Given the risk of this type of loans, percentages of coverage lower than 50% did not contribute to the appeal of both the microcredit operations and the loans granted to the SMEs. Low coverage was also the result of a prudential risk assumption policy adopted by the CGC, given the lack of NPL track record.

According to the information available, we identified six programmes currently managed by the CGC (Table 4.7).

As for the target of the guarantee, the table shows that the CGC supports programmes divided into six categories (Table 4.7), two of which are related to the size of businesses (start-ups and SMEs), two to the development strategy (reduction of poverty and modernisation of

Table 4.7 Key features of the main programmes managed by CGC (as of 2010)

Programme	Founder	Start Date	Purpose	Beneficiaries	Operating Methods for Implementation		
					Type of Funding and Amount of Fund	Loans Size/ Business Sector/ Assets	Coverage ratio
SME Fund[8]	Egypt government	1991 April 2003	Facilitate the access of SME to financing	SME	Soft loan: EGP 60 million[9] Trust fund: EGP 60 millions[10]	*Loans size:* min EGP 20,000 max EGP 1,4 million *Business Sector:* all *Type:* working capital or investment	Up to 75% (at the beginning up to 50%)
Health Care Providers Programme (HCPP)	USAID	1991	Facilitate the access of target group to financing provided by CGC's partner banks and NGOs specialised in this type of lending	Healthcare professionals (including physicians, dentists, veterinarians, pharmacists and healthcare facilities such as laboratories and clinics)	Trust fund: EGP 33.9 million (USD 10 million at that time)[11]	n/a	100% of loans up to EGP 100,000, and 65% to 75% of loans exceeding such amount

Continued

Table 4.7 Continued

Programme	Founder	Start Date	Purpose	Beneficiaries	Operating Methods for Implementation		
					Type of Funding and Amount of Fund	Loans Size/ Business Sector/ Assets	Coverage ratio
Small and Emerging Business (SEB) Support Programmes	USAID	2000	Facilitate the access of SME to financing through NGOs under contract with CGC to provide small and micro and group-focused micro-loan[12] services to MSMEs	Micro and SMEs	Trust fund: USD 8.2 million	n/a	100% of the NGO's overdraft with its bank
Poverty Alleviation and Employment Generation programme (PAP)	Italian government	1998	Raise the living standard of micro-entrepreneurs in the Giza Governorate by increasing their incomes	Micro	Trust fund: EGP 2.7 millions	n/a	100% of the NGO's overdraft with its bank
Industrial Modernization Program Credit Guarantee Fund (IMP CGf)	EU[13]	2005	n/a		n/a	n/a	n/a
Energy Efficiency Improvement and Greenhouse Gas Reduction (EEIGGR)	UNDP	2005	n/a		n/a	n/a	n/a

the sector) and two to specific sectors of the economy in Egypt (healthcare and energy).

With specific regard to microcredit, it must be noted that, according to the available data, it is not possible to identify exactly the funds providing the guarantees for the micro-borrowers; if we exclude, in fact, the two funds dedicated to healthcare (though some medical professionals could be considered micro-entrepreneurs) and energy, theoretically all other programmes could be used to provide the micro-loan guarantees. Surely intended for the development of microcredit is the SEB program, for which the CGC – in cooperation with USAID – is committed to start the programme with 30 so-called lending units, initially only in the Great Cairo area, then extending it to the whole national territory. In particular, the CGC here plays the following role in the programme:

- It supports start-up and operating costs of the lending units up to the break-even point.
- It provides technical assistance for the lending units' resources.
- It offers a 100% guarantee on the micro-loans granted by these lending units.

The beneficiaries of these programmes are NGOs.

In terms of supply, the CGC offers four products: individual loan guarantees, loan portfolio guarantees, securitisation and factoring (for bigger companies), aimed at financing both fixed-assets and working capital.

Generally, the guaranteed subjects pay the CGC a fee amounting to 2% of the loan value.[14]

The types of guarantees and the relationships between the CGC and banks underwent several changes over time:

- During the first phase, from 1991 to 1997, the CGC used to provide loan guarantees for each eligible loan against the payment of a commission.
- In the second phase, from 1997 onwards, the HCPP Fund also covered the bank accounts overdrafts of NGOs that used to provide loans to healthcare professionals; starting in 1998, the same occurred in the Italian programme, and since 2000, also for the SEB Fund dedicated to projects financing micro-enterprises.
- The third phase was characterised by a progressive shift from individual loan guarantees to bank portfolio guarantees.

In addition, during the third phase, between 2004 and 2005, the CGC proposed that the banks manage the whole credit portfolio guaranteed in outsourcing against a management fee; it is not clear how such a proposal was received.

According to a survey carried out by Bennet et al. (2005), the most active partner banks have mainly a commercial interest in CGC's "products" and have only residually shown a willingness to support the government policy to promote SMEs or other social projects. It is worth pointing out that such commercial interest is not related to any regulatory opportunities; as Basel II is not yet fully operational in Egypt, the CGC contributes to reduce credit risk without generating a risk-mitigation effect for the banks. In fact, loan reserve requirements for banks are established by the central bank beforehand and depend on the nature of the borrowers rather than the types of guarantees offered.[15]

While the relationships between banks and the CGC develop during the guarantee provision process, there is hardly any direct relationship (if so, it is quite marginal) between the guaranteed subjects and the CGC. Banks, in fact, select the entrepreneurs who may benefit from the guarantees (a so-called ex post scheme) and perform the initial risk assessment. Even if potential borrowers contact the CGC directly, they would be referred to a partner bank.

The relationship between the CGC and NGOs is quite different; the provision of guarantees aimed both at facilitating access to credit for the NGOs in need to fund their activities, and to its own micro-loan portfolio for small and micro-enterprises.

In the first case, as indicated in Figure 4.1, the CGC guarantees the NGOs in their relationships with banks, by enabling them to obtain loans aimed at supporting micro-entrepreneurs. As previously mentioned, the

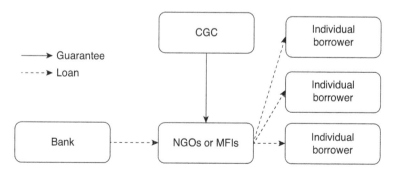

Figure 4.1   Institution-oriented approach used by CGC towards NGOs

NGOs' regulatory framework does not encourage banks to provide unsecured loans to them (Chemonics, 2007, p. 6). Moreover, banks must be expressly authorised by the CBE to grant loans to NGOs against guarantees in foreign currencies, which represent the main funding source for such organisations.

We can therefore say that the different programmes managed according to the different relations between the CGC and guaranteed subjects, can be considered *institution-oriented funds*, when they are aimed at facilitating financing for the NGOs', or *enterprise-oriented funds*, when banks grant loans to micro-enterprises.

As for the evaluation process, initiated upon recommendation of the banks, it basically regards the compliance with the criteria for the use of the fund, the characteristics of the borrowers and the projects to be financed. Generally, creditworthiness analyses from banks regard larger enterprises – unlike those from the NGOs – where it is possible to carry out a comprehensive assessment and acquire their credit score, in addition to consulting local credit bureaus and registries.

Applications for guarantees handled by the NGOs instead require a more careful evaluation by the CGC as well as an additional follow-up on the guarantees issued on the loan portfolio. In order to increase the exchange of information, a CGC representative attends the meetings of the NGOs' credit committees. Moreover, the NGOs are monitored and assessed by the CGC through portfolio monitoring and a monthly online reporting system.

The CGC is not subject to the supervision of the Central Bank or any other financial regulatory authority; however, it is supervised by the *Egyptian Central Auditing Organization* (CAO) and monitored by the financing intermediaries as well as, obviously, by the Ministry of International Cooperation (MIC). Thanks to the direct involvement of

Table 4.8 Main characteristic of the guarantees by enterprise size: taxonomy

Type of enterprise	Micro	Small	Medium
Application	NGOs and Banks	Banks	Banks
Fee (% of total outstanding loan)	2%-3%	2%	2%
coverage ratio(risk taken by CGC)	100%	Max 75%	Max 75%
Guarantee ceiling (EGP)	–	Up to 1 million EGP (170,000 USD)	Up to 2 million EGP (340,000 USD)

Source: Own elaboration of Rope (2011).

Table 4.9   Main goals reached by CGC towards MSMEs

Reference Year	Number of Guaranteed Enterprises	Amount of Outstanding Guarantees*
From start to 2003[17]	18,654	192
2009	44,481**	949.5***
2010[18]	156,518	EGP 1.5 billion

Note: Data excludes results of HCPP, EEIGGR Programmes, * EGP million, ** of which EGP 34.7 million to micro-enterprises, *** of which 40,501 to micro-enterprises

Source: Own elaboration.

the GoE in the creation, support and partial supervision of this company, the CGC operates as a quasi-governmental body rather than a private entity.

From an organisational standpoint, the CGC is structured through seven departments and employs a total of 200 workers, 36% of them assigned to the guarantee department. Through its seven branches located in Northern Greater Cairo, Southern Greater Cairo, Alexandria, Tanta, Ismaileya, Minia and Assiut, the CGC operates in all 26 governorates in the country. Thanks to its structure, the CGC can reach a great number of small and micro-enterprises (Table 4.9); however, fragmented data do not allow for a comprehensive and specific evaluation of its support to the microcredit sector. Anyway, from its foundation to 2012, the CGC granted guarantees for a total value of over 10 billion EGP, enabling MSMEs to access loans for 19 billion EGP.[16]

Cooperative Insurance Society for Small Enterprises

The other institution operating in the credit guarantee sector to facilitate loans to the MSMEs is the *Cooperative Insurance Society for Small Enterprises* (CIS). The CIS was created by the *Social Fund for Development* (SDF) in 1999 with a capital of 10 million, under the Insurance Supervision and Regulation Law (Law No. 10 of 1981) with the objective of offering insurance-products characterised by favourable conditions ("with appropriate and cost-effective terms and conditions"), including insurance programmes covering micro-loans granted by NGOs. As an insurance company, CIS is subject to the EFSA (former Egyptian Insurance Supervisory Authority – EISA) supervision.

At present, the CIS guarantees 80% of bank loans against the payment of a fee in the amount of 1% of the loan value. Since CSI is a cooperative, in order to benefit from its programmes, beneficiaries must become its members by purchasing shares (100 EGP per share).

For each EGP 10,000 obtained by the beneficiaries, the latter are entitled to a share in the company, which pays an annual dividend. The company is currently making a profit and, unlike in the beginning, it has now extended its guarantee services to professional associations and external loans.

As previously mentioned, the CIS was created and operates under the SDF; this means that the financial intermediaries participating in the SFD programmes (which provide for the use of this instrument) must use the CSI guarantees. In addition to this inevitable competitive advantage, the "imposing" presence of the SDF did not allow the CIS to operate efficiently: in fact, by operating essentially through an individual model of guarantee and the support of the SDF, the CIS is perceived as obliged to provide guarantees – and it actually does so. Consequently, despite the high credit risk coverage offered by the CIS, banks often require borrowers to come up with additional guarantees, almost in contrast with CIS's mission, which should facilitate access to credit for microenterprises and, at the same time, reduce any information asymmetries. This issue is partly highlighted by the fluctuating volumes managed in the period 2006–11, with activity close to zero between 2009 and 2010 (Table 4.10).

The document on the National Strategy for Microfinance (p. 12) is critical towards both organisations, CGC and CIS, at least until 2004; the final document, in fact, remarks on their failure to achieve significant objectives in terms of facilitating access to bank loans for the NGOs.

Alongside the guarantees CGC and CIS provide, there are other guarantees or co-guarantees provided by international development agencies (or supranational entities) such as KfW Development Bank and African Development Bank (AFD), which have already started or are in the process of activating credit guarantee programmes aimed at channelling NGOs' funds, seen as microcredit catalysts. Fragmented data on these guarantee funds does not allow for an in-depth analysis of their operations.

Table 4.10   Evolution of CIS main figures (2006–11)*

	2006–07	2007–08	2008–09	2009–10	2010–11
Investments	75,333	81,808	47,922	0	67,299
Paid-up capital	3,948	27,248	29,767	0	30,184
Capital reserve	683	9,249	(70,054)	-	7,382

Note: * EGP000s

Source: Own elaboration on EFSA data, 2012.

4.4 The microcredit guarantee funds and institutions in Italy: main features

As part of the microcredit programmes implemented in Italy so far, guarantee funds were often activated to mitigate, more or less incisively, the micro-borrowers' credit risk.

In particular, research carried out in 2011 by *Ente Nazionale per il Microcredito* (Italian National Public Agency for Microcredit, p. 89) showed that the presence of the guarantees seemed to be a decisive element in determining the provision of loans, even more so than the economic-financial assessment of the business projects. Also, access to microcredit in Italy seems to be governed by a purely insurance logic.

The guarantee funds are generally created through resources made available by public organisations, banks and banking foundations, chambers of commerce and other private institutions. The use of the European ESF funds for this purpose is extremely limited, as was already pointed out, Guarantee funds often have a mixed public-private nature, although their managers usually come from the private sector. They often coincide with the same intermediaries that allocate the loans and collect the guarantee funds deposited in earmarked current accounts.

The promoters of the microcredit programmes, as shown by a recent survey (*Ente Nazionale per il Microcredito*, 2011, p. 89), are mainly represented by local government authorities, such as provinces and regions, regional finance companies and, especially in the Convergence Regions, religious organisations, which play a vital role in the microcredit supply chain thanks to their large knowledge of the local contexts; less relevant is the activity of the bank foundations in the sector. As for the territorial coverage, the prevalent model privileges a local dimension, often coinciding with provinces and municipalities, rather than regional or national size (Table 4.11).

Table 4.11 Territorial coverage of microcredit promoters

Territorial Coverage	Number of Promoters
National	3
Regional	4
Provincial	6
Municipal	3
TOTAL	16

Source: Based on Ente Nazionale per il Microcredito (2011).

In 38% of cases, the microcredit programmes implemented have purely social or charity purposes, while those specifically aimed at promoting self-employment and entrepreneurship amount to 32%; 29% of the interventions are characterised by mixed purposes, while a negligible 1% represents measures implemented "for education purposes only" and aimed at financing training courses or studies. The situation sharply changes if we consider only the so-called Convergence Regions, where most programmes aim to promote self-employment and entrepreneurship (*Ente Nazionale per il Microcredito-Italian National Publi Agency for Microcredit*, 2012). Many of them require the creation of guarantee funds.

Several microcredit programmes with guarantee funds activated by public entities are dedicated to immigrants (who are traditionally more affected by financial exclusion).

In total, around 3,800 requests for microcredit were received at a national level in the period 2005–10, for a total volume of 31,600,000 EUR. 2,100 of these, amounting to around 27,000,000 EUR, were forwarded to the banks for financing; the percentage of requests sent to the banks out of the total number of applications received amounts to 56%, which is 85% of their total amount[19] (Table 4.12).

The requests for microcredit applications in the period 2005–10 and specifically concerning immigrant micro-entrepreneurs amount to

Table 4.12 Comparative analysis between requests for microcredit from immigrant micro-entrepreneurs and total requests for microcredit (2005–10)

Requests for Microcredit	Requests Approved		Requests Sent to Banks		Ratio %	
	Number (a)	Amount* (b)	Number (c)	Amount* (d)	c/a	d/b
A. Requests exclusively from immigrants	1,164	12,826,974	703	9,696,058	60.4	75.6
B. Total number of requests (microcredit for enterprise support and social microcredit)	3,796	31,595,894	2,132	26,937,609	56.2	85.3
Ratio % A/B	30.7	40.6	33.0	36.0		

Note: * *EUR*

Source: Based on Ente Nazionale per il Microcredito (2011).

30.7% of the total, as for their number, and to 40.6%, as for their total amount, as indicated by the 16 promoters. If we consider the requests sent to the banks, such percentages amount to 33% and 36% respectively. The average amount of the requests sent to the banks is quite limited, also in light of the maximum limits allowed by the new legislation on microcredit introduced by Legislative Decree No. 141 of 2010.[20] In fact, it emerges that micro-loans specifically concerning immigrant micro-entrepreneurs show an average amount of around 13,800 EUR, basically identical to non-migrant micro-entrepreneurs. This amount is still far higher than for social microcredit, which is a little more than 3,000 EUR.

Although the overall figures result from different average amounts according to the programmes (they vary from a minimum of 5,000 EUR to a maximum of 21,000 EUR), we can assume that the micro-loans requested are just enough to start a small artisanal or business activity in an advanced economy like Italy (Table 4.13).

Many banking intermediaries that participate in microcredit programmes, when determining the creditworthiness of the applicants, only rely on subjective evaluations; very few of them make use of credit scoring techniques. And even when they do, microcredit operations are not treated distinctly from others; this means that these operations are examined according to the same scoring systems used for small amounts of ordinary credit. This appears to be a further distortion within the above evaluation process; it is quite clear indeed that microcredit is characterised by a number of peculiarities that necessarily call for a dedicated and specific assessment methodology.

Information on the guaranteed subjects, collected in the preliminary investigation phase, in the majority of cases is not structured in an electronic database. There seem to be no systems/methods for the exchange

Table 4.13   Main business sectors involved

Business Areas	Immigrant Micro-entrepreneurs (%)	Micro-entrepreneurs in General (%)
Commerce	53	39
Handicraft	34	35
Constructions	24	–
Restaurants	22	–
Services to individuals	9	16
Services to companies	3	–
Tourism	–	5

Source: Based on Ente Nazionale per il Microcredito (2011).

of information on the borrowers between the owners/managers of the guarantee funds and the microcredit promoters.

The creditworthiness of micro-entrepreneurs and information sources used are not frequently revised and updated. The decision about whether to allocate credit or not seems to follow, in general, that of the microcredit promoters, while in other cases it is parallel/concomitant or preventative to this The guarantee funds in Italy are often created as monetary funds, which usually grant collaterals characterised by a very high percentage of the loans (up to 100%). This means that, in general, no leverage ratio is applied on the initial dimension of the fund or, when applied, it is quite low (between two and five).

All this limits the effectiveness of the funds as well as the optimisation of the benefits for the operators participating in the microcredit chain. So far, no one seems to worry about the compliance of the guarantees with the regulations on prudential management of the banks; this will certainly be a topic of discussion for the elaboration of any microcredit policy in the future.

Today, most banks that participate in microcredit programmes with guarantee funds do not seem to have an internal organisational structure – roles/functions expressly dedicated to microcredit. Tutoring beneficiary of microcredit is often carried out in collaboration with the local MFIs. Actually, the presence of organisational roles and functions dedicated to microcredit could be the turnkey for activating a more stable and cooperative relationship between immigrants and promoters, thus favouring the growth of micro-businesses, reducing the risks for banks and ensuring – at least theoretically – the attainment of important cost economies (in particular, in the case in point, information and purpose-based economies, in virtue of the development of cross-selling). Furthermore, such organisational structure could allow to obtain important soft information for evaluating the risk of the microcredit beneficiaries and their entrepreneurial projects, given the fact that management costs, especially the ones related to monitoring, are way too high; moreover, they are aggravated by the scarce amount of information on the enterprises and business sectors to support, including a reduced presence of local networks supporting immigrant entrepreneurs.

A particularly controversial aspect of the programmes examined is related to the definition of their beneficiaries, which it is often unclear; several microcredit programmes seemed to indicate a number of beneficiaries at the beginning, but then, as a matter of fact, their resources were made available also to other subjects.

Actually, for a correct management of the programmes and risks, their beneficiaries should be specifically determined by indicating exactly the requirements they should meet during the screening of their requests. Unclear, obscure or undetermined procedures obviously do not favour screening, monitoring and reporting of the programme results; often information is available only on the number of approved projects within a given programme.

Management cost data of microcredit programmes with guarantee funds are unknown; the aforementioned survey (*Ente Nazionale per il Microcredito*, 2011) identified some of the management costs declared by the promoters of microcredit programmes dedicated to micro-enterprises; they run from a minimum of 400 EUR to a maximum of 570 EUR (including legal and consulting fees, communication and marketing activities, in addition to the management costs associated with the relationships with the applicants).

Data on microcredit criticalities recorded so far (as of 2010) are on average higher than those identified at a national level, where, in any case, the credit quality was more affected by the weakness of the economy. At a national level non-performing loans accounted for 1.2% in 2008 to 2% in 2010 compared to the total number of loans; substandard loans instead increased from 2.1% to 3.3% in 2010.

In the Annex 1 you can find an overview of the operating characteristics of some microcredit programmes promoted by the Apulia Regional Administration that make use of guarantee funds as their financial instrument; among the Convergence Regions in Italy, Apulia is the most capable in making use of the EU structural funds to implement microcredit programmes to support its economy (*Ente Nazionale per Microcredito*, 2011, p. 89).

In the Italian microcredit guarantee sector there is also another player (a public one): the Central Guarantee Fund (FCG), established in 1996 with Law No. 663 and managed by *MedioCredito Centrale*. It offers access to credit by supplying direct guarantees to financial intermediaries, co-guarantees with other funds/guarantee intermediaries favouring lending companies and, finally, counter-guarantees supported by other funds, mainly those of welfare entities.

Access to the FCG guarantees is essentially limited to financially stable SMEs. The guarantees cover a percentage of the loans between 50% and 80% and a commission is required for their allocation, which is higher for larger companies (further discounts are expected for women's micro-enterprises). In recent years, the FCG played a key role in the allocation of public guarantees on small loans (in many ways similar to microcredit).

Within the vast guarantee activity carried out by the Central Guarantee Fund, the government decided to reserve a specific position for low-amount operations[21] (although not completely similar to the concept of microcredit according to the new regulatory framework) by setting forth a number of simplified requirements. Low-amount operations are given priority during the preliminary credit assessment procedures and undergo a simplified creditworthiness analysis. The low-amount operations carried out by the FCG, on the other hand, are exclusively aimed at enterprises active for at least two years and judged financially and economically sound. The commissions for allocating the guarantees are very low and vary between 0% for micro-businesses employing mainly women[22] and 0.25% of the amount guaranteed by the fund for micro-businesses not located in one of the protected regions.[23] These commissions are lower than those established for small and medium businesses, due to a specific policy aimed at promoting this delicate group of enterprises, which are distributed throughout the Italian territory, are generally under-capitalised and lack adequate financial resources.

In particular, since 2009, the fund Management Committee has adopted more flexible assessment criteria and introduced a number of simplified procedures aimed at allowing the Central Guarantee Fund to work more closely with the slumping economic context.[24]

Data available (Central Guarantee Fund Management Committee, 2012) highlight that, in 2011 and 2012, the fund granted guarantees mainly to micro-businesses (60.5% of the total operations, Table 4.14, 4.15). With regard to business sectors, industry is the area producing the highest number of requests accepted (26,720 operations), followed by commerce (20,350 operations). Even though the second half of 2012 was characterised by an increasing use of the above instrument by businesses whose financial levels were higher, the average value of the guarantees granted and the collateralised loans continued to drop (respectively 65,700 EUR and 133,400 EUR at the end of 2012 against 79,900 EUR and 151,000 EUR in 2011). In addition, an increase of requests for low-amount loans was recorded (up to 100,000 EUR: 43,326 requests received, 70.6% of the total). Furthermore, from a territorial point of view, the majority of the requests accepted concerned mainly enterprises located in the North (48.5% of accepted requests) and in the South of Italy (31.2%).

Within the total granted requests, counter-guarantee interventions represented the prevailing amount (67.3% of the total, with 41,309 operations), followed by requests for direct guarantees (32.5% of the total, with 19,984 operations) and co-guarantees (115 operations). Comparing the data relating to the same period of the previous year, we can observe a higher increase of requests for direct guarantees (12.8%) than counter-guarantees (10.2%). Counter-guarantee operations bear the highest amount of loans granted, equal to EUR 4.8 billion, while direct guarantees account for EUR 3.3 billion.

Out of 41,309 requests for counter-guarantees, the majority of the operations, equal to 36,099 units (87.4% of the total) are granted upon first request, while the additional ones are 5,210 (12.6% of the total).

Guaranteed women-led businesses stood at 25% of the overall operations. The economic activities are mainly included in the retail business, with the exception of cars and motorcycles, personal goods repair and home appliances. 49% of the guarantees granted were directed to support such activities, while 13% went to hotels and restaurants. The commercial sector had the highest number of requests to access the fund, accounting for 78% of the fund-guaranteed operations. The type of guarantee adopted was mainly counter-guarantees, used in 64% of the cases, while direct guarantees were used in 35.8% of the cases. There were hardly any requests for co-guarantees.[25]

These low-amount guarantee operations carried out by the Central Guarantee Fund, though similar to microcredit operations, show some elements differing from the definition of microcredit according to the Italian legislation, specifically article 111 of the Consolidated Law on Banking. However, a number of adjustments and innovations are expected for the public guarantee activity in the microcredit sector in the near future.

Table 4.14 Number of requests received by size of business (years 2011–12)

Year	Micro-Businesses	Small Businesses	Medium Businesses	Others
2011	35,061	15,980	4,140	25
2012	37,142	18,859	5,370	37

Source: Based on Central Guarantee Fund Management Committee (2012).

Table 4.15 Loans granted in thousand million EUR (years 2011–12)

Year	Micro-Businesses	Small Businesses	Medium Businesses
2011	2.5	3.5	2.3
2012	2.3	3.5	2.3

Source: Based on Central Guarantee Fund Management Committee (2012).

As a matter of fact, the "Save-Italy decree" of December 2011 introduced, among others, a number of innovations on the guarantees for the microcredit industry. They included the requirement to reserve a portion of the available funds managed by the FGC to guarantee interventions in favour of microcredit, according to article 111 of the Consolidated Law on Banking, aimed at promoting entrepreneurship. For the creation of the above-mentioned reserve and the definition of its resources, the Italian Ministry of Economic Development should soon issue a nonregulatory decree.

Several microcredit programmes are active in Italy (Table 4.16). The weight of the Convergence Regions (Campania, Calabria, Apulia and Sicily) in them is quite relevant, often greater than or equal to other geographical areas. Overall, more than a third of the total initiatives started up nation-wide were concentrated in the South of Italy in 2012 (*Ente Nazionale per il Microcredito*, 2012).

Limits of the microcredit guarantee fund sector in Italy

Generally, the main criticalities detected in the microcredit programmes activated in Italy are related to the following:

• first of all, a serious deterioration in the use of EU funds for the implementation of the above programmes (especially in the period 2007–11[26]) in the South of Italy (with different degrees) and also the achievement of results below expectations.[27] It is a peculiarity in common with many other European countries that scarcely participated in the EU programmes defined by the European Commission (Jeremie, Progress and Jasmine), probably due to a lack of knowledge at local level and a widespread difficulty of local microfinance institutions to meet EU requirements and parameters;

Table 4.16 Geographical distribution of microcredit initiatives

Geographical Areas	Microcredit Initiatives	Distribution %
North west	15	19.2
North east	17	21.8
Centre	19	24.4
South convergence region	18	23.1
South no-convergence	9	11.5
Total	78	100.0

Source: Based on Central Guarantee Fund Management Committee (2012).

- lack of transparency and clear information on microcredit programmes. There is little readily available information on the project results in terms of credit volumes provided, technical characteristics, credit performance and guarantees, terms and conditions applied to loans, and so on. With a few exceptions, there seems to be a strong reluctance to publish the microcredit programme results; likewise, it is hard to obtain a clear picture of the whole projects (in terms of subjects involved, roles and responsibilities, business sectors involved). The microcredit programmes activated in Italy often lack the use of effective communication methods to disseminate information to the public (information is available on different websites, including some obsolete ones, often overlapping and unclear); communication is often fragmented and limited to a few basic pieces of information. There are few indications on the roles and responsibilities of the subjects involved in the programmes (who considers the applications, who disburses the loans, and so on); equally unclear are the operating methods of several programmes (interest subsidies, provision of subsidised loans, guarantees); data on monitoring of the programme performance is almost never available;
- no centralised and institutional monitoring of the microcredit programmes;
- inadequate or missing assessment of the social-economic impact of the microcredit programmes activated. This assessment seems to be present, albeit low-quality, in programmes activated through EU structural funds, but it must necessarily be improved to be used as an instrument for effective decision-making;
- incorrect determination of roles and responsibilities (who is in charge of what) of the various subjects involved in the microcredit programmes (public institutions, chambers of commerce, banks, guarantee intermediaries);
- some programmes appear to include generic and unspecified objectives; for instance, in some cases, co-financing of innovative projects in partnership with other national, European and extra-European entities and promoted by regions, government and the EU, is combined with the promotion of enterprises, with a particular focus on social enterprises. In other cases, social objectives are mixed with support to enterprises, which should be pursued through different methods and instruments; several programmes are then indistinctively addressed to financially excluded micro-enterprises and families, while others are generally directed to youth, unemployed and innovative start-ups created by young or women entrepreneurs.

Scarcity of instrumental and complementary microcredit services: a few programmes indeed combine the provision of micro-loans with coaching and tutoring services (although the reference legislation considers them as constitutive elements of any microcredit activity). Besides the technical support during the pre-investigation phase, a few programmes show awareness to support the start-ups through training, technical assistance and monitoring of the newly created business. The projects promoted by public entities – except for a few cases – do not provide for partnerships with organisations able to provide coaching, mentoring and tutoring services.

4.5 The microcredit guarantee funds and Institutions in Spain: main features

The credit guarantee system in Spain was considered relatively stable until the early 2000s, having contributed to improve the financial management of micro-enterprises. However, soon some weaknesses started to emerge, mainly due to the kind of products offered and the incapacity of monitoring the credit risk of the guarantee intermediaries and, therefore, generating large credit lines, that is a multiple of the assets used as collaterals, combined with the inability of assessing atypical enterprises.

Guarantee funds were used in the period 2000–09 within state-sponsored programmes participated also by Savings and Loans banks and large commercial banks. The main programmes that activated guarantee instruments were: ICO (*Instituto de Credito Oficial*) Microcredit Line 2002–05, Microcredit *Programme para Emprendedoras y Impresaria del Instituto de la Mujer* (2001).

ICO microcredit, with its activity related to the guarantee system, represented a mediation tool between partner banks and micro-enterprises. From an operational point of view, micro-enterprises in need of financing would submit their requests to the *Social Microcredit Financial Institutions, SMFIs*, which would then carry out the creditworthiness analysis in order to approve micro-loans guaranteed by ICO Microcredit Line. SMFIs did not limit its activity to creditworthiness analysis, but provided also counselling, tutoring and technical support services. The use of counter-guarantees provided by the European Investment Fund (EIF)[28] to the banks, to be enforced in case of default of the micro-enterprises, allowed the banking system to use insurance methods as risk mitigation instruments as well as risk diversification of their portfolio, by turning individual risk into collective risk.

The intent of improving the micro-enterprises' capacity to access credit through the use of guarantee funds initially produced a number of advantages, through the involvement of some large commercial bank, in particular BBVA, Santander Group and *Banco Popolare*, which would provide 60% of the guaranteed loans (out of a total of 15.1 million in 2002). As a matter of fact, this system did not improve the efficiency of the microcredit chain with regard to the capacity of detecting and monitoring the credit risk assumed by the banks. Following the reduction of the guaranteed portion of the loans from 80% to 50%, both for the first and second protection level, banks, in fact, stopped financing these programmes as they were deemed to be too costly and risky. In other words, the small size of loans generated high credit management costs and required significant capital provisions to offset NPLs. Generally, operations would not make any profit. The stringent terms and conditions of the loans, due to the limited profit capacity of the borrowers, could also have had a negative impact on the solvency of the micro-entrepreneurs, which, according to Martínez Estevez (2005), resulted in NPLs rate close to 35%.

Considering the other two aforementioned programmes, we must stress that the fact that they were supported by EU institutions certainly contributed to achieving balanced conditions for the banking intermediaries involved in the programmes, both by favouring the volume of operations through credit lines provided by the Council of Europe Development Bank – like in the agreement between "La Caixa" and EIF – and also by reducing the loan portfolio risk through the transfer of the credit risk to the EIF – like in the MAP[29] (Multi-Annual Programme for Enterprises and Entrepreneurship). In the latter, the EIF used to cover 75% of the defaults generated by loans granted for social purposes and enterprise development – provided that the guarantees were granted for a maximum amount of EUR 1,668,000 and a value not greater than 11.25% of the portfolio.

Evolution of the public guarantees: the Spanish Guarantee Fund

Within public and private partnerships involving entire local communities, a number of operating solutions have recently been introduced or are investigational in Spain, as in the case of Madrid. Drawn from US experiences, all actors operating in Madrid involved in the business development, both private and public, are focused and collaborate to provide and guarantee funds and support for microenterprises to succeed (see Annex 2).

Another successful experience of public and private partnerships at the local level is represented by the Foundation CP'AC (*Fundacio Privada per la promocio' de l'Autooccupacio de la Catalunya*), which has created a microcredit fund in collaboration with the government, namely the Ministry of Labour and Welfare, the European Social Fund and ICO, involving a network of local operators and stakeholders, such as young entrepreneurs[30] (between 18 and 35 years of age) excluded from the traditional banking system.

This government guarantee fund is activated through financial resources provided by the Ministry and EIF to finance microcredit programmes for employment. The fund operates according to a German-inspired model revolving around the collaboration between the fund itself, banks and a number of *instituciones microfinancieras* (MFIs) certified by the fund; this model is aimed at improving the efficiency of the whole microcredit chain as well as providing microcredit support services. The operational scheme is summarised below:

- Applicants present their business projects to one of the certified MFIs;
- The MFIs assess the projects and carry out the preliminary investigation to identify potentially fundable projects, which are then granted loans by the partner bank and guaranteed by the fund;
- The bank signs a loan agreement with the micro-enterprises, without being involved in the assessment and credit risk assumption process, then disburses the loans to the borrowers, who shall periodically repay them, including interest, following an amortization schedule.

In order to minimize the operating risks, the MFIs must provide collaterals to the banks granting the micro-loans, by creating a cash earmarked deposit amounting to the loan portfolio value in order to fully cover the first losses in the event of the borrowers' default.

However, the Spanish Microcredit Fund intervenes to cover the exceeding portion of the first loss guaranteed by the cash deposit and within the limits of the portfolio's nominal value. We can therefore observe that the guarantees, in this case, end up covering the full credit risk of the loan portfolio.

The agreements between the banks, institutions and the Spanish Guarantee Fund indicate loan ceiling, operating costs and loss recovery methods in case of insolvency of the enterprises. From an economic standpoint, the Spanish bank periodically transfers to the fund the difference between the instalments repaid by the borrowers and the fund's management costs. The fund periodically pays the MFIs a commission to cover operating costs and risk against the operations as well as a share of the capital amortised and repaid in order to replenish the provision, net of the expenses incurred by the fund.

A percentage of the resources allocated is used to partly cover costs related to development and support actions for the beneficiaries (technical support, training and tutoring), which are deemed to be key for the success of any microcredit initiative (Box 4.1).

Box 4.1   Support actions carried out by microcredit institutions

These actions are carried out by the certified microcredit institutions that make the initial screening of the projects and the support provided during the start-up phase of the projects. In particular:

1. Selection of the beneficiaries – The institutions perform an initial screening as well as support potential beneficiaries:

- In the definition of the business project;
- In the preparation of the business plan;
- In planning the activities.

2. Micro-enterprise assessment – Microcredit institutions also assess the subjects' creditworthiness by preparing reports on their financial reliability during the preliminary investigation phase, a task traditionally performed by banks. The decision follows an attentive financial and economic analysis of the projects.

3. Training – Subjects who are granted financing, or whose assessment process is nearly finalised, benefit from training courses organised by the MFIs and aimed at improving their business and management skills, with in-depth sessions covering the following areas:

- Enterprise funding sources;
- Business management;
- Accounting and cost analysis: basic principles;
- Tax and social contributions; and
- Marketing and communication.

4. Coaching and tutoring – Following the provision of the loans, the financed subjects are coached by the certified MFIs both during the enterprise creation phase and its development. Coaching/tutoring takes place through periodic meetings with the beneficiaries and visits to their business premises. This process is based on *business coaching* techniques aimed at developing business potential and achieving results and objectives in a timely and constant fashion.

The financing bank supports the MFIs in monitoring the loan repayment schedule.

Microcredit and SGR guarantee

The mission of the *Sociedades de Garanzia Reciproca* (SGR) consists of supplying guarantees and counselling services to its member enterprises. Within such activity, the SGR manage guarantee funds to facilitate access to subsidised credit for micro-enterprises.

Before examining the technical characteristics of these guarantees, we must briefly illustrate the main features of the SGR. Currently, the system includes 23 intermediaries with mixed capital, their business association CESGAR (*Confedaracion Española de Sociedades de Garantia Reciproca*) and CERSA (*Compañía Española de Reafianzamiento*), a state-owned entity specialising in the provision of counter-guarantees. According to the SGR bylaws, we find two types of institutions here: local SGR and national SGR.

Currently, the first group includes 20 SGR. These guarantee intermediaries operate exclusively within the communities where their registered offices are located; the remaining three SGR belong to the second group and operate in specific business sectors, in accordance with their by-laws. From a territorial point of view, the SGR cover all of the autonomous communities, with the exception of "La Rioja" (Panetta and Lo Cascio, 2012).

The SGR and counter-guarantee companies were turned into no-banking financial intermediaries, since 1994 and 1996 respectively, subject to the BoS[31] supervision. Their legal status of regulated financial intermediaries entailed relevant consequences in terms of prudential supervision, risk containment and capital requirements, which resulted in improved efficiency of both their operations and the guarantee system itself, therefore contributing to their appeal for banks and enterprises.

This institutions release financial guarantees to facilitate access to microcredit for micro-enterprises and self-employed workers; the guarantees are released to the banks providing loans with maturity between 1 and 5 years, in a maximum amount of EUR 25,000, for financing working capital or multi-annual investments. Their costs include administration expenses and the SGR membership fee.

As for the preliminary investigation, the SGR scrutinizes the business plans submitted by the entrepreneurs as well as other documents required for creditworthiness analysis. Once the preliminary investigation is terminated, a committee resolves on their acceptance and informs the bank, specifying the size of the guarantee granted and its maturity. The key phases can be identified in the assessment, counselling and monitoring of the guaranteed activity.

Table 4.17 Key features of the credit guarantee scheme and guarantee product for microcredit: SGR

Start Date	Purposes	Ownership	Product	Beneficiaries	Business Sectors	Operating Methods for Implementation					
						Guarantee/ Loan Size	Type loans	Maturity	Coverage ratio	Fee	Other cost
2003	Granting guarantee that facilitate SMEs' access to credit and to provide assistance	Mutual	Guarantee for microloans	Independent Self employed Liberal profession Micro-enterprise	All	Max: EUR 25,000	Working capital Investment	Between 1 to 5 years 5 years	100%	1%	Administrative Cost: 0.50% Other Cost: Social contribution

Source: Own elaboration on data OECD, CFE/SME (2012)1/FINAL and Company Financial Statements.

Table 4.18   Guarantee portfolio (as of 2012)*

Size of Loan	SGRs' Guarantees	CERSA Counter-Guarantees
Microcredit	15,740,948	10,162,798
<60,000	5,886,282,238	1,793,075,682
>600,000	5,902,023,186	1,803,238,480

*Note: * EUR*

Source: Own elaboration on CERSA data (www.cersa-minetur.es).

It must also be noted that the SGR do not limit their assessments to the solvency of the borrowers but focus on the analysis of the projects. This requires specific skills and expertise as well as the use of an objective evaluation system, which conversely requires investments in technology and training of personnel, a process quality certification system and an updated information database.

However, the guaranteed micro-enterprises tend to have a much riskier profile than other businesses. One of the weaknesses of this system lies in the limited number of micro-enterprises able to access such guarantee instruments: that is, on average, no more than 2.6% of all associated enterprises, given the limited resources provided by SGR, 65% of which is counter-guaranteed by CERSA. Data as of 31 December 2012, reported in Table 4.18, confirm this.

The SGR are participated by local communities that inevitably influence their governance with an impact on their risk assumption and volume of operations. The counter-guarantee system plays a relevant role within the microcredit chain. Its activity can be summarised as follows:

- The autonomous communities grant counter-guarantees at a regional level and the government at a national level;
- CERSA grants counter-guarantees;
- Counter-guarantees are granted by the European Investment Fund to CERSA.

As for the first point, some SGR are able to access these counter-guarantee schemes and thus transfer the credit risk to the public sector. These counter-guarantee schemes all show similar features: they counter-guarantee risks originating from specific areas or regions; they are meant to be used as complementary instruments in conjunction with other public guarantees; they are automatically/semi-automatically activated; and, mostly, they are interest-free.

CERSA's activity has a strong impact in economic and capital terms. Every year or two, CERSA establishes the requirements to access its counter-guarantees and the business areas involved. Hence, policymakers can use this guarantee system as a powerful political and economic tool, by channelling resources into priority business sectors and areas that are deemed to be key for economic development.

Credit risk plays an important role for the SGR, which monitors it through the Q index, namely the ratio between the annual increase of funds and the increase of insolvencies and amortised risks. For the whole maturity of the loan, this index cannot exceed the loan by over 6%. This index recorded average values lower than 2.7% until 2007, probably due to the favourable economic conditions before the crisis and an excessively prudential policy by SGR. In 2006, it was decided that the Q index would not be applied to the financing of innovative projects, a clear signal that the SGR intended to encourage such operations.

The credit risk assumption by the SGR makes them more similar to banks, as they operate following a health and prudential management logic, which is not always compatible with the development of the entrepreneurial fabric. However, the SGR have proven their capacity to support local enterprises over time, with a particular focus on start-ups. According to CESGAR data, in 2012, 29% of the guarantee operations provided by SGR were dedicated to financing of start-ups.

On the other hand, the SGR highlighted an important methodology related to their capacity to turn their available information into evaluation models allowing them to correctly assess the credit risk of enterprises. Such principle of healthy and prudential management is applied by CERSA as well as all the SGR; it complies with all restrictions and limits these institutions are subject to in their role of regulated intermediaries.

Yet, CERSA's prudential policy in terms of capital provisions to mitigate credit risk was not enough to support enterprises during the economic crisis.

Supporting the guarantee funds managed by the above intermediaries through public contributions could be a good way to channel public resources into new industrial projects and employment policies.

The possibility for SGR to extend the range of their guarantees depend on their net capital, which can be increased through capital contributions by their partners or private and public contributions, which anyway are getting increasingly lower. Besides the operational aspect, it is clear that the increase of their net assets was ensured also by the contributions provided by the various regional government administrations and the participation of public entities in the operations carried out by such intermediaries, thus increasing their solvency and business volumes.

If, on one side, the current guarantee system can be considered sufficiently evolved and structured to improve the management of the enterprises that access to it, both through capital contributions and reduction of borrowing costs, some weaknesses are emerging in times of economic stagnation, mainly due to the reduced signalling capacity of the system with regard to the credit risk assumed by the banks. At present, the credit process is unable to correctly report all operations in progress and provide an accurate estimate of losses related to non-performing loans and critical situations, in particular those concerning start-ups that operate in technology innovation and atypical businesses for their areas.

4.6   The microcredit guarantee funds and Institutions in France: main features

The French microcredit system is characterised by government/public support to all operators in the industry (also through subsidies), with the objective of ensuring the functioning of different networks supporting enterprises (see Section 3.7) operating in the country. In this perspective, the government intervenes on both secured and unsecured microcredit, but while in the secured microcredit sees only a marginal[32] government intervention, in the unsecured the public hand plays a primary role (Figure 4.2).

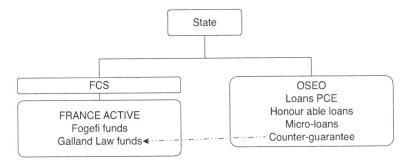

Figure 4.2   The guarantee system in France

Source: Own elaboration on Banque de France (2010).

The current structure of the microcredit guarantee system in France was established by the Planning Law for Social Cohesion No. 2005/32 (known as "Borloo Law"),[33] which, among other things, created the *Funds de Cohésion Sociale* (FCS), managed by the CDC and funded through the European Social Fund (ESF). The FCS is unincorporated and operates through a Steering and Fund Monitoring Committee (Cosef) and a Certification Committee (CAFCS). Its mission is to promote social[34] and enterprise microcredit by providing guarantees on loans granted by banks and MFIs to unemployed individuals who intend to start a business. In order to access the fund, these would-be entrepreneurs must make use of the coaching services provided by the major support operators/networks in the country.

The fund has basically two objectives:

- Developing microcredit for the creation of micro-enterprises and *microentreprice d'insertion* (These are micro-enterprises involved in the production of goods or provision of services that employ economically or socially disadvantaged subjects or individuals who lost their jobs.)
- Promoting individual micro-loans. In this case, the fund provides 50% of the guarantees on loans granted by banks to subjects traditionally excluded from traditional banking services, in order to support their personal, social or business projects. The CDC signs collaboration agreements with the MFIs and local and national microcredit support networks to promote personal microcredit.

The total amount of loans guaranteed by FCS in 2012 was EUR 103,7 million (Figure 4.3, black line on the right scale), a 7% increase compared to 2011, while the total number of guarantees provided was 16,720 (Figure 4.3, grey line on the left scale), a 5% increase compared to 2011.[35]

Microcredit for enterprise support

The microcredit for enterprise support is covered by guarantees granted by the Fogefi funds (*Fonds solidaire de garantie pour l'entreprenariat féminin et l'insertion*) as well as by the funds established by what is known as "Galland Law" (hereinafter "loi Galland"), included in the FCS, and more specifically,

- The public existing funds merged into the Fogefi funds
- The local "loi Galland" funds

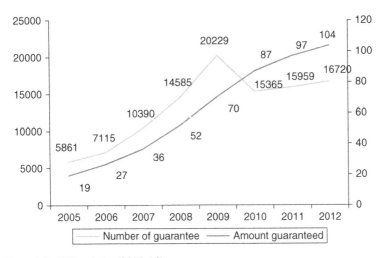

Figure 4.3   FCS activity (2005–12)
Source: Own elaboration on Banque de France (2013).

Both managed by France Active.

Since 1991, France Active has been providing guarantees for micro-credit, and in 1995 it started to operate through the financial company France Active Garantie (FAG), which acts as a guarantor of the loans. Over the time, France Active, through several agreements signed with the main banks operating in the loan market in France, has become a significant intermediary between entrepreneurs and banks. For this reason, and given also the high consideration it enjoys, France Active can greatly influence decisions underlying the provision of loans to subjects affected by economically and socially adverse conditions.

The Fogefi funds

With the objective of promoting the creation, development and recovery of enterprises, the French government channelled three specific funds into Fogefi, each focusing on specific business areas:

* *Fonds de Garantie pour la création, la reprise ou le développement d'entreprises à l'iniziativa des femmes* (FGIF) was created in 1989 and funded by the government and FSE. FGIF is a fund dedicated to the creation and development of enterprises led by women entrepreneurs, including micro-enterprises, regardless of their legal status and business sector. Public guarantees cover medium-term bank loans

granted to fund the purchase of goods or capital investments, and are complemented by the provision of counselling services. The amount of the guarantees provided, which varies according to the loans (the minimum loan amount must be EUR 5,000) cannot exceed 70% of the loan value and, in any case, must be no higher than EUR 27,000. The maturity of the loans must be between two and seven years. Enterprises must pay a guarantee fee equal to 2.5% of the guaranteed amount.

- *Fonds de Garantie pour le Développement des Ateliers Protégés* (FGAP), created in 2002, is financed by the government and France Active. It is dedicated to companies and micro-enterprises that intend to start or expand activities dedicated to protected segments and covers loans granted both for financing working capital and fixed-assets. Guarantees cover over 50% of the loan value and vary according to the type of loans, whose amounts can fall between

  - EUR 15,000 and EUR 120,000 and between 2.5 and five years for financing working capital.
  - EUR 7,500 and EUR 500,000 and between 2.5 and 15 years for financing fixed-assets.

For fixed-assets financing, the percentage covered cannot exceed 70% of the investments. The FGAP provides for the complementary possibility of using FAG and other guarantees, but it rules out the possibility of using personal guarantees. In other words, it allows co-guarantees up to a maximum of 75% of the loans granted, while the intermediary banks must inevitably assume the risk of the remaining 25%. A 2% commission of the guaranteed loans is applied, provided that the maturity of the loans is lower than or equal to three years; it is 2.5% if the loan is longer. Applications to access the FGAP can be directly submitted to one of France Active's local branches.

- *Fonds de Garantie pour l'Insertion Economique* (FGIE) is financed by the government. The fund aims to support start-ups aimed at economic development or integration, by guaranteeing loans provided for financing fixed-assets or working capital. The amounts of these loans are
  - EUR 15,000 and EUR 120,000 and between 2.5 and seven years for financing working capital.
  - EUR 7,500 and EUR 60,000 and between two and 12 years for financing fixed-assets.

The guarantees, which cover over 50% of the loan value, cannot exceed 70% of the investments for fixed-assets financing. FGIE, too, provides for the possibility of using the complementary FAG guarantees and other guarantees but it prohibits using personal guarantees; it admits co-guarantees up to a maximum of 75% of the loan granted, while the risk of the remaining 25% must be inevitably assumed by the intermediary banks. A commission of 2.5% of the guaranteed loans is applied. Just like FGAP, applications to access the FGIE can be directly submitted to one of France Active's local branches.

In 2012, Fogefi guaranteed a total amount of EUR 51.8 million (Figure 4.4, black line on the right scale), an 8% increase compared to 2011, while it released a total of 13,101 guarantees (Figure 4.4), a 5% increase compared to 2011.[36]

The "loi Galland" funds

As previously indicated, microcredit for enterprise development is covered by guarantees granted by the above Fogefi funds and the "loi Galland" funds. The 1988 "loi Galland", in particular article L. 2253–7, L. 3231–7 and L. 4253–3 of the Code of Local Government Authorities, authorised municipalities, provinces and regions to enter the capital of banks through limited liability companies whose business purposes is the provision of guarantees on loans granted to private enterprises, including start-ups. The same law authorises the local government authorities to

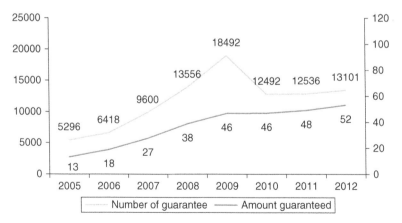

Figure 4.4   Fogefi activity (2005–12)
Source: Own elaboration on Banque de France (2013).

grant guarantees in the form of subsidies. Purposes, amounts and operating methods of the guarantee funds as well as terms and conditions for the repayment of the subsidies in the event that the fund modifies or ends its activity are established by specific agreements. The guarantees granted by the "loi Galland" funds cannot exceed 50% of the loan value, 65% in case of start-ups. Amount and maturity of the guarantees vary according to the local areas considered. The FCS interventions is aimed here at supporting local guarantee funds created by France Active and, within the "loi Galland" framework, at improving the financial provisions of the local communities.

In 2012, the "loi Galland" fund granted 3,382 guarantees (Figure 4.5, light grey line on the left scale) for a total amount of EUR 49.5 million (Figure 4.5, dark grey line on the right scale), which led to the mobilisation of loans worth over EUR 112 million (Figure 4.5, black line on the right scale). In 2012, the number of guarantees decreased by 1%, while the total value of the guarantees increased by 4%.[37]

Alongside the aforementioned funds, other guarantee funds operate in the microcredit sector in France; although not expressly dedicated to microcredit, they can be included in the microcredit sector as they serve small and micro-enterprises; more specifically, we refer here to the funds OSEO and SOCAMA.[38]

OSEO was founded in 2005 as a public development bank (it operates under the supervision of the Ministry of Economic Affairs, Finance and Industry) and not only provides guarantees on bank loans, but also on financing provided by business angels and private equity (Porretta and Bikoula, 2012) to MSMEs operating in the technology innovation and

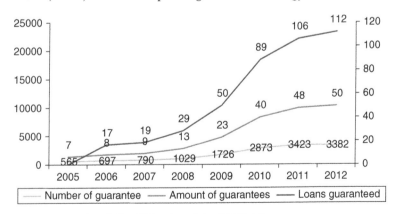

Figure 4.5   The "loi Galland" funds activity (2005–12)

Source: Own elaboration on Banque de France (2013).

export business. The guarantee fund OSEO is financed through public contributions (National Guarantee Fund), local government authorities, CDC and the EU. Its guarantees (Table. 4.19) reduce credit risk by 20% to 80%, according to the type of guaranteed loans and, anyway, always for medium- and long-term financing. Guarantees provided by OSEO are technically issued in the form of co-guarantees alongside other guarantee instruments provided by the lending banks.

SOCAMA, instead, is a mutual company (Société de Caution Mutuelle Artisanale) founded in 1917 to support artisans. Still today, its activities are mainly focused on craftsmen who are associated in 42 cooperatives that constitute this institution. SOCAMA, created by and for enterprises, provides guarantees for investments in equipment, business development, and company transfers/acquisitions. Its guarantees are only released in concomitance with loans granted by the Cooperative Banks. Table 4.20 shows the key features of the microcredit guarantees provided by SOCAMA.

With the purpose of providing some concluding remarks, we have relied on data published by Banque de France (2013) on the economic advantages of the microcredit sector (as a whole). Data recorded by the observatory show that in 2012, following a decline in the creation of jobs in 2010 and a recovery in 2011, the FCS activity led to the creation/consolidation of 33,716 jobs, registering a 20% increase if compared to the previous year. These figures are confirmed by impact studies carried out by Adie and France Active (2013 data), which, although reflecting the specificity of actions and their positioning, confirm and prove the usefulness of microcredit as a tool to facilitate the social and economic integration of the beneficiaries.

Table 4.19 Key features of the credit guarantee scheme: OSEO

Start Date	Purposes	Owner-ship	Product	Benefici-aries	Business Sectors	Guarantee size	Maturity	Coverage Ratio
					Operating Methods for Implementation			
2005	To granting guarantee that facilitate SMEs' access to credit	Public-Private	Loan guarantee	MSMEs	Construction Commerce Manufacturing Services	Limit: EUR 1.5 million	Max: 15 Average: 6	Min: 20% Max: 80%

Source: Own elaboration on data OECD, CFE/SME (2012) 1/FINAL, and Company Financial statements.

Table 4.20 Key features of the credit guarantee scheme: SOCOMA

						Operating Methods for Implementation						
Start Date	Purposes	Ownership	Product	Beneficiaries	Business Sectors	Guarantee/ Loan size	Type Loans	Maturity	CoverAge Ratio	Fee	Other Cost	
1917	To granting guarantee that facilitate SMEs' access to credit and to provide assistance	Mutual	Guarantee for microloans	Independent Self employed Liberal profession Craftsmen Shopkeepers SMEs	All	Max: EUR 30,000	Investment	Between 1 to 5 years	100%	1.5%	Administrative Cost: 0.50% Other Cost: Social	

Source: Own elaboration on data OECD, CFE/SME (2012) 1/FINAL and Company Financial statements.

The impact study carried out by Adie (a three-year survey focusing on the beneficiaries supported by the association) was aimed at assessing the impact of its operations,[39] among others, in terms of survival rate of the enterprises supported, permanence of the beneficiaries in the labour market and creation of new jobs. More specifically:

• The research showed that the micro-enterprise survival rate after two-three years from their creation is stable in compared to the 2010 levels, as 70% and 58% of the beneficiaries were still doing business after two and three years from their start, respectively.
• For the permanence in the labour market, 84% of the beneficiaries are still working, 63% of them continued their businesses, and 21% of them were hired as employees.
• With regard to creation of jobs, the study highlighted that micro-entrepreneurs financed by Adie created an average number of 0.3 jobs besides theirs (on an annual-basis, during the three-year period). This figure should be considered while taking into account that new workers are generally hired after the start of the business activity.[40]

The impact study carried out by Adie highlights the creation of relationships between the micro-entrepreneurs and the banks, which allows the former to access traditional credit. According to such research, the association helped three quarters of its beneficiaries access funding through progressive access to traditional financing sources and also by establishing trust-based relations with the banks.

The impact study prepared by France Active,[41] equally aimed at identifying the usefulness of the support provided in terms of loans granted, though mostly in terms of financial inclusion and creation of new enterprises, showed that 81% of the beneficiaries thought that the support and financing received from the association were key to establish solid relations with the banks, also considering that 58% of them had never submitted any projects to obtain loans before or, anyway, could not access traditional forms of funding. The survival rate after three years from start of the enterprises financed in 2009 was 78%, with an average of 2.5 jobs created.

4.7 Comparative analysis of the guarantee funds and institutions among African and European countries

As mentioned in the introduction, this section aims to answer the following questions:

1. What are the main operational features of the guarantee funds?
2. Is it possible to find out some similarities between the guarantee funds used in North African countries and those used in the European economies considered?
3. Do they contribute to the development of sustainable microfinance?
4. What are the implications for the financial and business systems in the countries analysed?

Unfortunately, the limited amount of information publicly available on the websites of the guarantee fund promoters/operators examined does not allow us to answer the above questions exhaustively, nor does it offer a clear picture of their main operational features (following the logical scheme indicated in Chapter 1). At this stage, we can just outline some general considerations that only start answering some of the questions, while leaving an open field to further developments of this work. Before presenting them, we think it appropriate to recall what lies behind the planning/design of the microcredit guarantee funds, in order to have a better reference for the following reflections.

Designing any guarantee fund:

- May entail some trade-offs between the main objectives such as outreach, additionalities and financial sustainability. For example, targeting riskier types of borrowers while applying strict eligibility criteria may result in a positive impact on additionalities, but, at the same time, it could reduce the outreach and lead to relevant losses. Similarly, very high fees may improve additionalities by discouraging banks to demand guarantees from good borrowers, but, again, it could limit the outreach as well as generate adverse selection effects. The optimal balance between these three objectives depends, to a fair extent, on the countries' social and economic conditions. For example, in countries characterised by serious shortcomings in their financial infrastructure and limited SME financing, high outreach and high additionalities may be achieved simultaneously, while more advanced economies may only increase outreach at the expense of sustainability and a limit impact in term of additionalities (Panetta, 2012);
- Means, first of all, considering the countries/regions/areas affected by clear economic and social problems;
- Implies deep knowledge of the regulatory framework and the state of the art of the financial system;
- Requires an exact definition of roles and responsibilities of the different operators involved (government/public entities, MFIs, banks, non-financial service providers, beneficiaries, and so on).

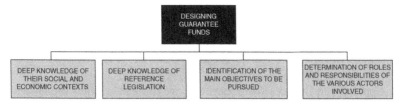

Figure 4.6 Designing guarantee funds: development guidelines

These are the guidelines for effective planning of guarantee funds (Figure 4.6).

From this perspective, it is clear that there cannot be a guarantee fund model valid for all social, economic and financial contexts; those analysed in this chapter are essentially tailor-made funds created according to the characteristics of certain geographic areas, business sectors or segments of population (women entrepreneurs, unemployed subjects, micro-enterprises involved in the export business, immigrants within certain age limits, associations, social cooperatives, individual or associated micro-enterprises, businesses willing to employ youth, and so on).

Hence, an erroneous comprehension of the guidelines to design guarantee funds may result in the activation of microcredit programmes and funds characterised by multiple criticalities, which are likely to undermine their long-term sustainability and survival; likewise, political interferences may prevent fund managers from carrying out their business following good financial practices as well as achieving the expected results. Some of the programmes mapped in this chapter were ended due to mismanagement or ineffectiveness of results due to exhaustion of the guarantee fund provisions (inadequate credit risk management); other criticalities may lie in the incorrect identification of the beneficiaries, application of inadequate multipliers and so on.

If, on one side, guarantee funds are essential to implement any microcredit programme, on the other one, their sole presence is not enough to ensure the achievement of the expected results and, therefore, their sustainability over time. This is why guarantee funds should always be designed by professionals who have a deep understanding of the local social and economic contexts as well as the reference legislation, in order to optimize their operating structure through an accurate identification of roles and responsibilities of the different actors involved, thus developing an efficient and solid system able to ensure long-term sustainability of the services provided to subjects excluded from the traditional banking circuit. To answer question No. 3 above, theoretically, the activation of guarantee funds can surely help develop a sustainable microfinance model, yet business practice shows that the actual sustainability of such initiatives should be assessed case by case.

The analysis to come will firstly compare the guarantee schemes of the three North African countries, where microcredit guarantee funds have been in place for a longer time.

Generally, in the countries examined, we can observe that the importance of the guarantee schemes is related to their economic structure, characterised by the widespread presence of MSMEs, which, in spite of their relevance in terms of economic development, GDP growth and creation of jobs, often cannot access traditional credit.

The provision of guarantees in those countries may be an additional incentive for investors to target smaller businesses; nevertheless, it must be pointed out that in the three African countries considered, most (or all) micro and small enterprises are family-owned.

Guarantee schemes were created to facilitate access to credit for many businesses unable to access the traditional banking circuit. These micro and small enterprises are usually started with money from family and friends; they are often under-capitalised and excluded from commercial financing channels. International donors (and the EU Commission) have already poured several million EUR into these countries to start or support such guarantee funds. While their importance is acknowledged, they need to be improved and supported by policymakers, provided there is a better understanding of their operations and financial support provided to local economies. The origin of most of the guarantee funds analysed is undoubtedly one of their common features; another common aspect is the role played by governments and international donors/agencies in their creation (as they are often the promoters or funders of microcredit initiatives).

The government intervention in the sector can be justified in light of information asymmetries and high credit risks associated with small and micro-enterprises. The ultimate objective of any public intervention indeed is to increase the creation of capital dedicated to economic and productive activities, in order to promote the competitiveness of their economic systems. This is confirmed by the mission of several funds, which is often quite extensive, such as in Morocco, where the above schemes are created to support export or entrepreneurship. Our analysis mapped a number of funds pursuing specific objectives (employment, self-employment, internationalisation of enterprises, export) under the direction of international donors, which promote such initiatives following well-established standards and practices applied to many developing countries.

More in detail, funds in Egypt are financed by government and international donors, while in Tunisia and Morocco they are mostly state-owned. The results of our analysis (Table 4.21) highlight that the main differences between the funds seem to lie in the limits imposed on targeted

Table 4.21 North African countries: a brief comparative analysis

		Egypt	Tunisia	Morocco
Credit guarantee scheme	Institutions/ Fund name (start date)	CGC (1989), managing 6 guarantee funds CIS (1999)	National Guarantee Fund (1981) Sotugar (2003)	CCG (1949)
	Nature of Institutions/ Fund	Programmes managed by specialised institutions; Mutual companies (supervised financial institution)	Programmes managed by specialised institutions	Programmes managed by specialised institutions
	Funding of the microcredit fund managed	Mixed with majority international donors and government of Egypt	Mixed with majority donors	Mixed with majority donors and government of Morocco
Beneficiaries		MSMEs and NGOs individuals	MSMEs, individuals	MSMEs, individuals and MFIs
Operating methods for implementation	Max loan size	n/a	n/a	4,000,000
	Max loan maturity	n/a	n/a	n/a
	Business sectors	All	Handicraft, agriculture, fishing	All
Coverage rate	Min	65%	50%	50%
	Max	100%	90%	100%
Fees charged	Min	2% of the total outstanding loan	0.6%	0.5%
	Max	3% of the total outstanding loan	3%	2%
Guarantee management	Operational mechanisms	Loan guarantee Loan portfolio guarantee (portfolio only for micro-loans)	Hybrid: n/a	Loan guarantee Portable guarantee Loan portfolio guarantee
	Leverage ratio	Up to 2.5	n/a	n/a
	Use of credit scoring model	Limited	n/a	n/a

firms and the loan size of the beneficiaries. In Morocco and Tunisia, there is no limit to the firms' size, and the maximum loan ceiling is well above the international average. This may encourage banks to use the guarantees to provide larger loans to larger businesses, thus weakening the additionalities of such schemes. It seems that only Egypt limits the use of the guarantees to support micro-enterprises, a circumstance that should be examined through careful data reading of the operational features of the guarantee schemes, their portfolios and relationships with the banks and the enterprises supported.

The above table summarises some of the operational features of the guarantee funds examined and highlights the following:

- They are mostly public instruments funded by public resources largely provided through international circuits;
- They target beneficiaries of any size (with the exception of Egypt, where the use of guarantees is normally restricted to smaller firms) operating in different business sectors of traditional and developing economies, with the exception of Tunisia, where these measures are mostly limited to support handicraft, fishing and agriculture;
- They are used to mitigate the risks of relevant loans (such as in Morocco) or loans whose amounts are undetermined;
- They provide for high loan coverage, from a minimum of 50% to a maximum of 100%, low financial leverage and fees that may reach up to 3% of the loans granted;
- They do not include the use of specific scoring systems for creditworthiness analysis of the beneficiaries.

With regard to credit risk mitigation instruments, we can observe that loans secured only by movable collaterals are not widely used, due to the inability of the banks to secure their rights over the assets through a collateral registry as well as to enforce security interests in movable property.

This problem is particularly acute for the micro-loans provided in Morocco and Tunisia, where it may not make much economic sense to execute collaterals on very small outstanding amounts if the recovery costs are relatively high. Movable property is usually accepted as a secondary type of collateral as well as a complement to fixed assets (real estate property), which are also not entirely fit to secure micro-loans. Loans secured by receivables and inventory are even scarcer. None of the MENA countries boasts modern legislation on secured transactions.

To complete the analysis, coverage ratios should maintain incentives for effective loan provision and monitoring while providing sufficient protection against default risk. The coverage ratio needs to provide sufficient protection against credit risk, while preserving incentives for the banks to screen and monitor borrowers.

In the countries covered by our study, the coverage ratio ranges from 50% to 100%; banks usually require higher coverage to extend loans to riskier borrowers. Many guarantee funds mapped in this chapter extend such coverage by charging higher fees.

As for the fees, we can observe that commissions are quite low in Tunisia, regardless of the risk profile of the subjects guaranteed. Commissions are charged against the provision of guarantees according to a percentage of the loans; this system implies that commissions follow the values of the loans guaranteed, instead of the risk profile of the loan beneficiaries; these circumstances could jeopardize the long-term economic sustainability of some schemes.

In the North African countries, roles and responsibilities of the actors involved in the guarantee chain seem to be clearly defined; these systems are also characterised by a strong degree of centralisation. This follows a functioning and organisational logic (subjects involved, roles and responsibilities) already experimented with in many other countries.

However, the absence of proper legislative frameworks in the above economies does not allow the creation of an effective link between operations, guarantees and beneficiaries, including the use of modern risk mitigation instruments that comply also with the legislation on financial intermediaries. Not enough information is available on the scoring systems used for creditworthiness assessment, which would improve the overall monitoring of lending. A common trait of the funds operating in these countries is also the participation of international donors and organisations in the guarantee schemes, at least in some of them. Yet, the same countries are also characterised by limited investments of resources in credit risk analysis; credit risk management is scarcely encouraged as well. The provisioning policies against credit risk are not always adequate; in some cases, this would justify outsourcing the preliminary investigation phase to banks. Yet, this constitutes an intrinsic weakness of the system and make the MFIs unable to provide banks with adequate credit risk information.

With the exception of Egypt, the guarantee provision system is affected also by other weaknesses, mostly related to the scarce variety of products supplied as well as a lack of instrumental and supporting services that allow micro-enterprises to successfully implement their business projects.

With regard to Egypt, the funds' operating mechanism generates a limited leverage effect that is able to act as a multiplier of public resources, with the result that, although guarantee funds are deemed an effective industrial policy instrument, donors, following a prudential approach, have maintained a limited cost-benefit ratio, reflecting the fact that fund management is rarely accompanied by credit risk management. As known, in the guarantee funds, the greater the financial leverage, the higher the credit risk assumed by them; high leverage undermines the sustainability and balance of the guarantee funds, and this is why normal business practice (on average the microcredit sector is riskier than ordinary credit) establishes a low financial leverage, also due to the incapacity/impossibility of assessing the beneficiaries' creditworthiness through specific methods. Low financial leverage is another common aspect between the guarantee funds operating in North African countries.

Guarantee funds play an increasingly important role in the microcredit sectors of Europe, too, especially following the international financial crisis. The absence of a specific regulatory framework, especially in Spain, does not help identify their objectives and mission. Actually, this is a recurrent issue. In European countries, in fact, we can observe that generally funds have target objectives and beneficiaries very distant from each other. Usually business and social objectives are mixed together, instead of being pursued with different methods and instruments, as it should be. Many programmes indiscriminately target micro-enterprises and families unbankables, while others are dedicated to youth, unemployed subjects, start-ups created by young or female entrepreneurs or innovative start-ups. Although the European Commission indicates some guidelines for the use of the structural funds, their use to activate microcredit programmes in the countries examined (with the support of guarantee funds) is left to the discretion of the single regional government institutions. Our study highlights also the "facilitating" role played by the guarantee systems in the microfinance sector. These funds, in fact, provide guarantees to micro-loan beneficiaries in order to replace / cover the lack of collaterals, where needed. Yet, what occurred in the European countries analysed was that guarantee schemes partly made up for such purpose because of the scarce interest to support microcredit by banks; the latter, in fact, deem microcredit a scarcely profitable business, one that involves high operating costs, high risk profiles and difficulties reaching a critical mass, and, therefore, implement economies of scale and the sustainability of the sector. A clear example is given in Spain, where banks engaged with microcredit activities only when public guarantees ensuring total micro-loan coverage were available.

The EU stimulated the use of such funds through subsidies aimed at funding microcredit programmes, structural funds or microcredit guarantee schemes. The role played by the EU in promoting this sector has been particularly relevant in those countries where it compensated the lack of counter-guarantees at a national level.

If we compare the operating methods of the different funds, we can see that the guarantee funds show clear differences in the way they are set up and operate. These differences are mainly due to adjustments to their operating environment.

Deficiencies in creating a proper enabling environment have motivated government interventions designed to expand financing systems dedicated to micro and small enterprises. Government interventions may be justified when it takes time to build an effective enabling environment, or where some groups are difficult to reach, despite the presence of efficient financial infrastructure and regulations. Traditionally, such interventions included credit guarantee schemes, direct lending and lending provided by state-owned financial institutions. The relevant presence of the policymakers (usually acting as promoters) is a common feature shared by the guarantee funds operating both in European and African countries.

In the three European countries examined (Table 4.22), the guarantee funds are promoted by central governments (Italy and France), local government authorities, chambers of commerce, banks and private subjects (Italy) or the entrepreneurs themselves, who take the initiative of guaranteeing each other's loans following a mutual assistance scheme (Spain).

Table 4.22 summarises some of the operational features (research question No.1) of the guarantee funds examined and highlights the following:

- There is a good degree of participation of private actors in the sector (both as promoters and financrial backers of microcredit programmes supported by guarantee funds), despite the strong government presence (yet less evident than in the African countries, where the microcredit system is mostly centralised). Public initiatives are largely determined, as for their extent and operating methods, by EU policies on microcredit. Very often, public institutions are the main actors seeking partners to support projects and create a virtuous circle: public

Table 4.22   European countries: a brief comparative analysis

		Italy	Spain	France
Credit Guarantee Scheme	**Institutions / fund name (start date)**	Central Guarantee Fund (1996); Many local funds (2003–12)	SGR (1994, active in microcredit since 2003) CERSA (1994) ICO (SME Guarantee facility 2001), Foundation CP'AC	France Active Garantie (1988); OSEO (2005); SOCAMA (1917); Many local funds
	Nature of institutions / fund	Programmes managed by specialised institutions	Programmes managed by specialised institutions (public agency, development bank, public financial institution); Mutual companies (Supervised financial institution); Bank	Programmes managed by specialised institutions (Financial institutions, development bank); Mutual companies (Supervised financial institution)
	Funding of the microcredit fund managed	Public funds (national and local), banks and banking foundations, chambers of commerce or other private institutions	Public funds (national and local) and EU	Public funds (national and local) and EU
	Beneficiaries/ client/targeting	MSMEs	MSMEs and Individuals and MFIs	MSMEs and MFIs
	Operating methods for implementation	25,000	SGR: 25,000 EUR	500,000
	Max loan size			

Max loan maturity			For working capital: between 1 to 5 years / For investment than 5 years	15 years
	Business sectors	All	All	All
Coverage rate	**Min**	50%	SGR: 100% (for microloans) CERSA: 75%	20%
	Max	100%		100%
Fees charged	**Min**	0%	SGR: 1%	0.5%
	Max	25%		2.5%
Guarantee management	**Operational mechanisms**	Loan guarantee	Loan guarantee	Portable guarantee / Loan guarantee / Loan portfolio guarantee
	Leverage ratio	n/a	n/a	n/a
	Use of credit scoring model	n/a	n/a	n/a

institutions, in fact, also following the appeals from associations, try to involve banks, associations and guarantee funds in a sort of "social agreement", where the banks sign a memorandum of understanding to apply special credit terms and conditions to the targeted subjects, while the associations carry out selection and monitoring and, along with the public institutions, provide assistance and training services to support the projects.

- Non-profit associations, acting as main providers of non-financial services, including coaching and support to prepare requests for loans, largely participate in guarantee schemes.
- In some cases, the targeted beneficiaries are not clearly defined; in other cases, the target is excessively restricted (with regard to business sectors or geographic areas):
  - Micro-enterprises, especially the ones operating in the social economy, micro-enterprises creating jobs;
  - Individuals who have lost or are at risk of losing their jobs, or who have difficulties entering or re-entering the labour market; individuals facing the threat of social exclusion, or vulnerable subjects in a disadvantaged position who are, therefore, unable to access credit market; subjects willing to start or further develop their own businesses, including self-employment initiatives;
  - But also MFIs (in France); In this case, the credit guarantees issued by an institution-oriented guarantee fund secure loans taken by NGOs or microfinance institutions.
- Guarantee funds are used to mitigate credit risk related to loans whose size is now almost standardised at a European level (25,000 EUR for business micro-loans, 10,000 EUR for social micro-loans) and target a micro-enterprise model defined quite homogeneously in all countries analyzed;
- They include high coverage ratios, ranging from a minimum of 20% (for France) to a maximum of 100%, low financial leverage, and fees that can reach up to 2.5% of the loans granted;
- They do not provide for use of specific scoring systems for creditworthiness analysis purposes. Given the absence of the beneficiaries' credit history, accounting records and business plans, the assessment of their risk profile is a critical aspect in the chain. In addition, a lack of structured databases specifically dedicated to the microcredit industry does not help. The limited size of loans and, consequently, reduced profit margins for financial intermediaries do not motivate them to develop adequate scoring systems for the sector, as the latter

is considered undeveloped and not particularly appealing. Unlike the African countries, the European countries examined did not start any initiatives to create national databases for the industry; in this perspective, a joint effort between banks and MFIs is needed to elaborate specific methods for standardised risk profile assessment for all MFIs.

Also in the three European countries, coverage ratios should preserve incentives for effective screening and monitoring of borrowers while providing sufficient protection against default risks. In general, higher coverage ratios are applied to riskier types of borrowers; yet, European countries also need to improve the capacity/possibility of assessing such risk. Setting a higher coverage ratio for riskier types of borrowers is an option to enhance additionalities while providing some flexibility – less risky borrowers can benefit from the guarantees but with lower coverage ratio and lower fees.

Provided that fees should be related to risk exposure and contribute to the financial sustainability of the guarantee scheme, linking the price of the guarantees to risk exposure is a basic insurance principle that should generally be adopted by all guarantee schemes. In the funds analysed, fees range from 0% (minimum value for Italy) to 2.5% (maximum value for Italy and France) of the loan value.

With regard to operational mechanisms, guarantees can be delivered in the form of individual or portfolio guarantees. According to the individual option, each loan application is assessed and approved by the guarantee scheme. The portfolio approach is more flexible instead, as it allows banks to extend guarantees without consulting the guarantee scheme. Each bank receives a guarantee allocation, which can be used for a number of eligible firms.

As for the types of guarantees provided, France, which boasts a long-standing experience in the sector, already activated portfolio guarantees; this is not the case in Italy and Spain. Both approaches have their own advantages and limits. The main advantage of the individual approach is its potential to improve credit risk control and ensure financial sustainability. In the case of banking systems with less SME lending experience, the individual approach adds another important value, namely its capacity to provide information and technical support to banks during the decision-making process.

Under the individual guarantee scheme, the guarantor individually screens each and every client of the guarantee fund. Guarantee schemes, thus, are able to develop direct contact with entrepreneurs.

Each entrepreneur applying for a credit guarantee is evaluated before any guarantee is granted. Clearly, this is a very labour-intensive activity. In a portfolio guarantee scheme, instead, the guarantee scheme does not look at the credentials of each and every applicant. Instead, it authorizes banks to attach a credit guarantee to any client that fulfils certain eligibility criteria. Banks simply inform the guarantee fund, usually on a monthly basis, of the new loans approved. Portfolio guarantee schemes are obviously less labour-intensive than individual guarantees, since screening of clients is performed by banks only; while involving higher risks for the guarantee schemes, they are also able to substantially slash down operational and transaction costs. This is an advantage for the guarantee funds, although they have a lot less control over the quality of its guaranteed portfolio. Portfolio schemes can only work if the guarantee funds trust the capacity of their partner banks to evaluate the entrepreneurs applying for loans.

Effective credit risk management carried out by the participating banks and the scheme itself may have a substantial impact on the sustainability of such guarantee schemes.

In our opinion, guarantee funds should be subject to high prudential standards and supervision, whether regulated by special legislation or general regulations for financial institutions. If portfolio guarantee schemes comply with high prudential standards, financial supervisory authorities could consider guarantees as credit mitigation instruments for provisioning and capital funding purposes.

The use of counter-guarantees as a form of reinsurance may significantly increase the outreach, as it can multiply the capacity of the guarantee funds. Counter-guarantees are commonly used in Europe, both at supranational (for example EIF) and national levels. In the three European countries examined, public counter-guarantees are currently used. While they can be useful to extend the outreach, their use needs to be carefully considered and matched by adequate regulation and supervision of the guarantee funds.

In a nutshell, guarantee funds are strictly tailor-made instruments of economic policy. Yet, their functioning can be undermined by a variety of factors. If, on one hand, they are an essential complement to any microcredit programme, on the other hand, their sole presence is not enough to ensure the achievement of the expected objectives. First of all, it is necessary to study the social and economic contexts they operate in, optimize their operating structure and identify the roles and responsibilities of the different actors involved, so as to develop a solid and effective sector able to ensure long-term sustainability of the microcredit programmes activated.

Annex 1: Some of the microcredit programmes of the Apulia Regional Administration

Table A1.1 Some of the microcredit programmes of the Apulia Regional Administration

MICROCREDIT FOR ENTERPRISES IN THE APULIA REGION

Start date	May 2012
Normative reference	Regional Council resolution No. 892 of 9 May 2012
Purposes	Micro-entrepreneurship Micro-enterprises created by no more than five years and active for at least six months or start-ups created by individuals in economically or socially disadvantaged conditions
Beneficiaries	Economically or socially disadvantaged individuals, women, youth, immigrants, ex-convicts, disabled, former drug addicts, subjects at risk of social exclusion, long-term unemployed subjects (6/12 months)
Operating methods for implementation	Guarantee rotation fund of the Apulia Regional Administration; unsecured loans in minimum amounts of 5,000 EUR and maximum amounts of 25,000 EUR with fixed interest rates corresponding to 70% of the EU rate
Microcredit operators involved and their role within the programme	n/a
Entities/institutions involved and their role within the programme	-Apulia Regional Administration: guarantee fund supported by FSE funds -Puglia Sviluppo: technical management -Banco di Napoli and another bank to be identified: loan disbursement -Employment Centre Network (under implementation: hospitality, initial coaching)
Monitoring and main operating results	The project is being launched
Website	www.sistemapuglia.it; www.pugliasviluppo.eu

Continued

MICROCREDIT FOR THE PROVINCE OF LECCE

Start date	2007
Normative reference	Provincial Council resolution No. 305 of 01.09.2006
Purposes	Creation of micro-enterprises in the form of one-man companies or firms
Beneficiaries	Unemployed women; high school or university graduates no older than 35 years of age; long-term unemployed individuals no older than 40 years of age; immigrants residing in the province of Lecce
Operating methods for implementation	Guarantee fund of 150,000 EUR; loans up to 25,000 EUR
Microcredit operators involved and their role within the programme	Cooperativa di Garanzia Unità artigiana salentina
Entities/institutions involved and their role within the programme	-Department for Economic Planning of the Provincial Administration of Lecce: requirements assessment, preliminary investigation -Cooperativa di Garanzia Unità Artigiana: loan disbursement -Local employment centres of the Provincial Administration of Lecce: technical support for applications -Assessment Committee consisting of 3 representatives of the cooperative and two of the Provincial Administration of Lecce
Monitoring and main operating results	n /a
Website	www.provincia.lecce.it

SOCIAL MICROCREDIT OF THE PROVINCE OF LECCE

Start date	2011
Normative reference	Provincial Council resolution No. 288 of 27.10.2010
Purposes	Support to families affected by economic hardship
Beneficiaries	Citizens resident in one of the municipalities of the Province of Lecce for at least 6 months and with total family income, according to IRPEF (personal income tax withholdings), of no less than 7,500 EUR and not higher than 21,000 EUR. The ISEE (equivalent financial situation index) income limit must not be greater than 10,000 EUR
Operating methods for implementation	Guarantee fund; subsidised personal loans between 5,000 and 10,000 EUR
Microcredit operators involved and their role within the programme	n/a
Entities/institutions involved and their role within the programme	-Department for Social Policies and Equal Opportunities of the Provincial Administration of Lecce: requirements assessment, preliminary investigation -Unicredit: creditworthiness analysis, loan disbursement
Monitoring and main operating results	n/a
Website	www.provincia.le.it/web/10716/513

"BARNABA – DARE CREDITO ALLA SPERANZA" (Barnaba – Grant credit to hope)

Start date	2003
Normative reference	n/a
Purposes	To create jobs and generate income
Beneficiaries	Weakest segments of the young population residing in the diocese area, Italian youth or immigrants between 18–35 years of age, associations, social cooperatives, one-man micro-enterprises or partnerships, companies willing to employ youth
Operating methods for implementation	Guarantee rotation fund at the Banca Etica of Padua

Continued

"BARNABA – DARE CREDITO ALLA SPERANZA" (Barnaba – Grant credit to hope)

Microcredit operators involved and their role within the programme	Counselling centres of the Caritas of Andria
Entities/institutions involved and their role within the programme	-Caritas of the Diocese, Pastoral Social and Labour Office and Pastoral Office for the Youth of the Diocese of Andria: promoters -Caritas counselling centres: education to use of money and solidarity -Caritas of the Diocese: loan guarantor, moral and ethical guarantor of the subjects identified as beneficiaries, coaching -Banca Etica of Foggia: loan disbursement
Monitoring and main operating results	32 guarantees were granted in the period 2003–09 (40% to women and 60% to men)

Year	2004	2005	2006	2007	2008	2009	2010	2011
Projects financed	4	4	7	3	4	2	4	4
Amounts disbursed	17,500	20,000	35,000	15,000	25,000	7,500	20,000	35,000

Credit repayment rate: 28% being regularly paid; 9% enforced; 19% partly repaid; 44% fully repaid

Website	www.caritasandria.it; www.progettopolicoro.it

"TOBIA" – MICROCREDIT PROJECT OF THE DIOCESE OF UGENTO

Start date	2010
Normative reference	n/a
Purposes	To create jobs and generate income
Beneficiaries	Weakest segments of the young population residing in the diocese area, Italian youth or immigrants between 18–35 years of age, associations, social cooperatives, one-man micro-enterprises or partnerships, companies willing to employ youth
Operating methods for implementation	Guarantee rotation fund created thanks to 50,000 EUR from the Italian Bishop's Conference, the bishop's personal allowance, priests and deacons, contributions from parishes, religious entities and institutes, donations from banks, companies, private and public entities, businesses or trade associations, besides offerings of the faithful

Microcredit operators involved and their role within the programme	Service centre of the Diocese "Progetto Policoro"
Entities/institutions involved and their role within the programme	Service centre "Progetto Policoro": tutoring, coaching and training; Caritas of the Diocese: loan guarantor, moral and ethical guarantor of the subjects identified as beneficiaries, coaching; Banca Etica: loan disbursement
Monitoring and main operating results	n/a
Website	www.diocesiugento.org/progetto_tobia

MICROCREDIT PROJECT OF THE FOUNDATION OF THE BANK DEL MONTE "DOMENICO SINISCALCO CECI"

Start date	2010
Normative reference	n/a
Purposes	Creation and development of micro-enterprises
Beneficiaries	Micro-enterprises with registered office located in the Province of Foggia. The following should be regarded as micro-enterprises: one-man companies, individual or cooperative companies with maximum 5 employees. Non-performing subjects are excluded
Operating methods for implementation	100,000 EUR-guarantee rotation fund created by the Foundation. 2x multiplier to be applied to the guarantee fund by Banca Etica
Microcredit operators involved and their role within the programme	Social cooperatives Consortium Aranea di Foggia – free technical assistance before and after loan disbursement
Entities/institutions involved and their role within the programme	Foundation of the Banca Del Monte Domenico Siniscalco Ceci: guarantee fund, technicalsocial assessment -Banca Etica: guarantee fund, preliminary investigation, creditworthiness analysis, loan disbursement -Consortium Aranea: technical support of the evaluation committee consisting of two members appointed by the foundation and one member appointed by Banca Etica
Monitoring and main operating results	13 loans were granted in 2010 for a total value of 122,000 EUR
Website	www.consorzioaranea.it; www.fondazionebdmfoggia.com;

Continued

MICROCREDIT PROJECT OF THE MUNICIPALITY OF MANFREDONIA

Start date	2011
Normative reference	Municipal council resolution No. 24 of 13.01.2010
Purposes	To tackle poverty and social exclusion by granting small loans to individuals with difficulties accessing traditional credit sources
Beneficiaries	Those in highly disadvantaged temporary situations
Operating methods for implementation	Guarantee fund; maximum loan amount is 3,000 EUR, to be repaid in 3 years
Microcredit operators involved and their role within the programme	Foundation Karol, 'SS. Redentore' voluntary association
Entities/institutions involved and their role within the programme	Municipality of Manfredonia, Bank of Campania branch of Manfredonia: technical assessment committee consisting of six representatives of the Municipality of Manfredonia, the Foundation 'Karol' and the Association 'SS. Redentore'. Each entity selected two women among bank experts, lawyers and social counsellors and voluntary associations to identify the beneficiaries.
Monitoring and main operating results	n/a
Website	www.comune.manfredonia.fg.it

MICROCREDIT PROJECT FOR ENTERPRISES OF THE FOUNDATION OF THE BANCO DEL MONTE DI FOGGIA

Start date	2012
Normative reference	
Purposes	To promote and facilitate access to subsidised credit for small enterprises affected by severe liquidity shortage
Beneficiaries	'Healthy' small artisanal enterprises having difficulties accessing traditional credit sources
Operating methods for implementation	Guarantee fund: 2% contribution for low-interest loans; maximum loans of 20,000 EUR to be repaid in 18–36 months with 5% interest rate
Microcredit operators involved and their role within the programme	n/a

Entities/institutions involved and their role within the programme	-Foundation of the Banca Monte di Foggia: financing entity -Italian General Federation of Commerce and Tourism -Provincial Administration of Foggia -Cofidi Business Operators of Capitanata -Banca della Campania
Monitoring and main operating results	n/a
Website	www.cofidifoggia.it

CREDIT TO THE FUTURE OF THE MUNICIPALITY OF MOLFETTA

Start date	2010
Normative reference	Experimental project "Credit to the Future" (local projects for youth, Department of Youth Affairs – Prime Minister's Office)
Purposes	To create enterprises
Beneficiaries	Youth between 18 and 35 years of age
Operating methods for implementation	150,000 EUR-guarantee fund created with the resources of the Department of Youth Affairs of the prime minister's office. Maximum amount of loans + 5,000 EUR for individuals and 10,000 EUR for companies
Microcredit operators involved and their role within the programme	n/a
Entities/institutions involved and their role within the programme	-Department of Youth Affairs of the prime minister's office: creation of the guarantee fund -The Municipality of Molfetta pays in advance to the bank the sums corresponding to interests and costs for each loan; it provides unconditional guarantee and undertakes to replenish the guarantee fund; collection and preliminary investigations of the requests for loans -Banca popolare di Bari: loan disbursement
Monitoring and main operating results	20 requests for loans processed, 18 of which were submitted by individuals and 2 by companies; 11 loans granted in 2010 for a total value of 60,000 EUR
Website	www.comune.molfetta.ba.it

Continued

EXPERIMENTAL MICROCREDIT GUARANTEE FUND OF THE MUNICIPALITY OF MONOPOLI

Start date	2010
Normative reference	Regional Law No. 19 of 10 July 2006; Municipal Council resolution No. 14 of 15.02.2010
Purposes	To provide financial support for periods of economic hardship that could result in delays in the payment of rent and, consequently, eviction; to facilitate access to rental housing by providing financial support to pay the monthly rent advances; to facilitate the purchase of furnishing and payment of utilities; to support expenses for housing requalification, small structural interventions and unexpected healthcare costs
Beneficiaries	Residents in the Municipality of Monopoli for at least three years or immigrants with regular residence permit in a situation of temporary economic difficulty, with ISEE (equivalent financial situation index) between 3,000 and 15,000 EUR
Operating methods for implementation	Guarantee fund of the Municipality of Monopoli, 2x multiplier; maximum amount of loan is 2,000 EUR, refundable in 36 months
Microcredit operators involved and their role within the programme	n/a
Entities/institutions involved and their role within the programme	-Municipality: guarantee fund -Banca di Credito Cooperativo of Monopoli: loan disbursement -Organisational Area No. 5 of the municipality: acceptance of requests and preliminary investigation -Social counsellors of the municipality: coaching and assistance to prepare the requests
Monitoring and main operating results	16 loans were granted in 2010 for a total value of 31,500 EUR
Website	www.comune.monopoli.ba.it

CREDIT TO WOMEN. MICROCREDIT OF THE PROVINCIAL ADMINISTRATION OF FOGGIA

Start date	2005
Normative reference	Provincial Council resolution No. 166 of 28.02.2005
Purposes	To create enterprises
Beneficiaries	Women to create enterprises or expand/modernise their businesses

Operating methods for implementation	200,000 EUR-guarantee rotation fund (100%) created by the provincial administration of Foggia and Etica Sgr
Microcredit operators involved and their role within the programme	n/a
Entities/institutions involved and their role within the programme	-Provincial administration of Foggia: collection of requests, preliminary investigation and guarantee fund -Etica Sgr: guarantee fund and loan disbursement
Monitoring and main operating results	70 applications received; 32 projects were financed for loans totalling 110,054 EUR
Website	www.provincia.foggia.it; www.eticasgr.it

MICROCREDIT of PERMICRO in Apulia

Start date	2012
Normative reference	n/a
Purposes	credit for families and creation of enterprises
Beneficiaries	Those who cannot access traditional bank financing in the Province of Bari
Operating methods for implementation	Guarantee rotation fund
Microcredit operators involved and their role within the programme	Permicro
Entities/institutions involved and their role within the programme	-Permicro: Technical support and coaching -BNL: loan disbursement
Monitoring and main operating results	n/a
Website	www.permicro.it

Continued

MICROCREDIT PROJECT OF THE MUNICIPALITY OF CASSANO

Start date	2012
Normative reference	
Purposes	To provide support for the creation of enterprises
Beneficiaries	Youth between 18 and 35 years of age
Operating methods for implementation	Guarantee rotation fund provided by the municipality, the association and the bank; loans between 1,000 EUR and 2,500 EUR to be refunded in 18 months with 6.5% interest rates
Microcredit operators involved and their role within the programme	Association Eticanonmente
Entities/institutions involved and their role within the programme	- Association Eticanonmente: guarantee fund creation and management, coaching and training - Municipality of Cassano: promotion and creation of the guarantee fund -Banca Popolare di Bari: loan disbursement
Monitoring and main operating results	n/a
Website	www.eticanonmente.it

PROJECT "OPEN AND SUPPORTIVE APULIA – RIGHT TO HOUSING, RIGHT TO CITIZENSHIP"

Start date	2010
Normative reference	Notice No. 1/2007 of the Ministry of Labour; agreement between the Ministry of Labour and the Apulia Regional Administration of 19.06.2008; 21.08.2008: protocol signed between the Apulia Regional Administration and provincial administrations
Purposes	To provide financial support to immigrants to facilitate access to housing, such as, for example, the creation of deposits for lease, rent support and common expenses, or costs related to ordinary maintenance of buildings
Beneficiaries	Registered immigrants residing in Apulia
Operating methods for implementation	Guarantee fund of the Apulia Regional Administration

Microcredit operators involved and their role within the programme	Provincial Asia (Social-Housing Intermediation Agencies)
Entities/institutions involved and their role within the programme	Provincial Asia: identification and selection of the beneficiaries through an assessment of the consistency of the projects submitted, their purposes and other criteria Banca Etica: loan disbursement Apulia Regional Administration and Apulia Institute for Economic and Social Research (Ipres): R&D and promotion of the programme
Monitoring and main operating results	n/a
Website	www.sistema.puglia.it

PROJECT TRUST AND SOLIDARITY FUND

Start date	2009
Normative reference	Social care microcredit
Purposes	Individuals and families affected by temporary and extraordinary economic constraints
Beneficiaries	Guarantee rotation fund; loans from 1,000 to 3,000 EUR to be refunded in 36 months
Operating methods for implementation	Caritas of Andria
Microcredit operators involved and their role within the programme	- Caritas of the Diocese Andria, Diocesan Office for Family, in collaboration with Banca Etica and "8x mille Chiesa cattolica italiana": promotion of the project
Entities/institutions involved and their role within the programme	- Caritas of Andria and counselling centres: identification of beneficiaries, coaching - Banca Etica: loan disbursement and monitoring - Ipres: R&D and marketing
Monitoring and main operating results	n/a
Website	www.caritasandria.com

Continued

MICROCREDIT FOR FAMILIES OF THE MUNICIPALITY OF PUTIGNANO

Start date	2011
Normative reference	Municipal council resolution No. 164 of 17.12.2010
Purposes	To provide support to families who cannot bear unexpected and extraordinary expenses needed for family stability
Beneficiaries	Families and/or subjects in situations of temporary economic hardship.
Operating methods for implementation	30,000 EUR-guarantee fund of the cunicipality; micro-loans from 1,000 to 5,000 EUR to be refunded in 36 months
Microcredit operators involved and their role within the programme	Local voluntary associations (not specified)
Entities/institutions involved and their role within the programme	- Municipality of Putignano: creation of the guarantee fund
	Assessment Committee consisting of a representative of the Social Service Office and two representatives of the voluntary associations engaged in social work
	Technical Committee made of two representatives of the associations and a representative of Banca Etica to assess the refunding capacity of the families
	Banca Etica: loan disbursement
Monitoring and main operating results	n/a
Website	www.comune.putignano.ba.it

Annex 2: Financial inclusion and guarantee funds: Madrid, a case study

Rising unemployment, large companies experiencing a shortage of labour, and the increasing difficulties of the SMEs to access credit are all critical factors that halt the development of the microcredit industry in a region like the metropolitan area of Madrid, characterised by a productive fabric mainly made of MSMEs. Micro-enterprises represent over 90% of the productive sector in Madrid, 15% at national level, and create between 25–50% of jobs among the active population. These are often extremely small businesses that are facing two important challenges: (1) access to credit and (2) the complexity of the administrative and legal procedures in the start-up phase.

Despite the failure of the microcredit programmes promoted by savings banks (with the exception of MicroBank la Caixa's program), micro and small companies in Madrid have the opportunity to benefit from a number of inclusive financial services (for example, *Avalmadrid*, the *Business Incubator Network* or *Fund Seed Capital of Madrid Emprende*). These are initiatives characterised by a limited range of operations though. Considering that the financial inclusion of thousands of micro and small businesses can contribute to job creation and economic growth in modern cities, some experts (see Rico Garrido et al., 2005), started to examine other successful models, such as the financial inclusion strategy towards micro and small businesses implemented in New York, in order to draw ideas to consolidate a financial system able to support the economic development of small and micro-enterprises and employment in the Madrid area.

The issues faced by micro and small businesses in the New York area were tackled through the implementation of a series of innovative partnerships between the public sector (i.e., federal, state and local levels), private banking and non-profit institutions. Specific public and private financial measures were put in place to resolve problems related to the convenience of starting a business. These solutions combined a number of new experimental projects, such as the Community Development Financial Institutions (CDFIs). The work of these semi-private institutions is catalysed by the support provided by the public sector (i.e. CDFI Federal Fund, US Small Business Administration, NYC Small Business Services Department), commercial banks, through the Community Reinvestment Act (CRA), and other entities from the private sector. In order to adopt and apply a similar financial inclusion model to the Madrid area, the following needs to be implemented:

- An adequate regulatory framework to recognise the social value of entrepreneurship and support adequate financial services dedicated to MSMEs;
- Market research to identify needs and criticalities in order to promote the creation of new businesses;
- A global strategy to support businesses, as defined above.

Credit access methods for MSMEs in New York

Also the MSMEs in New York meet multiple obstacles to accessing credit, as banks and financial intermediaries, for profitability reasons, usually grant loans in amounts of no less than 120,000 EUR (USD 150,000). However, the last few years saw the introduction of a number of innovative partnerships in the area between the government, banking associations and private non-profit organisations that could inspire similar solutions for Madrid. It is an effective and solid system aimed at actively supporting the creation of small enterprises with small financial needs. Its main objective is to drive the creation of jobs and economic growth of the city.

To comprehend this model of financial inclusion, we need to examine the relationships between public and private finance in the United States, as it constitutes a reference model for the policymakers.

Government Support

In the United States, public institutions play a fundamental role in facilitating the financial inclusion of small and micro-enterprises and self-employment, by promoting partnerships between public and private actors and the creation of a business-friendly regulatory framework that may help define the boundaries of this model. The Figure A2.1 summarizes the United States microfinance chain model and the kinds of public/private intermediaries involved.

Federal Level: CDFI Federal Fund

Created in 1994 and managed by the US Treasury Department, the CDFI Federal Fund represents the main funding source for the CDFIs. This fund plays a crucial role providing resources to the CDFIs, ensuring credit, capital and non-financial services to the most vulnerable communities in the country. It is a public entity whose objective is to create a greater critical capital mass dedicated to business development, also playing a role as a catalyst for private capitals.

Small Business Administration (SBA)

SBA is a federal agency created in 1950 to support entrepreneurs and small and micro-enterprises throughout the country. It is a synergic

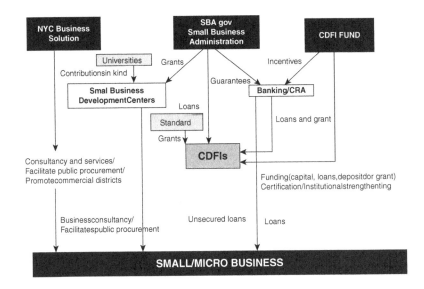

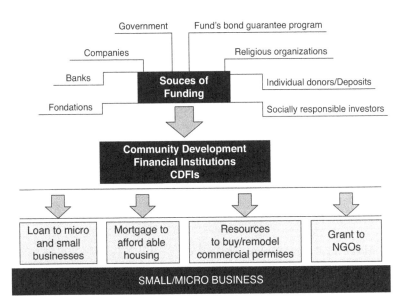

Figure A2.1 Simplified financial inclusion model

Source: Based on Rico Garrido et al. (2005)

tool which, combined with other forms of public intervention, promotes direct and indirect support measures for small and micro-enterprises by

- guaranteeing risk-sharing mechanisms to banks and providing loans to CDFIs and other microfinance institutions to increase direct credit to entrepreneurs;
- granting subsidies to organisations offering business consultancy to entrepreneurs, most notably the Small Business Development Centers (SBDC); and
- providing consultancy services to small businesses in order to help them obtain government contracts.

We will examine now some operational aspects that characterize the risk mitigation instruments granted by the SBA.

SBA loan guarantee

To cope with the difficulties of accessing funding sources most small and micro-enterprises experience, the SBA offers private lenders guarantees on loans granted to qualified small businesses.

The SBA creates a link between public support measures, effective guarantees, and access to credit for micro-enterprises, as it offers public guarantees on loans granted by private lenders to SMEs for an amount not exceeding 85% of the loans to cover the losses generated by the inability of the borrowers to meet their obligations. The advantages of this solution can be identified as follows:

- Transfer and reduction of credit risk;
- Creation of a readily available secondary market in which to sell the guaranteed portion of the loans;
- Exemption from the federal loan losses reserve requirement to which banks are subject.

Community Reinvestment Act (CRA)

In 1977, the United States federal government passed an act known as Community Reinvestment Act (CRA), which established an institutional and legislative framework for this inclusive financial system to operate in the country.

With this law, policymakers put in place a selective measure to supply bank credit to minority groups, as the credit crunch that affected these groups in the 1970s, according to some experts, was one of the reasons leading to urban decays in many American cities. The basic assumption here is that banks must reinvest the funding they collect to the benefit of such segments of the population. Such assumption represents the parameter defined as credit measured in CRA.

Local Level: NYC Small Business Services Department

The Small Business Service Department is a public body (specifically an operating arm of the municipal government of New York City) that provides assistance and support to small business owners, encourages neighbourhood development and connects employers to the workforce.

From this perspective, the NYC Small Business Services Department is an important stakeholder of the local productive micro-system, as it contributes to solve three main issues: (1) access to qualified workforce, (2) access to financial resources, and (3) simplification of the administrative procedures.

Community Development Financial Institutions (CDFIs)

An important role in the system is played by the CDFIs, which provide inclusive financial services (loans and business consulting) to small and micro-enterprises.

These are US Treasury-certified financial institutions (in particular certified by the Federal Fund CDFI) focused on community development; they cater to a target market, acting as financing entities; they provide development services, remain accountable to their communities and, technically, operate as non-government entities. These structures experienced a strong expansion following the creation of the Federal Fund CDFI and the introduction of the Community Reinvestment Act (CRA). They were given a further boost by the fund's bond guarantee programme, authorised by the Small Business Jobs Act of 2010 (P.L. 111–240).

Box A2.1 The fund's bond guarantee programme

The fund's bond guarantee program is designed to provide a low-cost source of long-term, patient capital to CDFIs.

Through the CDFI bond guarantee program, selected certified CDFIs or their designees will issue bonds that are guaranteed by the federal government and use the bond proceeds to extend capital within the broader CDFI industry for community development financing and for long-term community investments. The secretary of the treasury may guarantee bond issues having a minimum size of USD 100 million each, up to an aggregate total of USD

750 million. Multiple CDFIs may pool together in a single USD 100 million bond issuance, provided that each eligible CDFI participates with a minimum of USD 10 million. The bonds cannot exceed a maturity of 30 years, are taxable, and do not qualify for Community Reinvestment Act (CRA) credit. The CDFI bond guarantee program supports CDFIs that make investments for eligible community or economic development purposes. Authorized uses of the loans financed through bond proceeds may include a variety of financial activities, such as supporting commercial facilities that promote revitalization, community stability, and job creation/retention; housing that is principally affordable to low-income people; businesses that provide jobs for low-income people or are owned by low-income people; and community or economic development in low-income and underserved rural areas.

Financial inclusion in Madrid

Our brief analysis provided a picture of a financial ecosystem based on public-private partnerships, strong political and financial commitment from the government and private sector, and, finally, a solid and efficient microfinance network. The possibility of adapting this model to the Madrid context is currently being examined in order to build and promote an inclusive financial system aimed at supporting enterprises and creating jobs. Implementing such a model requires concrete actions to overcome the major challenges faced by the small and micro-enterprises in this geographic area.

Notes

* Although the chapter has been prepared by the authors jointly, Sections 4.1, 4.2, 4.4 and Annex 1 have been written by Pasqualina Porretta, Section 4.3 has been written by Ida C. Panetta, Section 4.5 and Annex 2 have been written by Paola Leone, whereas Section 4.6 has been written by Sabrina Leo. Paola Leone and Pasqualina Porretta have written Section 4.7.

1. http://www.ccg.ma.
2. http://tunisieopportunites.unblog.fr/2013/01/09/tunisie-les-mecanismes-de-garantie-des-credits/
3. Small and Medium Enterprise Development Project. Research Study on Credit and Credit Guarantees: Executive Summary. November 2005.
4. Among the nine shareholders, we have to consider the ex-officio presence of the Ministry of International Cooperation.
5. The Ministry of International Cooperation lent the CGC a 50-year, 60 million EGP loan – with a 10-year grace period. USAID signed an agreement with CGC for a USD 10 million guarantee fund to be disbursed over three installments. Through another agreement in 1992, this time with the SFD, the CGC was granted a EGP 10 million loan with a two-year grace period on interest. Nathan Associates, "Financial Reform for Small Business Development in

Egypt", USAID Policy Analysis/Office for the Government of Egypt, December 1997.
6. http://www.cooperazioneallosviluppo.esteri.it/pdgcs/italiano/iniziative/search_iniziative_ric.asp.
7. http://www.cgcegypt.com/about.html.
8. Since their creation, the first 4 funds have granted access to credit to 29,694 enterprises, for loans obtained in the amount of around EGP 2.5 billion. Until then, the cumulative repayment ratio for the same projects was 97%.
9. As of 31 December 2003, four annual instalments had been repaid, reducing the loan balance to EGP 54 million.
10. Of which EGP 20 million was received in July 2003.
11. Prudent investment management by CGC had resulted in a fund of EGP 77.9 million at the end of 2003.
12. For group lending, eligible loans are those from EGP 50 to EGP 500 (from EGP 500 to EGP 1000, the unit must refer the individual cases to CGC); eligible micro loans are from EGP 1000 to EGP 3000, and for small loans from EGP 3000 to EGP 25,000.
13. Being implemented by the MITD and the FEI with the EU as a major partner.
14. http://www.cgcegypt.com/.
15. In 2009, the Central Bank reduced the reserve requirements for the banks by 14% for their SME portfolio. This, however, does not necessarily affect the activities under the guarantee scheme.
16. http://www.cgcegypt.com/about.html.
17. Programmes considered: SME fund, PAP, SEB.
18. https://www.devex.com/projects/tenders/strategic-planning-for-credit-guarantee-company-cgc-in-egypt/62725.
19. We can notice here that most of the requests for microcredit examined (40% of them, 76% in terms of total amount) can be traced back to just two promoters that, operating through well-structured programmes at a regional level, show an operating capacity far higher than all other subjects.
20. As already mentioned in the chapter dedicated to the regulatory framework, this law establishes a loan cap of 25,000 EUR for enterprises and 10,000 EUR for social microcredit.
21. The sum of the low-amount operations must not exceed 20,000 EUR, but if certain conditions are met, it can also increase up to a maximum of 100,000 EUR. This sum varies depending on certain conditions certified by the bank: years of operation of the company, number of employees, turnover growth, and ownership of real estate assets. The microcredit regulations, however, establish a maximum amount of 25,000 EUR for financing micro-businesses.
22. The "one-off" commission is not owed for all operations relating to businesses operating in the areas admitted to the derogation, as per article 87.3.a of the EC Treaty for aid to regional purposes, businesses undersigning area contracts or territorial pacts, companies operating in the sector as provided for in ISTAT class 1991 60.25 (relating to some categories of transport companies) and companies taking advantage of the PON and POI Reserves.

23. For micro-businesses in protected regions, such as Campania, Calabria, Apulia and Sicily, commission is reduced and amounts to 0.125% of the sum guaranteed by the fund.
24. Before the amendments of 2009, companies should not show any losses in the previous two years of activity but, in light of the recent economic crisis, the MCC modified this requirement in order to ease the possibility to access the guarantee fund. FCG executive provisions, updated July 2012, part VI, section C-bis.
25. Data from 2009.
26. Report of the Ministry for Territorial Cohesion to the Parliament of 6 December 2012, http://www.camera.it/824?tipo=I&anno=2011&mese=12&giorno=06&view=&commissione=05c05.
27. It must be noted that at the end of the fifth year of planning for the period 2007–13, Italy received EU reimbursements amounting to 21.7% of the EU resources (6.1 billion EUR) compared to 36.1% (9.7 billion EUR) of the previous economic planning cycle related to the period 2000–06. Therefore, the slowdown of the current planning resulted in lower volume of reimbursements at the end of 2011, totalling 3.9 billion EUR.
28. With regard to micro loans, the "Spanish Institute for Women" (under the Ministry of Employment and Social Affairs), and the Directorate General for SME Policy (Ministry of Industry, Tourism and Trade) have been collaborating with the savings and loans bank, Caja de Ahorros y Pensiones de Barcelona (La Caixa), since 2001, in a microcredit programme aimed at providing financial support to female would-be entrepreneurs and business owners. This programme is co-financed by the European Social Fund and offers subsidised loans up to a maximum of 15,000 EUR with no collateral requirements. The total credit line available under its aegis is 6,000,000 EUR. The programme kicked off to an encouraging start, reflected not only by the number of women who used this service (328 in 2004) and who were granted micro loans, (209 in 2004, a 180% increase if compared to 2003), but also by the number of business women's associations that agreed to collaborate by providing full information and guidance as well as carrying out technical assessment of the projects submitted.
29. The multiannual programme for enterprises and entrepreneurship, in particular for SMEs for the period 2001–05, known as MAP, an acronym originating from the first two words of its English name (Multiannual programme for enterprise and entrepreneurship, and in particular for small and medium-sized enterprises-SMEs) was created by the European Council with resolution No. 2000/819/EC of 20 December 2000. The MAP objectives are as follows: (1) strengthen growth and competitiveness of businesses in an information-based and international economic context; (2) promote entrepreneurial spirit; (3) simplify and improve the administration and regulatory framework for enterprises, in order to promote R&D, technology innovations and the creation of new enterprises; (4) improve the enterprises' financial context, with a particular focus on SMEs; (5) facilitate enterprises to access support services, programmes and EU networks, including improvement of their coordination. Moreover, this programme is used to achieve the objectives set forth by the European Charter for small enterprises.

30. The beneficiaries are mainly unemployed individuals with professional experience or skills in their business area of choice.
31. However, it must be considered that SGR had been subject to the authorisation, supervisory and sanctioning system of the Spanish Central Bank since the introduction of Law No. 26/1998 of 29 July.
32. In case of unsecured loans, the government plays a marginal role because:

    Micro-loans (granted, for instance, by France Initiative) are provided by operators such as *Caisse des Dépôts et Consignation* (CDC) and local governments.

    Chambers of commerce and private partners provide guarantees on honourable loans.

33. Within the support of financial institutions and the development of microcredit, this law provided access to support services for the creation of enterprises and recognised self-employment as an instrument to enter or return to the business world.
34. Actually, social microcredit can be assimilated to consumer credit provided to low-income individuals, with amounts between EUR 500 and EUR 2,300.
35. Banque de France (2013).
36. Banque de France (2013).
37. Banque de France (2013).
38. It can be observed that a variety of institutions operate in the credit guarantee market; they are characterised by different legal status, target groups and operations (Porretta and Bikoula, 2012).
39. The method consists of telephone surveys targeting 1300 micro-entrepreneurs financed by Adie for the first time. The study was updated in 2013 (*Banque de France*, 2013).
40. According to the 2010 survey, we can observe that 29% of the new employees were recruited at the beginning of the activity, while 47% of them were recruited after one year.
41. The survey, updated in April 2012, was carried out by the provider A2S Communication on a representative sample of enterprises supported and financed by France Active and operating in 2009, namely 350 micro-enterprises and 190 social enterprises.

5
Nearly Conclusive Considerations

Paola Leone and Pasqualina Porretta

After having analysed the peculiar characteristics of the microcredit sector and the guarantee activity carried out by the MFIs in the countries examined, it is now time for some (almost) conclusive considerations.

Our research (a work-in-progress) highlighted the existence of different microcredit models and differences between guarantee schemes, which are country-specific and influenced by the legal contexts and historical background.

The main differences between the guarantee schemes are related to specific legislation, degree of government intervention, guarantee programmes, target market (multisectoral, monosectoral), guarantee products, guarantee beneficiaries, business sectors involved, leverage ratio, loan coverage, guarantee terms, conditions, commissions and so on.

Surprisingly the North African countries examined seem to have in place older legislation on microcredit than the European countries. This is surely due to their different social and economic contexts. However, we observed a relative "freshness" of the microcredit sectors in the three European countries analysed, which were deeply affected by the financial crisis and, consequently, characterised by a lower credit demand than in the past. In Spain, the regulatory framework is only at a design phase, while in Italy we are still awaiting the implementation decrees of the recently adopted regulatory framework.

However, there is no doubt that in order to develop the microfinance sector, regulators and governments in particular need to implement specific legislation and regulatory frameworks, consumer protection, and financial infrastructure. Also prudential supervisors can contribute to the growth of microfinance by defining clear requirements for microfinance institutions and guarantee funds. In our opinion, any microfinance regulatory framework should ideally define and cover all microfinance activities (direct loans, mortgages, deposits, micro-insurance, etc.), including their specific risks and business practice, especially in markets where modern banking systems have not been developed yet. An accurate definition of the sector would certainly contribute to a more timely and proactive supervision.

Microfinance regulations should, therefore, include punctual and simple standards for loan administration, NPLs management, write-offs, documentation and loan loss provisions that reflect the proximity to the customer, the success of collection practices, the use of guarantees or group lending practices, the informal nature of activities being financed and homogeneous and fast-rotating portfolios.

The mapping of microcredit operators provided herein according to available data showed that the North African countries are characterised by a low number of MFIs (Tunisia), relatively low (Morocco) or largely dominated by NGOs (Egypt); the European countries, instead, have MFI systems characterised by the presence of operators with different legal status and missions. Many of these provide non-financial services, such as coaching, tutoring, training and information. A common element between the European and African countries seems to be the public support enjoyed by the MFIs; in the African countries, such institutions benefit also from the support of some international donor agencies. From this perspective, it is important to point out that, in addition to the traditional role of ensuring the stability and efficiency of the MFIs through different forms of financial support (guarantees, capitalisation, and so on), governments can also contribute to greater access to credit by promoting a favourable legal and regulatory environment.

Microcredit programmes and guarantee funds seem to be operating in different ways. In the countries examined, a common trait is the presence of public guarantee schemes that guarantee and/or counter-guarantee the micro-loans, though operating according to different methods and regulations in their respective countries. Similarities and differences between the guarantee funds examined were outlined in Section 4.7.

All guarantee funds analysed share the objective of providing greater access to formal financing for micro and small enterprises, although there are clear differences in the way they are created and operate. These differences are related to adjustments to their operating environment. There is no single model that is deemed to work better than others. It is always a matter of creating the best type of fund for a particular context. When designing a guarantee fund, one has to take into account the existing financial landscape, the social and cultural conditions, and the prevailing rules and regulations. Then, there are parameters related to capitalisation requirements, provision of guarantees, terms of delivery and what kind of loans can be guaranteed. In addition, there are also distinct ownership structures.

Practically any guarantee fund combines features drawn from other types. In the three MENA countries analysed, for instance, the guarantee schemes operate as funded, non-mutual portfolio guarantee schemes in which ex-ante guarantees are delivered to enterprises. In the three European countries, instead, guarantee schemes may assume the form of unfunded guarantees, mutual or non-mutual individual schemes that provide ex-ante guarantees to institutions or individual entrepreneurs.

Guarantee funds, for example, can be promoted directly by governments to support economic growth in certain sectors. Or donors may fund them to create jobs or alleviate poverty in some areas. Or the entrepreneurs themselves might create them, guaranteeing each other's loans according to a mutual assistance perspective. The guarantee funds' most common objectives are small enterprise development, post-war economic recovery, youth employment, women's entrepreneurship and mutual assistance. In many cases, these overall objectives have proved too broad to cope with. Hence, they should be translated into clear eligibility criteria.

Besides the above differences, which can be ascribed to the different social and economic environments, it is possible to highlight some common traits, mainly related to a number of critical elements of the microcredit sectors and the credit guarantee schemes. Our research shows that several factors may compromise the efficiency of the credit guarantee schemes. Starting from an analysis of such weaknesses, it is possible to build more efficient microcredit sectors, regardless of their countries of origin. The following steps should be implemented:

- **A modern regulatory framework for the microcredit sector and the guarantee funds**:
  - As noted in the previous chapter, this is the starting point to develop any modern microcredit industry suitable to contribute to the national economy and improve the efficiency and effectiveness of MFI intermediation. This means to:
    (1) remove policies, red tape, infrastructures and legal barriers in the sector; (2) clearly define microcredit and microcredit operators; (3) establish supervision on the MFIs' activities and apply prudential norms to all aspects of their business.

- **Improved definition of the main features of microcredit programmes and the role of the operators involved:**
  - As underlined in the previous chapter, usually the goals of these programmes are not well defined, as well as the actions required, the players involved (role and responsibilities) and the expected results. This is a common trait to both North African and European countries. With regard to the operational planning, the agreed objectives should be defined in terms of expected results over specific time frames. In other words, "What is expected in terms of improved living conditions and improvement for businesses?" "Where and who is going to benefit from it?" Establishing the expected results on a preliminary basis is key to achieving an effective use of public funds. Correct management of the programmes, including their risks, requires a precise identification of roles and responsibilities of all the actors involved (fund managers, funders, beneficiaries, etc.); beneficiaries, in particular, should be clearly determined for credit risk management purposes, by indicating the requirements they should meet during the processing of the requests received.
- **Improved screening of potential beneficiaries and related credit risk analysis:**
  - An erroneous evaluation of the borrowers' risk profile can undermine MFIs' economic and financial sustainability. Commissions, premiums and provisions paid to the guarantee fund might not be consistent with the customer risk profiles. On the one hand, underestimating risks may result in unexpected losses and exhaust the provisioned resources. On the other hand, an overestimation of risk may lead to underutilising the fund, and this, in turn, might cause the fund managers to miss the expected sustainability and outreach goals. That said, credit excess or weak guarantees in a portfolio can undermine MFIs' sustainability, as happened for many MFIs in the surveyed countries (e.g., Morocco). It must be pointed out that it is not always easy to determine the risk profiles of microcredit borrowers, due to a lack of credit history and transparent bookkeeping procedures. Micro-borrowers' risk analysis proves to be difficult, given the absence of databases and project and credit scoring systems. Hence, a centralised database where all relevant information can be stored would be highly beneficial. This is what is happening in Morocco, where a new microcredit risk centre has been recently established. Anyway, the relatively small size of micro-loans and, as a consequence, their limited profitability is not an incentive to build efficient credit

scoring models. And this, in turn, explains why banks and fund guarantee managers tend to be very conservative towards micro-borrowers (especially in Tunisia and Morocco). Credit risk analysis plays a crucial role in the microcredit sector and the credit guarantee chain. Borrowers often lack formal financial statements, so loan officers help prepare documentation using expected cash flows and net worth to determine the amortisation schedule and loan amount. The borrower's character and willingness to repay is also assessed during field visits. Credit bureau data are not always available for low-income clients or for all types of microfinance providers, but when available, they are used as well. Credit scoring, when used, complements rather than replaces the more labour-intensive approach to credit analysis (BCBS, 2010, p. 10).

- **No duplication of activities within the credit-guarantee chain:**
  - It is not uncommon to see a given task assigned to different actors in the credit guarantee chain. This overlap of duties and responsibilities between different institutions ends up in unnecessary administrative burdens, which tend to slow down the overall guarantee granting process and generate higher costs. As a result, these guarantee schemes become less attractive to borrowers, since they cannot satisfy their needs in a timely manner. However, in Morocco, as previously mentioned, the financing banks are responsible for the evaluation process.
- **Clearly defined guarantee contracts:**
  - Litigation between guarantee fund managers and financial intermediaries would disrupt their relationship.
- **Consider that microcredit activities are strongly subsidised:**
  - Public subsidies and credit guarantee schemes can undermine MFIs' financial sustainability. This is the case of most institutions in Tunisia, although it is not uncommon to see heavily subsidised MFIs in Morocco, Tunisia, Italy or Spain, too. Subsidised MFIs tend to be poorly managed and unsustainable. Furthermore, the presence of public schemes in the microcredit sector discourages the implementation of modern and efficient risk management tools, not to mention the waste of public resources.
- **The role of policymakers in guarantee schemes:**
  - In Morocco and Tunisia, the government is the principal actor behind such guarantee schemes, since private financial institutions are less developed and unable to provide the necessary resources. In Italy or Spain, private guarantee funds are more common, although their use is limited for a number of reasons: limited amounts available, limited territorial outreach, poorly

designed targeting, absence of monitoring tools and scarce consultancy services. From this perspective, policymakers should provide or attract resources to fund such schemes and start microcredit programmes. They should monitor their performances and ensure that the results achieved are consistent with the expected goals. Moreover, policymakers should promote capacity-building[1] mechanisms in order to strengthen the sector and build long-lasting relationships between the different institutions. A more efficient use of the resources provided by national or international institutions is desirable as well. This is particularly true for the Italian and Spanish MFIs, which should take advantage of the funding initiatives (European Agricultural Fund, EIF, etc.) available under the new European policy framework 2020 (as far as they are compatible with the limits set for State Aid).[2] In particular, Spain results one of the countries that uses a lot of EU funds dedicated to microcredit, though this use is not always optimal. On the other side, the French microcredit sector is much more developed.

- **Development of further guarantee schemes funded through private and public resources:**
  - Our research underlined that usually, especially in African countries, the government is the main moneylender. However, it is equally important to stimulate private sector investments in serving low-income individuals and micro-enterprises. Microcredit programmes should be funded through both private commercial capital and public resources. Within the public sector, potential funders could include local governments, chambers of commerce, European programmes, and so on. Cooperation between the private sector and civil society (a G20 principle) is essential for far-reaching financial improvement. Private sector commitments, which may be backed by regulations or enforcement if the private sector is not sufficiently active in delivering them, can be an effective means of promoting financial inclusion and capability. Banks and MFIs can then assume a leading role in promoting financial inclusion, spurred on by competition, regulations and monitoring, in line with the current market opportunities. Commitments by regulators and governments must complement private sector targets (Douglas, 2011).
- **Sharing and disclosing credit information and filling the communication gap between the different actors involved in the microcredit programmes:**
  - Sharing information on the borrower's profile is essential to slash costs and overcome information constraints. By integrating microborrowers' information into credit bureaus, coverage and usefulness

of such data will be certainly improved. Financial institutions of all types may access new customers, while managing risks and costs more effectively. Communication and coordination between the different subjects involved in the microcredit programmes at various levels – promoters, funders, guarantors and so on – should also be improved. It is essential that MFIs maintain adequate records in accordance with accounting policies and internationally accepted practices; they should also publish information that fairly reflects their financial condition and profitability on a regular basis.

- **Encourage the MFIs to diversify their products:**
  - In the microcredit sector, it is important to offer guarantees (or other financial instruments) other than the traditional ones, such as the following:
    - Portfolio guarantees for certain banks with proven and efficient SME activities
    - Guarantees for long-term loans for specific activities (with long-term profitability) such as arboriculture, clean technology and sustainable energy, and so on
    - Guarantees for women entrepreneurs
    - Guarantees for innovative enterprises
    - Micro-leasing
    - Micro-insurance
    - Equity investment
    - Bond issuance
    - Debt financing
    - Contributions to risk funds and loans granted to start-ups
    - Different types of non-financial services and so on
- **Strengthening consultancy and coaching services:**
  - Microcredit programmes funded with public resources do not provide – with a few exceptions – adequate coaching services. This area should be further developed, especially in the African countries. Furthermore, microcredit programmes should be better advertised in order to reach a wider target of potential beneficiaries, who often lack the necessary financial culture to understand and appreciate them.
- **Development of monitoring activities and measurement of social and economic performance:**
  - Public subsidies and guarantee schemes reduce the need to monitor the programmes and their performance. If public support and guarantee schemes are often required to start a given microcredit programme, their presence alone might not be enough to achieve

the expected goals. For such purpose, it is necessary to build a monitoring system measuring the programme's efficiency and the use of public resources. From a methodological perspective, this translates into an integrated approach – from information to coaching – able to coordinate the efforts of all participants. This should be implemented in accordance with the objectives set within the Europe 2020 policy framework and reaffirmed by the European policy guidelines for the period 2014–20, which encourage member states to devote public resources to economic development and social cohesion in a timely and efficient manner. Hence, the expected results in the surveyed countries need to be clearly defined and disseminated, to both policymakers and end users, in order to lead to a true open public debate. These recommendations are true for emerging countries as well as for the European sectors, since our research has showed that the effectiveness and outreach of microcredit programmes in the latter is even more questionable. In any case, this is a delicate topic, which needs to be investigated further in order to substantially improve in the policymakers' programming efforts.

This research constitutes a work-in-progress and, as such, may be subject to changes and additions in the near future. In particular, this study highlights the importance of training and capacity-building in non-banking microfinance institutions, in order to improve the knowledge of different forms of raising and providing capital, such as equity investment, donations, bond issuance, debt financing, contribution to risk funds and start-up grants; we also believe that the exchange of best practices can play a valuable role in this sector.

Notes

1. This term refers to the obstacles faced by national and international institutions in setting up microcredit programmes and the solutions to overcome them in order to achieve measurable results.
2. State aid in the form of guarantees, governed by EU Communication of 20.6.2008, entitles a reduction in minimum commissions (safe-harbour premiums) under which aid is provided, that this, a reduction of 25% for SMEs and 15% for other companies; similar percentage reductions are granted on fair awards calculated in accordance with methods approved by the EU Commission. The maximum loan amount allowed under such guarantees must not exceed the cost of labour in 2008, including the fees to subcontractors' staff; the guarantees must be provided by 2010, for a portion of the loan not exceeding 90%, and on loans that finance investments in the likes of working capital; these fee reductions apply for two years from the granting of the guarantee.

Bibliography

Abdel-Baki, R., Cordier, C., Pistelli, M. and Zain S. (2010) *Arab Microfinance Analysis and Benchmarking Report*, Microfinance Information Exchange, http://www.themix.org/sites/default/files/2010%20Arab%20Microfinance%20Analysis%20Benchmarking%20Report%20-Final_3.pdf, accessed May 2014.

Aceña, P. M. (2003) "Las cajas de ahorros en la historia económica española", Revista Economistas, *Economistas*, 98, 26–34.

Allaire, V., Ashta, A., Attuel-Mendes, L. and Krishnaswamy, K. (2009) *Institutional Analysis to Explain the Success of Moroccan Microfinance Institutions*, CEB Working paper No. 09/057.

———. (2009) "The Success of Moroccan Microfinance Institutions: More Than Just Culture?" *CEB Working Paper No 09/057*, https://dipot.ulb.ac.be/dspace/bitstream/2013/53997/1/RePEc_sol_wpaper_09–057.pdf.

Allen, D. (2005) "Cohesion and the Structural Funds: Competing Pressures for Reform", in H. Wallace, Wallace, W. and Pollack, M. (eds.) *Policy-Making in the European Union*, 6th ed. (Oxford: Oxford University Press).

Andersen T. B. and Malchow-Møller N. (2006) "Strategic Interaction in Undeveloped Credit Markets", *Journal of Development Economics,* 80, 275–298.

Banque Africaine de Development (2009) *Programme d'Appui au Développement du Secteur Financier. Pays: Royaume du Maroc, Rapport d'évaluation,* October, http://www.afdb.org/fileadmin/uploads/afdb/Documents/Project-and-Operations/Morocco-%20%20PADESFI%20FR.pdf.

Banque de France (2013) *Rapport annuel de l'Observatoire de la microfinance. Exercice 2012*, Observatoire de la Microfinance.

———. (2012) *Rapport annuel de l'Observatoire de la microfinance. Financial year 2011*, Observatoire de la Microfinance.

———. (2008) *Rapport annuel de l'Observatoire de la microfinance. Financial year 2007*, Observatoire de la Microfinance.

BCBS – Basel Committee on Banking Supervision (2010) *Microfinance Activities and the Core Principles for Effective Banking Supervision*, February, http://www.bis.org/publ/bcbs175.pdf, accessed May 2014.

———. (2006) *Basel II: International Convergence of Capital Measurement and Capital Standards: A Revised Framework, Comprehensive Version*, June, http://www.bis.org/publ/bcbs128.htm.

Bechri et al (2001), "Tunisia's Lending Program to SMEs: Anatomy of an Institutional Failure?" *Small Business Economic*, 17, 293–308.

Belgaroui, M. H. (2005) *Performance et analyse des interventions des institutions de microfinance en Tunisie cas de la Banque Tunisienne de Solidarietè*, Université de Sfax, http://www.lamicrofinance.org/files/24285_file_performance_bts_Tunisie.pdf.

Bennet, F., Doran, A. and Billington, H. (2005) *Do Credit Guarantees Lead to Improved Access to Financial Services ? Recent Evidence from Chile, Egypt, India, and*

Poland, Department for International Development, London, Financial Sector, Policy Division Working Paper.

Bendig M., Unterberg M. and Sarpong, B. (2012) Overview of the Microcredit Sector in the European Union, European Microfinance Network (EMN) 2010–2011.

Bennardo A., Pagano M. and Piccolo S. (2009) *Multiple-Bank Lending, Creditor Rights and Information Sharing*, CEPR Discussion Papers, 7186.

Berger A. N. and Udell G. F. (2002) « The Economics of Small Business Finance: the Roles of Private Equity and Debt Markets in the Financial Growth Cycle », *Journal of Banking and Finance*, 22, 613–673.

Brana S. and Jégourel Y. (2011) *Breadth and Depth of French Microfinance Outreach: An Evaluation*, LAREFI Working Paper CR11-EFI/08.

Brabant M., Dugos P. and Massou F. (2009) Rapport sur le Microcrédit. Inspection Générale des Finances.

Carbo, S., Gardner, E. P. M. and Molyneux P. (2005) *Financial Exclusion* (Basingstoke and New York: Palgrave Macmillan).

Central Guarantee Fund Management Committee (2012) *The Guarantee Fund for SMEs. The Effectiveness of the Guarantee Fund in 2011*, Ministry of Economic Development.

CGAP – Consultative Group to Assist the Poor (2010) *The Rise, Fall, and Recovery of the Microfinance Sector in Morocco*, December, http://www.cgap.org/publications/ rise-fall-and-recovery-microfinance-sector-morocco.

——. (2003) *Disclosure Guidelines for Financial Reporting by MFIs*, July, http://www. cgap.org/publications/disclosure-guidelines-financial-reporting-mfis, access date may 2014..

Chemonics International Inc. (2007) *Microfinance Policy Forum: Third Meeting Report*, June.

Chemonics International Inc. and CGAP (2009) *Legal and regulatory environment for microfinance in Egypt. Diagnostic study with focus on NGO-MFI transformation issues*, June.

Cuzarenco A. and Szafarz A. (2013) *Female Access to Credit in France: How Microfinance Institutions Import Disparate Treatment from Banks*, CEB Working Paper n. 13/037, October 2013.

CECA – Confederación Española de Cajas de Ahorros (2005) "Situación del Microcrédito en las Cajas de Ahorros Españolas", in *El Libro Blanco del Microcrédito* (Madrid: FUNCAS).

Curran, L. (2005) "Financing microfinance loan portfolios", *Small Enterprise Development*, 16 (1), 42–49.

Daley-Harris, S. (2009) *State of the Microcredit Summit Campaign Report 2009*, Microcredit Summit Campaign, http://www.microcreditsummit.org/uploads/ socrs/SOCR2009_English.pdf.

Deelen, L. and Molenaar K. (2004) *Guarantee Funds for Small Enterprises. A Manual for Guarantee Fund Managers* ILO (International Labour Organization), http:// www.ruralfinance.org/fileadmin/templates/rflc/documents/1126268365900_ Guarantee_funds_for_small_enterprises.pdf, access date may 2014..

Degryse H., Lu L. and Ongena S. (2013) *Informal or Formal Financing? Or Both? First Evidence on the Co-Funding of Chinese Firms.* http://ssrn.com/abstract=2023751 or http:// dx.doi.org/10.2139/ssrn.2023751, accessed May 2014.

Douette, A., Lesaffre, D. and Siebeke, R. (2014) *SMEs' Credit Guarantee Schemes in Developing and Emerging Economies. Reflection, Setting-up Principle, Quality Standards* (Bonn and Eschborn: Deutsche Gesellschaft für Internationale Zusammenarbeit (GIZ) GmbH), http://www.aecm.eu/servlet/Repository/giz-study-on-smes-credit-guarantee-schemes.pdf?IDR=553.

Douglas, P. (2011) *Financial Inclusion in the Middle East and North Africa, Analysis and Roadmap Recommendations,* World Bank Policy Research Working Paper, No. 5610.

ECO – European Consultants Organization (2010) *FEMIP Study in Support of the Implementation of the Mediterranean Business Development Initiative (MBDI* – Final Report), http://www.eib.org/attachments/country/study_in_support_of_the_implementation_o_mbdi_en.pdf.

EIF – European Integration Fund, Ministry of Interior, Ministry of Social Policies in collaboration with *Ente Nazionale per il Microcredito,* (2011) *A. M. I. C. I. Access to microcredit for immigrant citizens. The Italian model,* http://www.microcreditoitalia.org/images/amici/download/libro_amici.pdf.

EFSA – Egyptian Financial Service Authority (2010) *Microfinance in Egypt Brief Overview of Current Status,* April.

EBI – Egyptian Banking Institute and SFD – Social Fund for Development (2005) The National Strategy for Microfinance in Egypt, December.

*Ente Nazionale per il Microcredito-*Italian Public agency for Microcredit (2012) *Monitoring of the Integration of Work Policies with Local Development Policies of Productive Systems Regarding Microcredit and Microfinance,* Annual report.

EQI – Environmental Quality International (2004) *Small and Medium Enterprise Development Project. Research Study on Credit and Credit Guarantees: Executive Summary,* November.

ESBG – European Savings Banks Group (2009) *ESBG Comments on Microcredit in Europe,* Position paper, http://www.esbg.eu/uploadedFiles/Position_papers/026%20-%20ESBG%20Microcredit.pdf.

Estapé-Dubreuil, G. and Torreguitart-Mirada, C. (2010) "Microfinance and gender considerations in developed countries: the case of Catalonia", *Management Research Review,* 33 (12), 1140–1157.

Estevez, A. M. (2005) *El programa de micro crèditos del ICO,* Perspective del Sistema financiero, No 84,, fundaciòn de las cajas de Ahorros, Madrid.

European Union Regional Policy (2006) *Regions and Cities for economic Growth and creation of new Jobs: An overview of the Regulations 2007–2013 for the on Cohesion policy and the Regional Policy,* Inforegio Factsheet 2006 http://ec.europa.eu/regional_policy/sources/docoffic/official/regulation/pdf/2007/publications/memo_en.pdf.

European Commission (2008) *Guidelines for EC Support to Microfinance,* EuropeAid Co-operation Office.

European Parliament (2009) *Report with recommendations to the Commission on a European initiative for the development of micro-credits in support of growth and employment, 2008/2122(INI),* http://www.europarl.europa.eu/sides/getDoc.do?pubRef=-//EP//NONSGML+REPORT+A6–2009–0041+0+DOC+PDF+V0//EN.   January   29, 2009, A6–0041/2009, Session document, Committee on Economic and Monetary Affairs, Zsolt László Becsey, Rapporteur.

Expert Group Report (2006) *Access to Finance for SMEs of the North Africa Region and the Middle East,* February, (Bruxelles: European Communities).

Fundación ICO (Instituto de Crédito Oficial) and Fundación Cajasol (2012) *Programa de microcréditos para la inserción social promis manual de aplicación*, Majo, http://www.fundacionico.es/fileadmin/user_upload/MICROCREDITOS/ PROMIS_Manual_de_Aplicacion.pdf, accessed May 2014.

García, A. and Lens, J. (2007) *Microcréditos. La Revolución Silenciosa* (Barcelona: Ed. Debate).

Ghatak, M. and Guinnane, T.W. (1999) "The economics of lending with joint liability: theory and practice", *Journal of Development Economics*, 60 (1), 195–228.

Gobierno de Españ ia and Ministerio de Empleo y Seguridad Social (2013) *Jornada La micorfinciqas en Espana: empulso en el nuevo periodo de programmacion del Fondo Social Europeo (2014–2020)*, Madrid.

Gutiérrez Nieto, B. (2005) »Antecedentes del microcrédito. Lecciones del pasado para las experiencias actuales », CIRIEC-España, *Revista de Economía Pública, Social y Cooperativa*, 51, 25–50.

Gutiérrez-Goiria, J. (2009) *Microfinanzas y desarrollo: situación actual, debates y perspectivas*, (Bilbao: HEGOA).

Harper, M. (ed.) (2003) *Microfinance. Evolution, Achievements and Challenges* (London: ITDG Publishing).

Hartungi, R. (2007) "Understanding the success factors of micro-finance institution in a developing country", *International Journal of Social Economics*, 34 (6), 388–401.

Intesa San Paolo (2010) *South Mediterranean countries: growth and business opportunities in the relationships with the European Union*, Study and Research Division, Monica Bosi, ed. http://www.group.intesasanpaolo.com/scriptIsir0/si09/ contentData/view/eos005.pdf?id=CNT-04-000000003F27F&ct=application/ pdf.

Italian National Institute for Microcredit (2012) *Monitoring of the integration of labour policies with policies for local development of the productive systems with regard to microcredit and micro-finance*, Annual internal report.

Jain, S. (1999) "Symbiosis vs. Crowding-out: the Interaction of Formal and Informal Credit Markets in Developing Countries", *Journal of Development Economics*, 59, 419–444.

Jain, S. and Mnsuri, G. (2003) "A little at a time: the use of regularly scheduled repayments in microfinance programs", *Journal of Development Economics*, 72 (1), 253–279.

Jayo, B., Rico, S. and Lacalle-Calderón, M. (2008) *Overview of the Microcredit Sector in the European Union 2006–2007*, EMN Working Paper No. 5, (Paris: European Microfinance Network).

Jose, R. Pin, Gallifa, A. and Susaeta, L. (2008) *Microcredit in Tunisia: Enda Inter-Arabe*, Iese Occasional Paper, Op. No 8(11).

Karlan, D. and Apple, J. (2011) *More Than Good Intentions: How a New Economics is Helping to Solve Global Poverty* (New York: Penguin).

Karlan, D. and Zinman, J. (2007) *Expanding Credit Access: Using Randomized Supply Decisions to Estimate the Impacts*, Working Paper No 108, (Washington, DC: Center for Global Development).

La Torre, M. (2005) »Microfinanza e Finanza Etica », *Bancaria*, No. 10.

La Torre, M. and Vento, G. (2006) *Microfinance* (Basingstoke and New York: Palgrave Macmillan).

——. (2005) Per una nuova microfinanza: il ruolo delle banche, *Bancaria*, No. 2.

Lacalle M. and Rico, S. (2012) *Microfinace in Spain: Impact and Recommendations of the Future*, Cuadernos Monográficos, Collection of monograph, No. 18, (Madrid: Foro Nantik Lum de MicroFinanzas).

Lammermann, S. (2010) "Microcredit in France: financial support for social inclusion", in B. Jayo Carboni (ed.) *Handbook of Microfinance in Europe. Social Inclusion through Microenterprise Development* (Cheltenham: Edward Elgar Publishing Limited).

Lazar, D. and Palanichamy, P. (2008) *Micro Finance and Poverty Eradication* (New Delhi: New Century Publications).

Ledgerwood, J. (2000) *Microfinance Handbook* (Washington, DC: World Bank).

Leone, P., Panetta, I.C. and Porretta, P. (2013) "Credit Guarantee Institutions, Performance and Risk Analysis: An Experimental Scoring", in J. Falzon (ed.), *Bank Stability, Sovereign Debt and Derivatives* (Basingstoke and New York: Palgrave Macmillan).

Leone, P. and Porretta, P. (2012) "Comparative Analysis of Mutual Guarantee System", in P. Leone and Vento G. A. (eds.) *Credit Guarantee Institutions and SME finance* (Basingstoke and New York: Palgrave Macmillan).

Littlefield, E., Morduch, J. and Hashemi, S. (2003) "Is microfinance an effective strategy to reach the millennium development goals?" *Focus Note,* January, CGAP, Washington.

Mahmud, S. (2003) "Actually how empowering is microcredit?", *Development and Change*, 34 (4), 577–605.

MicroBank (2012) *Datos básicos,* www.microbanklacaixa.com, January 2012.

——. (2012) *Annual Financial Statements, years 2011,* http://www.microbanklacaixa.com/deployedfiles/microbank/Estaticos/PDFs/Informe_Anual_2011_ANG.pdf . (2013) *Annual Financial Statements, years 2012,* http://www.microbanklacaixa.com/deployedfiles/microbank_v2/Estaticos/PDFs/Informe_Anual_2012_en.pdf.

Ministry of Finance (2011) *Vision concertée pour le developpement de la micro finance en Tunisie 2011–14.*

MIX and Sanabel (2012) *2011 Middle East and North Africa Regional Snapshot,* http://www.sanabelnetwork.org/UserFiles/file/Publications/Transparency%20Publications/2011%20MENA%20Regional%20Snapshot_EN.pdf.

Navarro, J. D. (ed.) (2013) *La importancia de una legislacion microfinanciera para el desarollo del sector en Espana,* Foro de Microfinances – Cuadernos Monográficos (20), 6–12 (Madrid: Fundación Nantik Lum; Universidad Pontificia Comillas).

——. (ed.) (2011) *Conclusions from the First National Meeting on Microfinance and Reflections on the Principal Issues Addressed,* Cuadernos Monográficos ((6) (Madrid: Fundación Nantik Lum; Universidad Pontificia Comillas) .

OECD (2012), *SME and Entrepreneurship Financing: The Role of Credit Guarantee Schemes and Mutual Guarantee* (Paris: OECD Publishing).

Otero, M. (1999) "Bringing Development Back into Microfinance", *Journal of Microfinance*, 1 (1), 8–19.

Panetta, I. C. (2012) "An Analysis of Credit Guarantee Schemes: Suggestions Provided by Literature", in P. Leone and Vento G. A. (eds.) *Credit Guarantee Institutions and SME finance* (Basingstoke and New York: Palgrave Macmillan).

Panetta, I. C. and Lo Cascio, C.(2012) "The Guarantee System in Spain", in P. Leone and Vento G. A. (eds.) *Credit Guarantee Institutions and SME Finance* (Basingstoke and New York: Palgrave Macmillan).

PlaNet Finance (2008) *National Impact Survey of Microfinance in Egypt*, May, http://www.sfdegypt.org/c/document_library/get_file?uuid=d11593f0–46b6–49d3-b64d-2eab2c0e6f12&groupId=10136.

Porretta, P. and Bikoula I. G. (2012) "The Guarantee System in France", in P. Leone and G. A. Vento (eds.) *Credit Guarantee Institutions and SME finance* (Basingstoke and New York: Palgrave Macmillan).

Rico Garrido, S. E., Lacalle-Calderòn, M., Màrquez, J. and Duràn, J. (2005) *Microcredit in Spain*, (Madrid: Foro Nantik Lum; Universidad Pontificia Comillas).

Rico, S. (2009) *Microcrédito Social: una evaluación de impacto, Observatorio de la Inclusión Social*, (Barcelona: Colección Herramientas para la Inclusión, Caixa Catalunya Obra Social).

Roodman, D. and Morduch, J. (2009) *The Impact of Microcredit on the Poor in Bangladesh: Revisiting the Evidence*, Center for Global Development, working paper, No 174.50.

Roper, S. (2011) *Credit Guarantee Schemes: A Tool to Promote SME Growth and Innovation in the MENA Region. Report and Guidelines*, MENA-OECD Investment Programme Working Paper.

Saadani, Y., Arvai, Z. and Rocha, R. (2011) *A Review of Credit Guarantee Schemes in the Middle East and North Africa Region*, Financial Flagship, World Bank.

Sanabel Network (2010) *Microfinance Industry Profile: Egypt*, http://www.microfinancegateway.org/gm/document-1.9.49876/Microfinance_Industry_Profile%20-_Egypt.pdf.

Schreiner, M. and Colombet, H.H. (2001) "From Urban to Rural: Lessons for Microfinance from Argentina", *Development Policy Review*, 19 (3), 339–354.

Sebstad, J., Neill, C., Barnes, C. and Chen, G. (1995) *Assessing the Impacts of Microentreprise Interventions: A Framework for Analysis*, USAID Managing for Results Working Paper No 7, USAID/Centre for Development Information and Evaluation, Washington D.C.

SEEP Network (2000) *Learning from Clients: Assessment Tools for Microfinance Practitioners*, AIMS, Washington D.C.

World Economic Forum, the International Bank for Reconstruction and Development/The World Bank, and the African Development Bank (2009) *The Africa Competitiveness Report 2009*, (Geneve: World Economic Forum).

Wright, K. and Copestake, J. (2004) "Impact assessment of microfinance using qualitative data: Communicating between social scientist and practitioners using the QUIP", *Journal of International Development*, 16, 355–67.

Ziadi, L. (2005) « La microfinance en Tunisie: une dynamique du développement durable », *Esprit critique*, Hiver 2005, 7 (1), 15–33, http://www.espritcritique.fr/0701/esp0701article02.pdf.

Zohir, S. and Matin, I. (2004) "Wider Impacts of Microfinance Institutions: Issues and Concepts", *Journal of International Development*, 16, 301–30.

Index

CPSIA information can be obtained at www.ICGtesting.com
Printed in the USA
LVOW05*0000030115

421309LV00002B/4/P

9 781137 452986